Surrogate Motherhood

SURROGATE MOTHERHOOD

Martha A. Field

Harvard University Press
Cambridge, Massachusetts
London, England
1988

This book is printed on acid-free paper, and its binding materials
have been chosen for strength and durability.

Library of Congress Cataloging-in-Publication Data

Field, Martha A.
  Surrogate motherhood / Martha A. Field.
     p.   cm.
  Bibliography: p.
  Includes index.
  ISBN 0-674-85748-8 (alk. paper)
  1. Surrogate mothers—Legal status, laws, etc.—United States.
2. Contracts—United States.   I. Title.
KF540.F53   1988
346.7301'7—dc19   88-17459
[347.30617]   CIP

To Maria

who first taught me the joys of mothering

Preface

My aim in writing this book has been to sort out the legal issues involved in the surrogate motherhood debate so that a layperson can understand them. In most states it has not yet been decided what rules will apply to surrogacy. It is my conviction that the legal solution to the surrogacy problem rests on value judgments that are yet to be definitively made. It is the task of the public generally, and not just of lawyers, politicians, or courts, to resolve those issues of value.

In the first four chapters I set out a spectrum of positions that might be adopted to deal with surrogacy and the reasoning that might support them. In the last five chapters I offer and defend the resolution I prefer: contracts made before birth should be unenforceable in the context of surrogate motherhood, just as they already are in the context of adoption. Moreover, a mother who withdraws from a surrogacy contract should be entitled to retain custody of her child without having to prove to a court that she would be a better parent than the biological father.

I am grateful to several people for helpful conversations: Mary Joe Frug, Phillip Areeda, Ruth Bourquin, Clare Dalton, Sylvia Law, Martha Minow, Marjorie Schultz, Kathleen Sullivan, and Lloyd Weinreb. I also benefited from help from two excellent secretaries: Caroline Martin and Deborah Thomas. And I could not have produced the book without several wonderful student assistants: Deborah Kravitz, Valerie Sanchez, Michael Stein, and especially Francesca Ortiz.

Contents

Contents

Surrogate Motherhood

. . . by the action of Modern Industry, all family ties among the proletarians are torn asunder, and their children transformed into simple articles of commerce . . .

—Karl Marx and Friedrich Engels,
Manifesto of the Communist Party

Introduction

In 1980 Denise Thrane, a divorced mother of three in her late twenties, agreed by contract to bear a child for Mr. and Mrs. James Noyes. She lived in California and they lived in New York, but Mr. Noyes's sperm was ejaculated, frozen, and flown to California, where Ms. Thrane was artificially inseminated. The contract specified that Ms. Thrane was not to receive any fee, although her medical expenses would be paid.

As her pregnancy advanced, Ms. Thrane changed her mind about surrendering the baby, and even before the child was born, the Noyeses took her to court, seeking a declaration thay they were entitled to custody. The case was settled on the eve of trial: the Noyeses backed down, leaving custody with the natural mother. Having learned that Mrs. Noyes had had a sex change operation to become a woman,[1] Thrane could credibly threaten exposure and damaging publicity; and in a court battle she might have been able to win custody on the basis of the child's best interests.

In 1982 Judy Stiver, a twenty-six-year-old housewife in Lansing, Michigan, agreed to bear a child for forty-six-year-old Alexander Malahoff and his wife, for a fee of $10,000. Stiver was trying to make money for a vacation with her husband, Ray, and for improvements to their house. Malahoff, who lived in New York, had wanted the child to strengthen his marriage, but he and his wife separated during the pregnancy.[2] The case became an example of the horrible possibilities such arrangements can entail when the baby was born with a handicap and both parents renounced the child. (The handicap was microcephaly—a smaller-than-normal head, which is usually indicative of retardation.) The natural mother said she felt no maternal bond for the baby, but she agreed to intravenous antibiotics to combat a life-threatening infection. Malahoff, however, instructed the hospital to "take no steps or measures to treat the strep infection or otherwise care for the infant."[3] The hospital obtained a court order authorizing doctors to treat the baby, and the infection was cured, but the baby had no home to be released to from the hospital and was placed in foster care.

The Stivers and Malahoff then went on Phil Donahue's television show to discuss their situation, and during the broadcast the results of their paternity tests were released for the first time: the surprise announcement was that Judy Stiver's husband, and not the sperm donor, was the father of the child; she had had sexual intercourse with him several days before the insemination.[4] The money for the fee, still in escrow, was returned to Malahoff; the Stivers became the baby's custodians and took the infant home; both parties went to court complaining of breaches of the contract; and both parties filed complaints against doctors and lawyers for not telling the Stivers to abstain from sex during the relevant period.[5]

Some Americans may have remained unaware of these early human dramas, but virtually everyone in the United States became acquainted during 1987 with the plight of Mary Beth Whitehead and "Baby M." Mrs. Whitehead, a twenty-nine-year-old housewife in Brick Township, New Jersey, was married to a sanitation worker, Richard, and had two children, a twelve-year-old son, Ryan, and a ten-year-old daughter, Tuesday. In a long and complex contract drafted by Noel Keane—a lawyer who practices in New York and Michigan and who had also represented the Noyeses and Mr. Malahoff—Whitehead agreed with William and Elizabeth Stern to be inseminated with William's sperm and to bear and deliver the child to them, surrendering her own parental rights. Whitehead was to be paid $10,000.

The Sterns are a professional couple who live in Tenafly, New Jersey. William Stern was a forty-year-old biochemist and his wife, who is called Betsy, a forty-one-year-old pediatrician. The Sterns had been married for twelve years and were childless. They had postponed childbearing at the outset of their marriage for financial and career reasons. Later Dr. Stern ruled out pregnancy because she had a mild case of multiple sclerosis and she heard of a colleague's wife with a similar condition becoming temporarily paralyzed when pregnant. The Sterns did not attempt to adopt. They did not talk with any adoption agencies but believed that they were unable to adopt because they were in their late thirties by the time they were seeking a child and also because they had different religions—Jewish and Methodist. Moreover, William said that he feared that an adopted child might have AIDS. He also said that he did not want a foreign child (referring to a Korean) because "the child would be different and therefore . . . would have more psychological difficulty."[6]. And Betsy said that she had misgivings about private adoption because "they would in some way need to convince a woman to relinquish her baby."[7]

Although Whitehead promised in the contract that she would form no bond with the baby, she knew in the delivery room that she could not give up her daughter. "Seeing her, holding her, she was my child."[8] "I signed on an egg. I didn't sign on a baby girl, a clone of my other little girl."[9] Whitehead refused to accept the $10,000 fee, which was to be paid to her upon delivery of the child to the Sterns, and which had been placed in escrow.

Baby M was born on March 27, 1986. The name on the birth certificate is Sara Elizabeth Whitehead, and that is what her mother's family calls her, but to the Sterns she is Melissa Stern. Baby M spent the first three days of her life in the hospital with her natural mother; then Whitehead handed her over to the Sterns in compliance with the contract. Within twenty-four hours Mary Beth Whitehead appeared on their doorstep saying that she needed to be with her baby and asking to keep the infant at least for a week. The Sterns agreed, and Baby M was taken to the Whiteheads' home in Brick Township, where she stayed for five weeks despite the Sterns' pleas for her return. At that point the Sterns in an *ex parte* hearing obtained a court order from the New Jersey

Superior Court awarding them temporary custody. The White-heads left New Jersey with the baby to avoid complying with the court decree, with Mary Beth Whitehead explaining that "she would not feel whole" if she gave up her child.[10] William Stern hired a private investigator to locate the Whiteheads, and in August the investigator found them staying with Mary Beth's mother in Florida. Along with FBI agents, he removed Baby M from the mother while her siblings and grandmother looked on. A month later the New Jersey judge continued custody in the Sterns but allowed Mary Beth Whitehead to visit Baby M for two two-hour sessions each week in a supervised setting.

The case proceeded to a much-publicized trial, entailing six weeks of testimony and half a million dollars of legal bills. A few days after Baby M's first birthday Judge Harvey Sorkow announced his decision: he granted permanent custody to the Sterns and ruled that Whitehead was to maintain no further contact with her daughter.[11] The New Jersey Supreme Court agreed to expedite the appeal and granted Whitehead visitation of two hours weekly pending the final outcome. In the meantime Whitehead divorced her husband, got pregnant again, and married Dean Gould, the father of the unborn child. Then on February 3, 1988, the New Jersey Supreme Court announced its decision: it affirmed the trial court's award of custody to the Sterns but held that paid surrogacy contracts are illegal in New Jersey.[12] That decision settled the legal status of such contractual arrangements in New Jersey, although that state's legislature is free to alter the result. But in most other states the issue remains open.

Even before the New Jersey Supreme Court decision, Whitehead had found a purpose in the role she was playing, claiming "that she has been chosen by God to show people not to do surrogate mothering."[13]

These and other cases have caused great heartache and disruption for the parties, but during the past decade many similar arrangements have been carried out according to plan, some quietly, others with much publicity. The practice of a woman's bearing a child for another couple in this way has come to be known as "surrogate motherhood," although the term is a misnomer: the "surrogate" is in fact the natural, biological mother—she both gives the egg and bears the child. Although she is the actual mother, she is in some sense acting as a "surrogate wife" for the sperm donor.[14]

Although the term is new, surrogate motherhood has been practiced for a long time. In the Bible, when Sarah, Rachel, and Leah were infertile, they gave their handmaids—Hagar, Bilhah, and Zilpah—to have babies for their husbands (Genesis 16:1–4,15; 30:1–10). Undoubtedly throughout our history there have been occasions when persons unable to have children persuaded sisters, friends, or strangers to have a baby for them. In the past decade, however, the practice has become widespread and is fast becoming a booming industry. The typical fee paid a surrogate has long been said to be $10,000—an estimate that is low. And in major cities nationwide there are now profit-making surrogacy centers, many of them run by lawyers or doctors, to which people can apply if they want to employ a surrogate or if they want to serve as one. The centers advertise aggressively for surrogates, on college campuses and elsewhere. A center usually makes a substantial sum each time it engineers a surrogacy contract; $10,000 is a typical fee.[15]

Contract surrogacy emerged around 1976. By the end of 1981 about 100 children had been born of these arrangements, and by the end of 1986 about 500.[16] As surrogate motherhood comes out into the open and is heavily publicized, it comes to seem a more legitimate and more available alternative to people wanting babies. It also comes to seem an available solution to women with a need to earn a substantial sum of money.[17] Fifteen percent of women questioned in a January 1987 Gallup poll said they would consider becoming surrogates for the standard $10,000 fee,[18] and the movement toward surrogacy may have snowballed further since then.

The typical surrogate motherhood arrangement involves a couple who want but cannot have their own biological child because the wife is infertile. In the past the only recourse was adoption, which remains the most obvious and commonly used option. Adoption, however, is notoriously more difficult today than it was in the past.[19] And a couple may feel that even if adoption is possible they prefer to find a surrogate mother, so that their child will inherit the husband-father's genes.

The typical surrogate mother is a woman in her twenties who has previously had children.[20] Some surrogates are single, but many are married and live with their husband or with their husband and children. When a surrogate motherhood arrangement is made, the woman who agrees to be the surrogate is inseminated with sperm from the man of the infertile couple, typically by artificial insemination. The mother agrees that she will turn over to the infertile couple the child so conceived. Usually she also agrees to give up all parental rights, and the expectation is that the father's wife will then adopt the child. As a result, the infertile couple legally will be the child's sole parents.

Even within this typical surrogacy arrangement, many variations are possible. For example, a couple may make an arrangement through a surrogacy agency, or advertise on their own, or make an arrangement with a friend. The insemination can be accomplished either by sexual intercourse or by artificial insemination; if artificial, it may be performed through a doctor or by the parties themselves. The couple and the surrogate may meet and even become friends, or they may remain entirely anonymous. Except when the parents have retained anonymity, the degree of subsequent contact between the surrogate mother and the child can vary considerably, even though the surrogate gives up the child for adoption.

The following chapters focus on the typical surrogacy arranged by an infertile couple, but others also may utilize surrogacy arrangements. Contracts may involve a single man, a gay male couple, or even a single woman who longs for a child and wants to inseminate a surrogate with purchased sperm. Or a married couple may have decided for reasons of convenience rather than infertility that the wife should not become pregnant. As surrogacy increases, the issues surrounding it are fast multiplying. Even proponents divide on such questions as whether surrogacy should be limited to married couples with a fertility problem. They also differ on whether surrogacy should be regulated at all, or whether instead the parties should be able to control the terms of their own bargain. Moreover, the problems that inhere in surrogacy are becoming more obvious and are increasingly finding their way into the courts.

The most dramatic problem arises when the surrogate mother decides that she wants to keep the child, as Denise Thrane and Mary Beth Whitehead did. Whether she decides early or late in the pregnancy, at the birth, or after the child is born, the ultimate issue is whether she or the infertile couple have parental rights. One reason the issue is difficult is that all the principals may be very sympathetic people, and in this conflict they all have very sympathetic positions. By changing her mind, the mother is showing maternal feelings that are surely not reprehensible. Although she has promised to give up the baby, her change of heart seems more understandable than dishonorable. The couple, on the other hand, may have been trying for a long time to have a child and are excited and happy that this one is to be theirs. They have justifiably relied on the agreement with the mother—and one of them has supplied half of the baby's genes.

How is the law to respond to this kind of problem? A jurisdiction could actively regulate or prohibit the practice of surrogate motherhood, but very few states have taken positions on surrogacy or have any clear, articulated policy.[21] Even if a state's laws are silent on the subject, disputes unavoidably come to its courts. For example, if the mother does not turn the child over at birth, and if the contracting couple are unable to persuade her to change her mind, the couple have three alternatives: (1) though sad, they may accept her decision and thereby avoid litigation; (2) they may go to court to ask its help in obtaining custody; or (3) they may employ self-help and steal the child from the mother. In the last case the mother is likely to seek the courts' help in getting the child back and in preventing future kidnapping.

As courts face disputes about the parenthood and custody of the child, how is a judge to decide in a jurisdiction whose laws are silent on the subject of surrogacy? Although it might appear that the problem is the absence of applicable law, in fact the real problem is an excess of available bodies of law. Several different bodies of law arguably are applicable, and the various possibilities lead to different results. Contract law might govern, and it might support enforcement of the parties' bargain. On the other hand, existing laws against selling babies might render the agreement illegal and might even suggest that the parties could be subject to criminal sanctions (see Chapters 1 and 5). Or laws governing adoption might be applicable and might rule out paying for the surrogate and binding the surrogate by a contract executed before her child's birth (see Chapter 6).

As an alternative to relying upon the contract, the biological father can attempt to obtain custody under laws governing the rights of a biological father who is not married to the mother of a newborn baby. Or the biological mother instead could find this law advantageous, depending upon the facts and circumstances of the various parties and also upon the uncertainties of how this law will be interpreted and will develop (see Chapters 8 and 9). Finally, state provisions concerning the rights and obligations of sperm donors could govern, in cases in which the surrogate has been artificially inseminated (see Chapter 8). A court is not, of course, limited to choosing between existing bodies of law; a judge who conceives of surrogacy as an altogether novel situation may consider it more appropriate to mold some new law to meet the needs of the situation. When a state's legislature has not made any rule, judges may fill in the gap and themselves make the law in the first instance. But at least initially, the judge may confront the problem by inquiring which of the existing bodies of law is most appropriate.

As well as considering how these existing bodies of law apply to surrogacy, the following chapters evaluate what policy we as a society should pursue in this novel area of human activity. The most important and difficult question is how society *wants* to treat surrogacy. Existing law is sufficiently flexible, and sufficiently subject to considerations of policy, that it could support any result. Lawyers may help elucidate how different possible results can be articulated, defended, and made to fit within the law. But they may not be the best group to decide what policy should be pursued.

The public should think critically about surrogacy and decide which of the sometimes-competing values at stake are most important. Popular sentiment concerning surrogacy varies enormously. On the difficult question of who should get the baby when the surrogate changes her mind, the prevailing view appears to be that "a contract is a contract"—that the surrogate should be made to abide by her promise to surrender the child (see Chapter 5). Yet there are many views, ranging from this policy of total enforcement to a preference for a total ban on surrogacy arrangements.

Surrogacy is most likely to be governed by state law, and as more states take positions on surrogacy, the rules will undoubtedly vary from one state to the next. One advantage of our federal system of government is this possibility of experimentation with a variety of systems when an issue is governed by state rather than federal law. On subjects such as surrogacy, about which we still have much to learn, such experimentation with a variety of approaches could be beneficial.

Yet if the public were intent upon preventing surrogacy, a federal law prohibiting it nationwide would be far more effective than allowing state-by-state resolution. Only if surrogacy were governed by federal law would there be a uniform nationwide approach. The choice of whether state or federal law will govern rests primarily with the Congress. A congressional enactment regulating or banning surrogacy will prevail unless the courts rule it unconstitutional. Without a federal enactment, the subject is left to the states. State legislative or judicial solutions will govern, unless the Supreme Court of the United States rules that the federal Constitution requires a particular result (see Chapter 4).[22]

One result of leaving surrogacy to be governed by state law is that people living in states that prohibit paid surrogacy, such as New Jersey, will not necessarily be denied the use of agencies and surrogate mothers in states in which it is legal. This lowest-common-denominator phenomenon—allowing the state with the least restrictive rules effectively to control the nation—is common in family law, where the lowest age for marriage, the least restrictive consanguinity rules concerning marriage, and the lowest requirements for divorce can often be used by people from all jurisdictions. If, for example, first cousins who want to marry live in a state such as Illinois or Oregon, where marriage between first cousins is not allowed,[23] they need only have the ceremony performed in a state such as Hawaii, Maryland, or South Carolina[24] that allows such marriages.[25]

Going out of state to avoid local prohibitions is not always an option, however, because some state provisions apply only to state residents; other people who wish to take advantage of those provisions must therefore first establish residency in that state. Divorce laws, for example, usually apply only to a state's own citizens;[26] and adoption, though fully available to nonresidents in some states,[27] is available only to resident prospective parents in others.[28] Still other states allow out-of-staters to adopt independently but not through an agency;[29] and a few allow them to adopt children with special needs but not other children.[30] Such provisions could easily be deemed to apply to surrogacy arrangements as well. Some people desiring to employ a surrogate have found it necessary to establish a residence in, and in some cases actually move to, a jurisdiction such as Kentucky where the courts have ruled that paid surrogacy is not illegal.[31] States also have restrictions on the export and import of children, which could sometimes be applicable in the context of out-of-state surrogacy.[32]

As well as surveying the range of plausible positions and the reasoning that supports them, I develop in the following chapters the position that seems to me to be the most just, the most workable, and the most compatible with the kind of society that we as a society should seek to develop. I would not oppose federal legislation prohibiting surrogacy. It is clear that on balance surrogacy is not a socially beneficial policy, although it does have the capacity to bring happiness to many childless couples and although some women find satisfaction by performing as surrogates. It is a close question whether surrogacy—at least paid surrogacy—should be made illegal. Even if it were made criminal to enter into a surrogacy arrangement, surrogacy would not altogether disappear, and it is possible that criminalizing surrogacy and thereby driving it underground would cause more harm than good. But whether or not a jurisdiction decides to make surrogacy arrangements illegal, I conclude that the surrogate mother should have the option to withdraw from the contract. She should not lose the option to change her mind until she freely gives the child over to the adopting couple. This proposal can find support in both adoption and contract law, but policy considerations, and not compulsion from existing legal rules or constitutional provisions, are the determinative factor in making surrogacy contracts legal but unenforceable.

Part I explores the various policy considerations at stake and the range of positions that the law could adopt concerning the effect of the surrogacy contract, as well as setting forth the proposal that surrogacy contracts be deemed legal but unenforceable. Part II discusses how custody and other issues concerning parental rights and the best interests of the child should be determined if the contractual provisions placing custody in the father and terminating the mother's rights are not enforced.

PART I

SURROGACY CONTRACTS

Enforcing surrogacy contracts like any others—like contracts for ordinary commercial services or for the exchange of a chattel—would most benefit the biological father and his wife. But it can be argued that contract law should not apply or should apply differently when a transaction involves conceiving, delivering, and surrendering a baby than when it involves barter of commercial services, or a chattel or a piece of land. In deciding what effect to accord to the surrogacy contract, a judge may look to contract law, constitutional law, and even criminal law, as well as to laws pertaining to adoption.

Contract law is a technical body of law with many rules, and disputants in surrogacy cases can frame many arguments that contract law, for one reason or another, compels the solution they happen to favor. Under traditional contract law, surrogacy arrangements would appear to be enforceable. But contract law makes exceptions for exploitation or unconscionability, and it is a familiar principle of contract law that public policy sometimes dictates that the parties' bargain not be followed or that it not be binding. Constitutional law also is indeterminate. Constitutional arguments can be formulated both to support the position that surrogacy contracts must be enforced and to support the position that they cannot be. Moreover, existing laws prohibiting baby-selling could be interpreted to encompass surrogacy arrangements, and even to make them criminal; or they could be held not to apply at all.

Despite an abundance of rules, existing law does not dictate the outcome. The ultimate issue society must face in deciding whether and how existing law applies is whether it wants to prohibit surrogacy contracts or, at the other extreme, to enforce them. Even if it avoids these extremes, it must decide whether to encourage or discourage them. In the absence of federal regulation, each state can decide for itself what policy to pursue with respect to contract law and surrogacy, and different jurisdictions are likely to adopt different policies.

The outcome will be decided by legislators or courts in accordance with their perceptions of appropriate policy. The most forceful arguments against surrogacy arrangements are that they violate public policy—that the balance of interests is such that society should invalidate the contracts. A conviction that they violate public policy could govern how contract and constitutional law apply. Reasons of public policy will probably also govern whether babyselling provisions are interpreted to apply to surrogacy. Policy determinations involve balancing society's perceived needs against the interests of the parties in making their own bargain, a process that requires both identifying those needs and evaluating their import.

Part I surveys both a range of plausible positions concerning the effect of the surrogacy contract and some considerations of policy that might influence which approach is chosen. Ultimately, it suggests reconciling the various interests by having surrogacy contracts treated as legal but unenforceable over the objection of the surrogate mother; the law would then treat surrogacy contracts the same way it now treats contracts to adopt a child.

Chapter One

Are the Contracts Illegal?

At one extreme of the spectrum of options, surrogacy could be made illegal, and even criminal. Should surrogate motherhood arrangements be viewed as illegal on grounds that they violate existing babyselling prohibitions? Alternatively, should legislatures enact statutes specifically prohibiting surrogate motherhood contracts? If so, should those few that are genuinely entered into for no compensation other than payment of expenses also be prohibited, or should surrogacy by unpaid volunteers be treated differently from surrogacy for a fee?

Babyselling

Because most surrogacy contracts involve payment of a substantial sum of money to the surrogate mother, in addition to her medical and perhaps living expenses during the pregnancy, they might be considered to violate prohibitions against babyselling. A few decades ago, many states did not criminalize babyselling. Senate hearings in 1955 showed how widespread the practice was, including extensive babyselling by prostitutes.[1] Today, a parent's surrender of a child for a fee—babyselling—is a crime in all states.[2] In addition, many states have "baby broker acts," which limit or prohibit compensation of intermediaries in connection with the transfer of a child. Surrogacy centers or attorneys who arrange surrogacy could be in violation of those statutes.[3]

Surrogacy contracts frequently describe the arrangement as one for services, for use of the mother's womb, in an attempt to avoid charges of babyselling. Proponents of surrogacy often also defend the contracts as involving pay for services in conceiving and carrying the child to term and not for the surrender of the child.[4] Others say that the arrangement involves "rent" and not the sale of a product.[5]

Obviously surrogacy contracts can be characterized either as contracts for services or as exchanges of money for a child. Whether a particular arrangement is punishable as babyselling should depend on something more substantial than the wording of any given contract. Similarly, whether the contracts should be viewed as void because they have an illegal purpose—the selling of babies—depends upon more than construction of the particular wording of a state's law. Arguments can easily be made either that surrogacy contracts violate laws against selling babies (because consideration is paid to the mother to have and turn over the child) or that these contracts are different from the babyselling at which the statute is aimed. The New Jersey Supreme Court followed the first approach, saying it had "no doubt whatsoever that the money is being paid to obtain an adoption and not . . . for the personal services of" the surrogate mother[6]: "It strains credulity to claim that these arrangements, touted by those in the surrogacy business as an attractive alternative to the usual route leading to an adoption, really amount to something other than a private placement adoption for money," which New Jersey law forbids as childselling and makes a "high misdemeanor."[7] The Supreme Court of Kentucky, however, has held that paid surrogacy arrangements do not constitute babyselling within the meaning of that state's law because the child was not conceived when the arrangement was made. Accordingly, the court said, the legislative concern with protecting expectant mothers from financial inducements to part with the child does not apply.[8] Or one might defend a babyselling charge by asking how a father can buy his own child (although even if this argument were accepted, a married father whose wife was to adopt the child could still be in violation of provisions forbidding payment of a fee to facilitate adoption).

The issue whether surrogacy arrangements constitute babyselling could come to the courts either in the form of a criminal prosecution for babyselling or in the form of a civil suit like *Baby M* in which it was argued that a surrogacy contract should not be enforced. And in Kentucky the issue arose when the state attorney general attempted to revoke the charter of a corporation engaged in the surrogacy business, on the ground that its activities were illegal. When a case occurs, logic will not select for a judge which approach to follow; instead the judge will be heavily influenced by her or his own views concerning whether the state ought to prohibit these contracts or whether instead the contracts serve a socially legitimate purpose. Similarly a legislature must address the normative issue in deciding how to regulate these arrangements, if at all.

Unpaid Surrogacy

Some contracts, such as the one between Denise Thrane and the Noyeses, specify that no compensation (beyond medical expenses) is to be paid. In many cases it is difficult to believe that no compensation is contemplated. Such a provision may have been included simply to avoid charges of babyselling, and often some payment has in fact been made or is intended.

In jurisdictions in which surrogacy is illegal—either as such or as babyselling—false recitals of no compensation will have limited effectiveness: if neither party questions the contract and all wish to perform according to its terms, the recital may make the contract appear more legal than it is. But if either party desires to back out of the surrogacy arrangement and the contract is taken to court, either party will be permitted to show that the recital is false and that the contract is therefore illegal.[9]

In most circumstances a contract specifying no compensation understandably arouses suspicions. It is difficult to understand why a woman would agree to serve as a surrogate without compensation. There are, of course, circumstances in which it is easy to believe a recital of no compensation: some surrogacy arrangements involve a sister or a good friend.[10] But even among strangers, many motives besides monetary compensation can contribute to a decision to become a surrogate mother.[11]

A frequent claim is that surrogate motherhood applicants may be compensating for an experience in their past: "surrogate mothers may have guilt over a past abortion, gratitude over being adopted themselves, the need to re-enact their own childhood abandonment or other deep psychological factors."[12] Some surrogates are "looking for love and acceptance."[13] In addition, surrogates often report that they enjoy pregnancy—they enjoy the physiological changes that take place and they like the way they are treated when they are pregnant. The process of delivering a baby can be a wondrous, though painful, experience for some people, an experience they would like to relive, even if they are unwilling or financially unable to raise another child themselves.

Women who have performed as surrogates for strangers without compensation give a range of explanations. One such woman said that she wanted to experience the "perfect birth." She had given birth to a son, but had been disappointed that the birth took place at a hospital instead of at home, and that the baby was removed from her and her husband for a few hours after birth. "My husband and I have a private joke that we would like to give birth over and over again until we got it right, but what in the world would we do with all the kids."[14] Another woman who had never been pregnant reportedly became a surrogate without compensation because her fiancé had had a vasectomy and she "wanted the experience of having a baby."[15] Another woman reportedly wanted that experience because she was a gynecologist and thought that it would make her a better doctor.[16]

Surrogacy can also be an "act of love and generosity."[17] Women who apply to be surrogate mothers, according to psychologists, are likely to be people with a high degree of empathy for others. Many of them feel the pain of the couple unable to have children, and even paid surrogates are often motivated not only by money but also by a desire to help. As one pregnant surrogate expressed it: "I'm not going to cure cancer or become Mother Teresa, but a baby is one thing I can sort of give back, something I can give to someone who couldn't have it any other way."[18] That woman's contract provided for compensation of $10,000. Another woman decided to become a paid surrogate when she was working for three obstetricians who specialized in infertility: "I saw the disappointment and the anguish that [accompany] infertility . . . It was so unfair."[19] And another paid surrogate reported: "I think being a surrogate mother has made me a better person. Never a day goes by that I don't thank the Lord for my own kids."[20]

Surrogates claim that agencies play upon this empathy in recruiting them for service, appealing to their desires for self-sacrifice and for useful service. Recruiters flatter potential surrogates into agreeing, making them feel that because of their promise to perform they will be both important and saintlike.

In most cases, altruistic or other nonmonetary considerations may play a part, but money also is an important part of the decision.[21] Mary Beth Whitehead herself showed both motivations when she answered an ad to become a surrogate mother and wrote in her application that "she was motivated to join the program in the hopes of 'giving the most loving gift of happiness to an unfortunate couple' . . . and felt that the surrogate's fee would assist her in providing for her children's long range educational goals."[22] Although a primary motive is usually monetary, there are nonetheless at least isolated cases in which the consideration is in fact limited to medical expenses, even in contracts between strangers. Noel Keane, a lawyer who specializes in arranging surrogacy contracts, reports that when he first started his surrogacy practice he operated on the assumption that the practice was legal but that in Michigan, where his practice was centered, compensation could not legally be paid. Accordingly, he limited his search for surrogates-to-be to persons willing to serve without payment. It was much more difficult to find surrogates when they could not be paid, but volunteers were found. Even among strangers, a few surrogate mothers, empathic with the dilemma of a childless couple, do seek to help, perhaps partly for psychological reasons of their own. And if we are to believe Keane's report, most of these performed as agreed, without receiving more than medical and living expenses.

Even while Keane was finding surrogates to serve without fees, he was getting paid for his services; it was (and is) considered criminal in Michigan for the surrogate to be paid, but until recently there was no such prohibition on payment to the go-between. It is a bizarre system that allows the broker to be paid (as "lawyer's fees in connection with an adoption," for example), but not the mother who produces the child. Indeed, a jurisdiction concerned with commercialization of childbearing might more reasonably make the precisely opposite judgment—that it is most important to prevent the brokers from profiting off of these transactions. Thus in 1984 a commission in England chaired by Dame Mary Warnock called for a ban on commercial surrogacy but suggested sanctions only against the agencies arranging surrogacy, whether profit-making or not-for-profit, and "professionals and others who knowingly assist in the establishment of a surrogate pregnancy."[23] Since then, legislation has been passed in the United Kingdom in accordance with those recommendations, imposing sanctions on agencies but not on the surrogate mother or the sperm donor.[24]

Not even all "unpaid" surrogate mothers truly operate without any compensation. Some are genuinely volunteers and do not profit financially from the transaction at all. But when living expenses as well as medical expenses are provided, some potential surrogates find that the expense payments offered are generous enough to serve as compensation. Agencies surely attempt to present the payment of expenses as a monetary inducement. The following classified ad, placed by the Hagar Institute in San Francisco, is illustrative: "SURROGATE MOTHER wanted to bear child for infertile couples. Artificial insemination, must be healthy, 21, given birth to healthy child(ren). *Medical expenses & living expenses ($800) pd for 10 mos.*" (emphasis added).[25] A jurisdisction truly aspiring to remove financial inducements to surrogacy should prohibit payment of all but medical expenses.

Although it has sometimes been possible to find a surrogate without paying a fee, there are not nearly enough women willing to serve as unpaid volunteers to satisfy even the current demand for surrogate motherhood, much less the potential demand that its purveyors anticipate when some states legalize and regulate it. Lawyers who make surrogacy arrangements have considered it very important that payment to the mother be allowed, realizing that without payment surrogacy would be very limited.[26] Noel Keane, for example, brought suit in Michigan attacking the application to surrogacy of laws prohibiting a fee in connection with adoption, but he lost.[27]

While surrogacy's promoters understandably want fees to be legal, the approach that Michigan and New Jersey now are pursuing—allowing surrogacy, but only if it is not paid[28]—is a plausible resolution to the surrogacy controversy. A state seriously pursuing that policy could also strictly calculate the permissible amount of recompense for expenses.[29] New Jersey and Michigan permit payment only for medical expenses.[30] Such a position would substantially cut back on surrogacy. It also eradicates its commercial aspects, and reduces possibilities of exploitation, when combined as well with a prohibition on payment to intermediaries. Yet it would still allow surrogacy as an act of love. Surrogacy then, like other means of adoption of infants today, would become a procedure available only to the lucky few.

Detecting and effectively prohibiting under-the-table payments would of course remain problems—but those problems would also exist even if all surrogacy were outlawed and the whole practice driven underground (see Chapter 7). For those worried about surrogacy's potentially harmful effects on society, it would be advantageous for the law to prohibit at least commercial surrogacy. And courts can interpret babyselling prohibitions to accomplish this result even without enactment of any additional statutes.

Making only paid surrogacy illegal would, however, lead to an odd result if unpaid surrogacy contracts were enforceable: those few surrogates who actually agreed to perform without compensation would be the most vulnerable to losing their child if they changed their mind.[31] Although it certainly makes sense not to treat unpaid surrogacy as babyselling, it would be extremely strange to force the volunteer mother to give up her child while allowing the paid mother to keep hers, if she changes her mind, because her contract is illegal and therefore unenforceable. Although it makes sense for unpaid surrogacy to be legal when paid surrogacy is not, it makes no sense for it to be enforceable when paid surrogacy is not. Nonetheless, a bill introduced in the District of Columbia in March 1987 by Democratic council member John Ray would have mandated exactly that result: it would have prohibited payment but made the surrogacy contract binding.[32] The New Jersey Supreme Court, however, avoided the problem in its *Baby M* decision by holding that unpaid surrogacy contracts, though legal, are not enforceable against the natural mother.[33] This argument suggests that it is improper to enforce unpaid surrogacy contracts *when paid surrogacy is illegal,* but does not speak to the desirability of enforcing surrogacy contracts in general. Chapter 5 will consider arguments concerning the unenforceability of both paid and unpaid surrogacy contracts that are relevant in jurisdictions that do *not* make commercial surrogacy illegal.

Chapter Two

Exploiting Women and Commercializing Childbearing

One of the most serious charges against surrogate motherhood contracts is that they exploit women. It is difficult to assess with any confidence whether surrogacy contracts are exploitative and whether exploitation is a valid reason for prohibiting these arrangements.

Does it constitute exploitation for childless persons or couples to pay women to conceive and bear children for them? Certainly the usual situation will involve a couple of considerably greater financial means than the woman who agrees to be the surrogate.[1] A conservative estimate of typical costs to the adopting couple is $25,000: $10,000 for the mother, $8,000–10,000 for the agency that arranges the procedure, and the rest for miscellaneous items such as travel, medical expenses, maternity clothes, and possibly lost wages. Any of these costs can be considerably greater. When it is necessary for the adopting couple to establish residence in another state in order to qualify as adopters, the couple must have not only considerable finances but also considerable control over their own time. Many people have jobs that are not flexible enough to allow them to move to another jurisdiction.

This is not to say that only the affluent hire surrogates. There are some less well-to-do and blue-collar families who had children this way.[2] Some have spent their life savings and mortgaged their homes in order to do so. Others have found surrogates who would perform as unpaid volunteers. Nonetheless, surrogacy is used primarily by the well-to-do—a trend likely to continue if surrogacy is to develop as an industry—and paid surrogacy as a method of *obtaining* children is clearly not available to the truly poor. Certainly in most cases children are removed from the relatively poor and given to the more affluent.

Fees can vary, just as expenses can. Most surrogacy contracts specify the monetary compensation to be paid to the woman for her services in bearing the child. Although the standard fee for some years has been $10,000, advertisements placed by persons searching for surrogate mothers or by women offering to serve as surrogates often mention a much higher price. *Boston Magazine,* for example, in 1985 ran an advertisement by a couple offering $50,000 to a "tall, trim, intelligent woman between the ages of 22 and 35" to serve as a surrogate mother for them.[3] Today it should be possible for some women, if they are sufficiently healthy and attractive, to obtain $75,000 or $100,000,[4] and the current demand for surrogacy may be only incipient.

From one perspective, generous payment for a surrogacy arrangement makes it less exploitative, and the most oppressive contracts are the low-paying ones: one women in San Diego, who fought to keep her child, was paid $1,500 to be a surrogate.[5] And perhaps the most oppressive result of all is to allow surrogacy but prohibit the payment of any fee. Such a result fits into our tradition of noncompensation for women's work.

But from another perspective, higher fees make surrogacy arrangements harder to resist for women who have no other means of livelihood, or no other means of making substantial sums of money. Should we worry that Whitehead was to receive less than half the minimum wage—earning only $1.57 an hour by one calculation[6]—or should we instead worry that large sums of money may tempt women, particularly poor women, to act against their better judgment?

Feminists divide on whether the surrogate should be prohibited from entering into the agreement even if it is appealing to her.[7] Arguably she should be able to make a living this way rather than by performing some kind of work that is more distasteful to her. Indeed if a woman is well paid for her work as a surrogate— making, say, $50,000 in addition to expenses—and if it might take her three to five years to earn such an amount in other work that is available to her, the appeal of the surrogacy arrangement is quite understandable. Accordingly, some women have repeatedly served as surrogates, producing offspring for several different couples.[8] Perhaps, then, policymakers should focus on having surrogates properly paid—substantially more than $10,000—rather than on eliminating surrogacy. But generous payment would only exacerbate the double bind that surrogacy involves for poor women: "It might be degrading for the surrogate to commodify her gestational services or her baby, but she might find this preferable to her other choices in life."[9]

Rules prohibiting surrogacy *are* protectionist toward women, but they also accord best with the kind of society we want to live in. A common attack against those who would ban surrogacy is that they are advocating legislation for women in an ideal world, whereas women in the real world need these opportunities and should be able to take advantage of them. But to portray surrogacy contracts as representing meaningful choice and informed consent on the part of the contracting surrogate mother, rather than to see her as driven by circumstances, also reveals an idealized perspective and a failure to take account of realities.

Arguments that the law should protect women against being tempted into surrogacy by generous offers of money rest largely upon a conviction that having a baby is such a personal and almost sacred thing that it should be kept outside the marketplace. A system of agencies reaping profits by arranging for surrogate mothers and of surrogate mothers earning substantial fees by having babies commercializes childbearing to the detriment of us all.

Laws against babyselling or childselling similarly intertwine the goals of protecting the poor and preserving a society in which children are not objects of barter. They reflect a judgment that we do not want a society in which people in extreme financial difficulty are tempted to sell a child or children, if they are lucky enough to have one attractive enough to produce a generous offer from a well-to-do person. Stories of families trading their three-year-old for a shiny new Cadillac chill the hearts of most of us.[10] Even if all parties are content with this transaction, societal interests counsel against it. It may or may not be in the interest of the

who are against it? the infertile unhappy couples

cf. men

particular child to prevent the exchange (depending on the characteristics of both the selling and the buying parents and upon the character of the child's relationship with her or his natural parents). It *is* in the interest of children and families *in general* for the state to foster a sense of security about them and to remove temptation by not allowing sales of family members for money.

Just as poor people are not permitted to sell their children to meet their financial needs, perhaps they should also be prohibited from contracting to use their bodies to produce a child for someone else. Our laws against prostitution also prohibit women from selling their bodies in exchange for money—partly to protect them from exploitation, partly to defend a concept of a society in which sex is too personal a matter to be made available for hire.[11] Indeed surrogacy is sometimes called "reproductive prostitution." Jenny Cassem, a twenty-eight-year-old California mother of five, recounts that when she was performing as a surrogate mother a woman in her congregation labeled her "a high-class hooker." (She responded that Mary was a surrogate for God.)[12] Others claim that surrogacy lacks the immorality of prostitution, at least when it is accomplished by artificial insemination rather than by sexual intercourse.[13]

For women to sell themselves and the products of their bodies is not unique to surrogacy, prostitution, and childselling. During the eighteenth and nineteenth centuries, poor Frenchwomen "often sold not only their bodies, but, as their charms began to fade, even their teeth—to be made into dentures for the wealthy elite."[14] Barbara Katz Rothman has suggested that reproductive technology, including surrogate motherhood, is the first step toward a "developing ideology [in which] we are learning to see our children as products, the products of conception"; moreover, "when we talk about the buying and selling of blood, the banking of sperm, the costs of hiring a surrogate mother, we are talking about bodies as commodities . . . The new technology of reproduction is building on this commodification."[15]

Surrogacy contracts commodify women and their experience of childbearing when they offer partial fees for miscarriages[16] and when they attach "a Saks Fifth Avenue price tag" to one woman because she is intelligent and attractive, while another woman receives "a K-Mart price tag."[17] Dr. Lee Salk similarly deprived Mary Beth Whitehead of her status as a person when he insisted that she was a "surrogate uterus and not a surrogate mother."[18] As well as objectifying her,[19] Salk's description also reveals a remarkable tendency to look at a person solely in terms of the role she plays for the father.

A current issue that is somewhat analogous to surrogacy is whether people should be permitted to sell organs that others vitally need—such as a kidney—for an enormous fee. In discussions of surrogacy, the question often arises whether such sales of organs should be allowed, encouraged, or outlawed. Although there are obviously certain common issues with surrogacy, including the ethics of such a practice that is available only to the wealthy, there is more of an affirmative state interest in allowing the sale of organs, since presumably it makes possible the continuation of life for someone who is already in existence. There is a state interest in preserving lives in being, but there is no similar state interest at this time in encouraging more births. Even so, the accepted position is that "the purchasing of organs . . . is inappropriate because of the potential for abuse,"[20] a position that has left family members as the primary organ donors. That position is analogous to the one the New Jersey Supreme Court adopted in *Baby M* for surrogacy: sale and purchase are illegal, but donation is allowed.

One common issue with respect to prostitution, childselling, and surrogate motherhood is whether legally prohibiting such arrangements is too protectionist, when the arrangements are satisfactory to the people who enter into them. Why should women not be allowed to use their bodies—or sell their children—to make money rather than engage in other work, if that is what they want? "The right to be a prostitute is as important as the right not to be one. It is essentially the right to set the terms of one's own sexuality, plus the right to earn a good living."[21] It is patronizing to women, and a threat to their rights, for government or society to assume the role of protecting them from doing what they want to do. On this theory, a national association of surrogate mothers called Surrogates by Choice has been formed to promote surrogate motherhood and to protect women's right to play that role.[22]

But just as the practice of surrogacy is both exploitative and liberating, so are antisurrogacy laws both patronizing to women and also arguably necessary to help build the kind of society we want to live in. There are some types of things that our society does not want measured in terms of money. Society may want to do what it can to help people keep these in a personal sphere that is distinct from the commercial; indeed it may even compel them to do so, to the extent that it can. This approach could support an argument that surrogate motherhood contracts should be illegal, just as prostitution and babyselling are, although reasonable persons would disagree about just how compelling such an argument is.[23]

The next two chapters also consider various policy arguments that can be made for prohibiting surrogacy (and perhaps also other alternative reproductive techniques), but couples who need or want surrogacy would argue that the prohibition is questionable in view of surrogate mothers' own eagerness to enter into the arrangements and that any harm is sufficiently speculative that it is outweighed by the obvious benefit that surrogacy arrangements provide. For there is a clear benefit to couples who may not be able to obtain a baby, and who surely will not be able to obtain a baby with whom they have any biological connection, without a surrogate motherhood arrangement. This process of predicting future developments and balancing the potential detriments of surrogacy against its anticipated benefits will ultimately determine whether courts and legislatures make surrogacy legal or illegal.

Advocates of surrogacy want it to be recognized by law and regulated, and they anticipate a surrogacy boom when that occurs.[24] At the extreme, surrogacy could become more widespread and over time fully socially acceptable. In that scenario, there is some risk that surrogacy would create an underclass of breeder women. Women generally might acquire an option to decide whether to carry a child themselves or to use a surrogate to do it for them. One can imagine career reasons, medical reasons, reasons of convenience, or a simple fear of or distaste for pregnancy that would lead women to decide to forego pregnancy. Indeed surrogacy-by-choice could become such a norm that employers would pressure

future ?

women to employ a surrogate rather than allow their own pregnancy to inconvenience their employer or impede their career. Employers might, for example, confer health insurance that would cover hiring a surrogate instead of giving women maternity leave. Such a scenario may belong to the future, but even in the short term, surrogacy is likely to become much more widespread than it is, and its growth will undoubtedly influence popular attitudes about it.

If surrogacy is allowed and regulated, one issue that inevitably will be debated is whether it should be reserved for infertile childless couples or whether it should be more widely available. Surprisingly few of the current legislative proposals contain any provision limiting access to surrogacy,[25] but some people would limit access to married couples, or to infertile married couples. Even when the law imposes no rule, individual doctors or agencies arranging surrogacy may themselves decide to limit the availability of their services to married couples or to infertile married couples.

The same issue has long been recognized with respect to adoption. Many adoption agencies accept as adoptive parents only infertile couples,[26] although that practice has been subject to criticism.[27] That debate is informative, but the issue might be resolved differently with respect to the adoption of existing children than with respect to surrogacy, because adoption deals with a limited supply of available children. Even if agencies simply state a preference for infertile couples and do not eliminate others from consideration, the limited supply of healthy infants in this country means that infertile couples alone will succeed in adopting them. In surrogacy, by contrast, there is no inherent limit upon the number of "adopters," and all types of would-be parents can freely use surrogates, unless some regulation eliminates particular groups.

When the issue arises with respect to surrogacy, singles, gays, and couples with some reason for wanting surrogacy other than infertility will have an important stake in demonstrating the unfairness of limiting access to surrogacy to infertile couples. Some fertile women have medical conditions incompatible with pregnancy or carry genetic disease that would be harmful to a child. And some fertile couples with less need for surrogacy might nonetheless want access to it in order to increase their options. Moreover, some single persons, men and women, would not be able to have their own biological child in any other way; they need surrogacy as much as infertile couples do, if they are to have a child at all. The next chapter suggests that access to surrogacy and to the new reproductive technologies should not be limited to married couples or to married couples with fertility problems. But that proposal carries with it a potential for increased demand for surrogacy, which is troublesome to those worried about the exploitation and commercialization that surrogacy arrangements entail.

Today it is primarily the affluent who can afford to hire a surrogate. As interest in surrogacy grows and the surrogacy business develops, many may turn to Third World women to perform for a much smaller fee.[28] It is already not unusual for Americans to look abroad for surrogate mothers. Great Britain's recent ban on commercial surrogacy arrangements was in part a reaction to Americans' use of Englishwomen as surrogate mothers (see Chapter 5). And the possibility of using Third World women has already not escaped surrogacy's promoters.[29]

Chapter Three

Do New Reproductive Techniques Threaten the Family?

I t is sometimes difficult to identify exactly what it is about surrogate motherhood that disturbs people. Fears about commercialization of childbearing and childrearing obviously play a role, as do fears of exploitation of women and of the poor. But equally important is a fear that surrogacy involves an attack on our concept of the family.

The picture of a mother handing over her child and getting paid for it does not fit easily with current values or with conventional notions of family. Surrogacy is also destructive to families in more tangible ways. For example, it must inevitably harm the older children whom most surrogates have. How can a mother explain to her children that she is giving away or selling their newborn sister?[1] How can she make them believe that they do not also have a price tag? If the infant is "a clone" of one of her other children, as Whitehead said Baby M was, will that not have a powerful effect?[2] Often the surrogate's parents and even her in-laws are also very upset that their grandchild is being given away or sold, and the conflict can cause a permanent rift in the family. When Lisa Walters, a Wisconsin housewife, performed as a surrogate, her in-laws threatened a court action to remove her other two children on grounds of unfitness.[3]

Beyond such harms to family life, surrogacy poses threats to the family as we know it. Other new reproductive techniques are like surrogacy in this respect, and they also tend to undermine our concept of the family. Moreover, they can be used in connection with surrogacy and can increase its impact by making surrogacy useful to more people. Some would prohibit or regulate surrogacy as part of a general prohibition or regulation of new reproductive techniques, rather than devising rules for surrogacy as a distinct category. The following paragraphs describe some of the new techniques and the issues they pose and then examine their potential impact upon our conceptions of ourselves and our families.

For all of its social complications, surrogacy is technologically the simplest of the various alternative reproductive techniques in use today. In fact when it relies upon natural sexual intercourse between the surrogate-to-be and the man who desires a child, it uses no technology at all. Usually, however, surrogacy arrangements use artificial insemination as the means of impregnating the surrogate.

Artificial insemination, the oldest and simplest of reproductive techniques other than sexual intercourse, has been in use for more than a century.[4] The procedure, which involves depositing ejaculated sperm in a woman's uterus with a needleless syringe, is usually performed by a doctor, but it is sufficiently simple that individuals can perform it by themselves; some individuals in surrogacy cases have performed artificial insemination privately.[5]

Artificial insemination has most commonly been used apart from surrogacy, primarily by married couples. A woman may be inseminated with her husband's sperm (AIH) in order to improve her chances of conceiving, or with sperm from a third-party donor (AID) when the husband is sterile or does not wish to pass on his genes. Single women who want children also use AID. Usually when a doctor performs AID, the donor and the woman who is inseminated remain anonymous to each other. Some private inseminations also preserve the parties' anonymity; for example, a go-between can retrieve sperm from the donor without revealing the source to the donee or the donee's identity to the donor. But often when the insemination is privately accomplished, the parties are known to each other.

Some raise moral objections to artificial insemination: "to beget, without the possibility of a continuing father-child relationship, would be to withdraw biological potential from personal potential—to reverse the long process of evolution by which biological capacities have been humanized. In a defined sense, therefore, the donor's action, made possible by human science, is anti-human."[6] But artificial insemination is generally accepted as legally permissible; there is substantially more regulation of it than of other alternative reproductive techniques, and the rules are comparatively clear (see Chapter 8).

Certain difficult questions are common to artificial insemination and other modern reproductive techniques—for example, whether artificial insemination should be available to facilitate parenthood for anyone other than married couples. Many doctors today refuse to inseminate unmarried women, and in some areas of the United States, it is still difficult for single women to find doctors who will inseminate them.[7] But even where regulations or medical practices concerning artificial insemination are highly restrictive, they cannot easily mold social policy because artificial insemination is so easy to accomplish privately. In that way it is analogous to conventional sexual intercourse: State policy historically has been to limit to married couples sexual intercourse and the childbearing that results from it, but antifornication laws have limited effectiveness.

Newer, more controversial reproductive techniques raise social issues similar to those raised by surrogacy and also can be used in combination with surrogacy. So used, they make even more staggering the prospects for change.

A decade ago the first "test-tube baby" was born, and in vitro fertilization (IVF) showed its potential to revolutionize our view of our families and ourselves. The term *in vitro fertilization* usually refers to the process by which a doctor stimulates a woman's ovaries, removes several eggs in a procedure called a laparoscopy, and fertilizes them in a Petri dish. After the fertilization, there are several options. Two or three days later, when each egg has divided a few times—usually into four-, six-, or eight-cell masses—the doctor can transfer the eggs to the uterus of the woman providing the eggs, with the hope of producing a "test-tube baby" nine months later. Although thousands of babies have by now been born by use of this procedure, the success rate is low; as of 1986, of "over 120 IVF programs . . . in the United States . . . most

programs have not yet had a pregnancy and even the best programs have less than a twenty percent success rate per laparoscopy
cycle."[8]

A different use of the IVF procedure is to transfer the fertilized
ova to the uterus of a woman other than the egg donor. Doctors
have recently become capable of accomplishing such a transfer.[9]
"Ovum donation," as it is sometimes called, can be accomplished
either by in vitro fertilization or instead by fertilizing the ovum in
the donor, allowing it to develop a short time, and then washing it
out and transferring it to the uterus of the gestational mother. This
procedure has a greater success rate than in vitro fertilization. The
first baby so conceived was born in January 1984.[10] Neither in
vitro fertilization nor ovum donation has been regulated to date.

Either of these procedures, in which a baby is conceived with the
sperm and egg of husband and wife and carried to term by another
woman, raises questions about the meaning of the genetic tie that
are even more pressing than in the classic case of surrogate
motherhood. When the egg is donated by one woman and incubated in another, the intention might be either that the gestational mother would act as mother to the child, or that the egg
donor, perhaps unable to bear the child herself, would be the
child's mother. Indeed the term *surrogate mother* is more appropriate in this latter situation than in the context in which it is
typically used; when the parties intend the egg donor to act as the
mother, the gestational mother is more of a "surrogate." And the
resultant child, though carried to term by the surrogate mother,
inherits the genes of both the mother and the father of the couple
intending to act as parents after birth.

On October 1, 1987, a gestational surrogate in South Africa
gave birth to her own grandchildren. Their story illustrates the
complications that surrogacy can bring to traditional family structure, and it also shows the family values that surrogacy can serve.
Pat Anthony bore triplets from ova supplied by her daughter Karen and fertilized in vitro by Karen's husband's sperm. Mrs. Anthony is recognized as the legal mother in South Africa, even
though she has a weaker case for motherhood than the surrogate
who provides the egg as well as the incubation. Karen, the egg
donor, legally has three new siblings. But all plan for Karen and

her husband to adopt the children, so she will become their mother instead of their sister and Mrs. Anthony will change from mother to grandmother. And in a cartoon welcoming their birth, one triplet claims to be the others' uncle.[11]

Why not welcome these new developments? They are being used to *create* families for couples who could not procreate without them. Why, then, should they be seen as undermining our family structure? The Roman Catholic church, which objects to separating sex from procreation, says it threatens the sanctity of the traditional family unit for a third party to have "any role in donating or in gestating the child." From this perspective surrogacy is objectionable because one of the genetic parents will not be part of the child's family unit. But this objection does not explain *why* it is important that the childrearing function not be separated from the genetic tie. The reasons for the church's objections to creating babies without sex are less evident than its reasons for condemning sex without babies. And the practice of adoption, which the Catholic church supports, similarly involves separation of childbearing and childrearing.[12] (A response, of course, is that adoption is laudatory but is not analogous to surrogacy or other methods of creating children because it addresses the needs of children already in existence. Adoption therefore raises very different issues from the questions of what arrangements society should sanction for the creation of children and whether society should strive to keep the biologically related family as the norm.)

Modern reproductive technology is now being used to serve the desires of childless couples to achieve a nuclear family, but potentially it can make the traditional nuclear family even less of a norm than it now is. The threat to the nuclear family is a sufficient reason to many religious groups, political movements, and individuals for opposing surrogate motherhood. Others, conscious of the injustices and inequities the traditional family structure has wrought,[13] would laud the change in social structure that new reproductive approaches would entail. Whether preservation or destruction of the traditional family is the preferable goal,[14] it is important at least to isolate exactly what the objections to modern reproductive technology are.

The problems modern technology entails are various and profound. They challenge not only what remains of the traditional nuclear family as a norm, but even our ways of thinking about ourselves and our families. One set of problems concerns how to regulate the embryo conceived in vitro or the newly conceived embryo that has been flushed out of the egg donor. What limits should society place upon how long an embryo developing in a Petri dish can be kept alive outside the womb? If there are no limits, then if and when scientists develop the technological capability they will be able to create people in this way—a development that would fundamentally alter our conception of human life.

Today we lack the technology fully to develop a baby outside the womb. A basic issue that we face today is whether there is a moral obligation—and whether there should be a legal obligation—to transfer all fertilized ova to a receptive uterus. The case for transfer is that each of the fertilized ova represents "life" in some sense; if they can survive only through transfer to a woman's body, those who oppose abortion on "right-to-life" grounds would predictably also oppose death for any of these embryos, arguing that they should not be created in the first place unless transfer is assured. Some programs accordingly require transfer of all fertilized ova—at least all that are developing normally. That policy is not difficult for a program to follow as long as care is taken not to fertilize too many eggs, perhaps not even all that have been removed. Arguably, however, it is not necessary to regard the newly fertilized extracorporeal ovum as "life." The chances that any particular such ovum will actually develop to term are slight, even if the ovum is transferred to a uterus; indeed its chances of survival and development are much lower than those of an equally long-lived embryo conceived and carried inside its mother.

In vitro fertilization also raises abortion issues in a much more direct way. The birth on January 12, 1988, of the first American quintuplets conceived through IVF[15] opened up a different debate. The quintuplets—four girls and a boy—were born to Michele L'Esperance and her husband, Raymond, in Royal Oak, Michigan. All babies seemed healthy, despite having been delivered by caesarean section two months prematurely. Mrs. L'Esperance had needed in vitro fertilization because her fallopian tubes had been removed. Fifteen eggs had been taken from her ovaries; seven fertilized ova, selected on the basis of healthiness, were transferred to her uterus; and five had developed fully. This was an unusually high survival ratio.[16]

Although Mrs. L'Esperance was permitted to carry to term, doctors generally consider it risky for a woman to bear more than three or four babies at one time, and when they have transferred more than that number of fertilized ova to the mother and all ova seem to be surviving, many of those doctors will abort "the excess." Some doctors want to avoid such selective abortions, fearing they will produce controversy and cause IVF to be regulated. But on moral grounds they believe these selective abortions are unassailable, because their purpose is to preserve life—to enable the remaining fetuses to survive.[17]

It would be possible to avoid both this abortion debate and the ethical problems raised by the destruction of fertilized ova by not fertilizing more than four eggs at a time and then transferring them all. One cost would be that fewer women would produce a child in any particular cycle—even fewer women than do now. And even though programs can adapt to a mandatory transfer policy, there are difficulties in having such a rule. Inevitably, on rare occasions a woman who has given the eggs with the intention of having them implanted in her uterus will change her mind, or become ill, or even die. But the real problem with having a mandatory transfer policy is that it will severely restrict possibilities for research and experimentation.

Should we allow these embryos to be the subjects of experimentation and research? Research involving artificially conceived embryos can contribute to medical advances in genetic disease, infertility, cancer, birth defects, and other areas. It can help save other fetuses and also people already in existence. Brain tissue transplants from aborted fetuses have recently contributed dramatically to the treatment of Parkinson's disease, for example. But ethicists fear that such uses of fetuses could create personal and commercial motives for women to conceive and abort; fetuses would become "organ farms."[18] And if it is legitimate to perform research on embryos that exist outside a woman's body, it is important to decide also what limits should be placed on how an extracorporeal embryo may be treated, and how long researchers should be entitled to keep the embryos alive.

Positions vary concerning the legitimacy of embryo research. The Vatican condemns it. Many groups that have considered the issues—including Britain's Warnock Committee, the American Fertility Society's Ethics Advisory Committee, and the authors of the Waller Report in Australia—have decided that it should be permitted but should be subject to prior review and should continue for only fourteen days after conception.[19] Research is proceeding on this basis in the United Kingdom, but it has been effectively halted in this country by denying federal funding despite the favorable reports. Similarly, research—and even tissue and organ transplants—using aborted fetuses is legal here in the United States, but federal funding requires prior review, and there is currently a moratorium on funding experiments transplanting fetal tissue.[20]

The rationale for the fourteen-day line is that it normally takes about that long for a fertilized egg to implant naturally in the uterine wall. Before implantation, there is a reduced likelihood of an egg's survival; in addition, other physiological and neurological facts about this stage of development can justify allowing research before implantation but not afterward.[21] Moreover, the fourteen-day limit has the advantage of allowing a period for research but not too long a period. Some, however, suggest a later cut-off time for research, such as the time when the fetus begins to be sentient and capable of experiencing pain.[22]

Discussion of research on embryos produced in vitro usually assumes that there is no requirement that all fertilized eggs be transferred to a woman's body for development; research can obviously be more adventuresome if there is no worry about deleterious effects upon an embryo that might develop into a child. Advocates of such research assume that the duty that is owed an embryo that will be transferred to a woman's uterus is not present when there is no intention to effect a transfer;[23] in the latter situation, research can proceed unchecked—at least for a fourteen-day period.

There are some situations, however, in which doctors and scientists might want to perform research and experimentation upon an ovum and attempt to develop it to term—and those possibilities raise yet another ethical dilemma and another potential legal problem. One consequence of removing the embryo from the woman's body is the possibility for broad genetic experimentation and manipulation. At a minimum, it is foreseeable that parents may want the opportunity to decide, after genetic analysis of the various fertilized ova, which of the eggs should be transferred. It is already the practice even in mandatory transfer programs not to transfer "defective" eggs, even though treating newborn "defective" offspring less favorably than healthy offspring is constitutionally questionable.[24] It is a small step from this practice to diagnosing for hereditary disease before implantation, or even to allowing the parents to select the gender of their offspring.

If society is to allow research at all, it must also decide for what purposes it will allow embryos to be created. Today the usual purpose of IVF is to enhance the opportunity for pregnancy of the woman from whom the eggs have been removed. When using the procedure for this purpose, is it permissible to superovulate—to produce and retrieve more eggs than predictably will be used on the particular occasion? One reason to do so might be to avoid a subsequent laparoscopy if initial attempts at conception or implantation were unsuccessful. An additional purpose might be to produce extra ova and extra embryos for purposes of research. Indeed, apart from superovulating women who are undergoing laparoscopy anyway, is it permissible to arrange for egg donation from women who are not seeking pregnancy, when the principal aims are experimentation or research? Although current research on extracorporeal embryos is limited, the possibilities for mass production of Petri-dish embryos for a large scale program of research and experimentation exist, once the legal and ethical concerns are resolved. That development could possibly create a profitable occupation for women willing to sell their eggs.

Finally, is it permissible to store and preserve a fertilized ovum, either for future implantation or for future research? Modern medicine is capable of freezing a fertilized egg indefinitely, without any known harm to the embryo eventually transferred. It would be difficult to combine this practice with a mandatory transfer policy, since the contingencies that might make donors unavailable or cause them to change their mind about producing offspring are much more likely to occur over a period of years than during the forty-eight-to-seventy-two-hour period usually involved between IVF and transfer. But with or without mandatory transfer, the freezing and storing of fertilized ova raise a multitude of unprecedented legal questions and entanglements and could undoubtedly cause fundamental social changes. The time may come, for example, when there is a commercial market for frozen embryos created from the genes of celebrities.

One of the more obvious possibilities that embryo storage creates is transfer of the embryo after the parents have died. (The same possibility exists, of course, with frozen sperm, which can be used after the father has died. In 1984 Corinne Paipalaix, a twenty-two-year-old secretary from Marseilles, asked a sperm bank to turn over to her sperm deposited by her husband before his death from cancer in 1983. The issue was controversial, but a French court approved her request.)[25] Indeed, many years might elapse between the death of both the egg and sperm donors and the transfer of the embryo to the uterus of another woman. Issues about whether an embryo transfer after the donors' deaths is permissible, or even required, received much public attention a few years ago in the case of the frozen Rios embryos. In 1981 Mario and Elsa Rios of Los Angeles had gone to Melbourne, Australia, for in vitro fertilization. Three of Mrs. Rios' eggs were fertilized; one was transferred to her and resulted in a miscarriage; the others were frozen. Two years later, both Mr. and Mrs. Rios were killed in a Chilean plane crash, and they had left no instructions for disposition of the fertilized eggs. Is transfer mandatory, is it prohibited, or is it optional—and, if optional, who is to make the decision?[26]

Is the frozen embryo a person who can inherit when her genetic parents die, so that if later transferred and carried to term she will be heir? It is difficult to imagine how the law of estates could adjust to the resulting long-term uncertainties about whether or not heirs would be produced.[27] This is but one example; long-term storage has innumerable possibilities for jarring family relationships; this seems inevitable when a person born may have been parented by persons who lived many years before. One way to reduce the difficulties considerably, if freezing and storing are accepted, would be to consider the gestational mother the sole legal parent in the event of transfer, since she alone will necessarily be present at the time of birth. If it seems important to locate rights in one person—in order to have a clear rule, rather than deciding custody on a case-by-case basis—that person should be the gestational mother.[28] Whether or not that suggestion is accepted, the new biological techniques will compel society to consider—as both a philosophical and a legal question—the degree of importance to attach to genetic ties.

Embryo storage, experimentation, and research also dramatically increase the possibilities of altering the embryos' genetic characteristics. The need to formulate policies permitting, prohibiting, or otherwise regulating genetic experimentation becomes imperative.

Even apart from genetic manipulation, this combination of new biological possibilities has staggering implications for our social structure. Many of the problems posed by surrogate motherhood assume much larger proportions if IVF and embryo storage are also available. Most important, the ability to use women simply as gestational mothers dramatically increases the appeal of surrogacy. Parents entirely capable of producing their own biological child by themselves could acquire the option of producing a child who is genetically linked to *both* parents without the necessity of undergoing pregnancy or childbirth. If this possibility leads to a sharp increase in demand for surrogates, including gestational surrogates, the exploitation not only of the domestic poor but also of Third World women is likely to mushroom; it does not seem farfetched to imagine that there will one day be a thriving business of sending frozen sperm and frozen embryos around the world to be transferred to childbearers for the production of children for contracting couples.[29]

Many people who have no objections to the current use of modern reproductive techniques to bring happiness to childless couples would nonetheless be alarmed by some of the possibilities that the new technology offers. Current ethical objections to surrogacy reflect a reasonable prediction that the means we are now using to make the traditional family possible for those who cannot otherwise achieve it carry with them the seeds of destruction of the concept of family as we know it. Of course our views will undoubtedly change as practices change, and future generations will see these issues very differently.[30] It is reasonable to expect that such fundamental views as the merits of genetic manipulation, our notions concerning family, and even what it means to be human will develop and change. It seems inevitable that without regulation modern technology will take this course, and that if we leave technology and individual initiative unchecked, it will be difficult to contain the revolution that will follow.

This prognosis has led to a perceived need to develop rules to contain or at least to regulate modern reproductive techniques, including surrogacy. Rules are needed both for the short term and the long term, and the choices that are made may have profound implications for how society will develop. But the unusual and difficult aspect of devising regulations for these subjects is that society is largely ignorant of the subjects to be regulated. Eliminating the new technological choices, even if that could be accomplished, would cut off our knowledge and prevent society from learning what technologies can accomplish and what social problems they will actually involve. The need for experimentation with different approaches may weight the balance in favor of state rather than nationwide regulation. As with surrogacy, in the absence of federal regulation modern reproductive practices are governed by the varying rules of different states—or by the states' failure to formulate any rules.

Jurisdictions cannot decline to have any policy, because a choice of no regulation also has consequences. If the law remains silent, the resulting uncertainty may slow down modern reproductive techniques; on that theory, proponents of surrogacy have supported explicit legalization and regulation. But the absence of regulation also allows all reproductive techniques to develop unchecked.

With or without regulation, modern reproductive technology may sharply transform our future. Once technology has developed the capability of doing something that will add to the happiness of some people, it is likely that the new technological arts will be pursued. Even if we as a society tried to prevent the transformation that the new technology is bringing, we might not be able ultimately to stave it off. As long as some governments permit surrogacy or reproductive technologies, some people can travel to where they are available. Moreover, they can use the technologies from afar by simply transporting their sperm, egg, or embryo. Accordingly, it is likely that in time the new technology will bring the opportunity to many more people to become a biological parent. And for fertile women, conventional childbearing will become only one choice available out of many. Singles and couples will be able to choose whether to parent, whether to donate the genetic material for the child, and whether to undergo pregnancy, and those options will exist independently of one another. For Professor Marjorie Schultz, this transformation from a time when parenting is determined by fate and chance to a time when it will be determined by decisionmaking is a positive development. Accordingly, she suggests that contracts—mutually binding contracts—are an appropriate medium for decisionmaking concerning childbearing and childrearing.[31]

Conceivably, at some future time people will have very different attitudes toward childbearing than we do today, and they will consider it suitable for the law to recognize a contract that binds all parties at the outset to a custody determination that they, represented by counsel, have agreed to in advance. But even if this future is inevitable, there is no need to hasten it by enforcing surrogacy contracts today. Regulating and even limiting the new reproductive possibilities may mold the form they take and perhaps even substantially slow down the transformation they will bring.

Chapter Four

Constitutional Arguments— For and Against

Instead of deciding surrogacy issues on the basis of the law and policy of the states, judges could look for guidance from the U.S. Constitution. Constitutional arguments can be made on both sides of the classic surrogacy dispute involving the mother who changes her mind about giving up her child. Resolution of the constitutional issues will depend ultimately upon assessing and weighing the various factors at stake. Like decisions based upon contract and criminal law, constitutional decisions will take account of the parties' interests, the child's interests, society's interests, and the effectiveness of legalization and regulation as opposed to prohibition.

If the U.S. Constitution were held to protect surrogacy contracts, the laws and courts of the states would have to conform and surrogacy could not be unlawful. But if the Constitution were held not to protect surrogacy, any state could protect or prohibit it under its own constitution or laws. By contrast, interpreting the Constitution to make it *un*constitutional to enforce surrogacy contracts would create a rule of unenforceability that would prevail in all states.

Arguments That Surrogacy Contracts Are Constitutionally Protected

At the other extreme from being illegal, are surrogate motherhood contracts constitutionally protected, so that a state must allow them to be made and must lend its enforcement mechanisms to them at least on a par with other contracts? An infertile couple who arrange to have a baby through a surrogate might argue that any state interference with their surrogacy arrangement is unconstitutional.[1] The right to procreate is a "fundamental right" protected by the Constitution.[2] The father-husband—or the couple—are exercising this right in the principal way available to them, given the wife's infertility.

A common form of the constitutional argument is that the state denies the husband, or the couple, equal protection of the laws in violation of the Fourteenth Amendment when it does not allow them to reproduce through a surrogacy arrangement. Equal protection doctrine provides that the state may not arbitrarily draw distinctions between persons who are similarly situated, and it requires substantial reasons for any such distinction that interferes with a person's fundamental rights.

The couple might contend that it is discriminatory to prohibit surrogacy and thereby limit having children, at least children to whom they are biologically connected, to couples who can have children naturally. But the argument that the state has arbitrarily distinguished between couples it will permit to have children is difficult to sustain, partly because it is not the action of the state that has made the wife infertile. In one sense, the state has one rule for all—that all can have children naturally but not for hire—and that rule is probably not vulnerable to attack under the equal protection clause. Even though the couple are hurt by that rule, it is not unreasonable for the state to distinguish between pregnancy achieved naturally and pregnancy for hire, if they are substantially different things.

A more common equal protection argument attacks antisurrogacy legislation because it treats even couples who are infertile differently from one another. Since the state allows couples in which the man is sterile to have the biological child of the woman through artificial insemination, it is a violation of equal protection, according to this argument, for the state to prohibit an arrangement whereby a couple could have the husband's biological child when it is the wife who is infertile. As one advocate of surrogacy has claimed, artificial insemination and surrogacy are the same except for "the plumbing."[3]

The problem with this argument too is that what one kind of infertile couple must do to obtain the child they desire is significantly different from what the other type of couple must do. The state would be preventing the couple from arranging to have the husband's child, not because of any purpose to prevent them from having a child, but rather because of the burden such an arrangement places upon the surrogate mother. It is reasonable for the state to differentiate between surrogacy and artificial insemination in this respect because so much more is required of the surrogate mother than is required of the semen donor.[4] Whereas the surrogate mother must be artificially or naturally inseminated, become pregnant, carry the child for nine months, and undergo labor and delivery, the semen donor need only masturbate, ejaculate into a clean container, and hand over his sperm. The sperm donor typically does not even know whether his donation has resulted in offspring or not. The differing burdens on the sperm donor and the surrogate mother are reflected also in the amount of consideration usually paid: whereas the surrogate mother's recompense is generally in the thousands of dollars, the semen donor receives $50 to $100 for one specimen.[5]

These differences in effort and responsibility give the state adequate reason to distinguish between artificial insemination and surrogacy, even though the resulting rule harms couples with an infertile wife much more than couples with an infertile husband. A judge need not agree with a distinction to find it constitutionally valid. The judge need only believe that reasonable persons could make the judgment. One may reasonably believe that as a matter of policy the correct course is to make surrogacy arrangements available to couples who need them, but it is extremely difficult to sustain an argument that the opposite course would violate the constitutional guarantee of equal protection of the laws.

The trial judge in *Baby M* did, however, rely in part on the equal protection argument, ruling that it is constitutionally impermissible to distinguish between the sperm donor and the surrogate: "Currently, males may sell their sperm. The 'surrogate father' sperm donor is legally recognized in all states. The surrogate mother is not. If a man may offer the means for procreation then a woman must equally be allowed to do so. To rule otherwise denies equal protection of the law to the childless couple, the surrogate whether male or female and the unborn child."[6] But the New Jersey Supreme Court rejected the argument, stressing the differences between the sperm donor and the surrogate mother.[7]

A couple seeking to enforce a surrogacy contract can make essentially the same argument through use of the due process clause. As it has been interpreted during the past thirty years, the due process clause protects the right to procreate,[8] recognizes it as a right of considerable importance, and would not allow the state to burden it unreasonably. The New Jersey Supreme Court sharply restricted the due process argument in *Baby M.* The contracting father had argued that his constitutional right to procreate required enforcing the surrogacy contract, but the court ruled that his right of procreation was not relevant. According to the court, his right to procreate had been fully exercised when the surrogate was artificially inseminated and a child with his genes was produced. The right to the custody and companionship of that child had nothing to do with the right to procreate, the court ruled, and those rights could not determine the controversy in his favor, because the natural mother shared those rights equally.[9]

Any argument from the due process clause must therefore assert that there is a right to procreate a child of whom one presumptively has custody—a more difficult proposition than a simple right to reproduce oneself. But if a court accepted that construction of the due process right, that argument would seem preferable to the equal protection one, because the due process argument does not have to rely upon the weak analogies with artificial insemination, or with couples who have children naturally, that the equal protection argument requires. While escaping those analogies, the due process argument incorporates the same points that the right to have a child is very important to the contracting couple and that it is important that they have available this means of exercising it. To succeed with the argument, the couple must also maintain that the state does not have good reasons for prohibiting surrogacy contracts, which are entered into between willing parties.

The chief obstacle to prevailing with the due process argument will be the need to show that the state's reasons for prohibiting surrogacy are so insubstantial in comparison to the importance of the right to the infertile couple and others like them, that the state should not be permitted to prohibit the arrangement even if its legislature so desires.[10] The interests of women who want to be surrogates, if they are regarded as substantial, would also be a factor (see Chapter 2). In any event, the interests to be weighed in a due process analysis are the same as when a policy choice is being made in the first instance. The ultimate questions are whether the arrangement does real harm, whether it is the kind of harm the state should or is entitled to protect against, and whether the harm outweighs the interests of people who need or want surrogacy.

In assessing the needs of an infertile couple one persistent issue is how to view a desire to give one's own genes to a child rather than to have a child who is not biologically related. Should the state respect the desire to pass on one's own genes when it legislates on the subject of alternative reproductive techniques? Or is such a desire narcissistic and egotistical?

William Stern turned to surrogacy shortly after the death of his mother, his last living relative. Stern said he felt "compelled" to continue his family's bloodline, which was threatened with extinction because, aside from his parents, all his relatives had been killed in the Holocaust.[11] Another contracting father came to surrogacy explaining that it was important for him to continue his bloodline (and to have a son!) because he never really got to know his father, who had died when he was six.[12]

Whether one is sympathetic with these motives or not, a desire to reproduce oneself is never the healthiest motivation for wanting to have a child. And there are difficulties especially in the surrogacy situation when an important part of the motivation of the men who contract with the surrogate is the desire to hand down their genes. Unlike pregnancy within marriage, which usually involves the couple's desire to intermingle and duplicate the genetic material of both partners, the father in the surrogacy arrangement is focused upon only half the genes that will make up his child. If his daughter closely resembles her natural mother and not her father, will the father feel he got a bad bargain? If such a reaction is likely, then at least one aspect of surrogacy is likely to be systematically detrimental to many of the children so produced. Dr. Michelle Harrison asked similar questions in connection with the *Baby M* case:

> What happens when Sara is two or three or ten and acts impulsively or wants make-up or looks just like her mother? Will she forever have to deny behaviors which seem "like her mother"? Will the Sterns forever be looking for behaviors that are "like her mother"? Will they see Mary Beth in her strength, tenacity, passion? What is the impact of Sara now being the last of her father's heritage? To what lengths must she go to carry on her father's genes and how does she do so while having to deny her mother's? Who will be the grandmother to her children, Betsy Stern or Mary Beth Whitehead?[13]

Couples do, of course, pay some attention to the genetic material of the surrogate mother when they require medical testing and other screening. But except in the case of a surrogacy arrangement involving close friends, many of the contracting families do not really know the woman with whom they are contracting. Sometimes the explanation is a desire for anonymity, but even if the parties meet, they usually do not take the time to get to know each other. The Sterns, for example, picked Mary Beth Whitehead as their surrogate on the basis of her application, a photograph, and a restaurant dinner with Richard and Mary Beth.[14] It seems odd that the couples using surrogacy should pay so little heed to the other half of the genetic material, since they are almost necessarily believers in the importance of the genetic tie.

The terminology concerning surrogacy reflects the fact that the father is using the arrangement because it is important to him to reproduce himself. The woman is a "surrogate"—a surrogate uterus or a surrogate wife—to carry *his* genes. Professor Margaret Radin has pointed out that the characterization of surrogacy as a sale of services and not as babyselling suggests that the baby is not the mother's at all, but belongs to the father:

> If we think that ordinarily a mother paid to relinquish a baby for adoption is selling a baby, but that if she is a surrogate, she is merely selling gestational services, it seems we are assuming that the baby cannot be considered the surrogate's property . . . conceiving of the

"good" as gestational services . . . reflects an understanding that the baby is already someone else's property—the father's . . . The would-be father is "producing" a baby of his "own," but in order to do so he must purchase these "services" as a necessary input. Surrogacy raises the issue of commodification and gender politics in how we understand even the description of the problem. An oppressive understanding of the interaction is the more plausible one: women—their reproductive capacities, attributes, and genes—are fungible in carrying on the male genetic line.[15]

The terminology that characterizes the transaction as "rent"—as "provid[ing] a home in her womb for the child of another"[16]— similarly denies the mother as the biological parent of the child.

One suggestion occasionally made for regulating surrogate motherhood contracts relies on removing the biological connection between the contracting couple and the child. It would allow sperm banks to perform "surrogacy arrangements" in which couples could arrange for others to have a child for them, but a child who was not biologically related to them. This alteration of our current surrogacy scheme would greatly lessen legal complications that currently accompany surrogacy; it would be much clearer that the woman bearing the child could change her mind and retain custody.[17]

Such a change would, however, also remove a distinctive and important feature of the typical surrogacy arrangement. Just as the husband can argue that surrogacy arrangements should not be prohibited because of their importance to him (and his wife) in allowing them to come as close as they can to having a child in the way that fertile couples do, he could also argue that it hurts his (and his wife's) interests to remove the possibility of having a child endowed with his own genes. Indeed it is having his biological child that makes the surrogacy arrangement more attractive to them than any other ways that may be available of obtaining a newborn child.

Couples desiring to use a surrogate motherhood arrangement are far more likely to prefer a rule that the arrangement would fall through if the mother changed her mind before or at birth to a rule that the husband's sperm could not be used to inseminate her. In the first instance, the couple would protect themselves as best they could by attempting to select a mother (either personally or through a lawyer or agency) who seemed happy with the arrangement and unlikely to change her mind. In the latter situation, there would be no way the couple could legally use the arrangement to obtain a child who shared the husband's genes.

For the most part, then, the same questions control, whether we think of the issue in constitutional terms, or simply ask what a judge should decide in the absence of legislative guidance, or what a legislature should decide concerning the legality of the contracts. The main differences between the constitutional framework and the others are: (1) if the courts decide that due process protects the husband-father's or the couple's right to enter into this kind of contract, the courts' view will prevail no matter what the state legislature does—even if the legislature enacts an explicit statute to the contrary; and (2) accordingly, the benefits-harms balance must be much clearer to sustain the ruling if it is to be based on the Constitution than if it is to be decided simply as a matter of policy. A judge who thought it was a close question whether the harms of surrogacy arrangements outweigh the needs for and benefits of such arrangements might find as a matter of common law, or interpretation of existing legislative provisions, that such arrangements were permissible, but she or he would not find that a clear legislative declaration prohibiting such arrangements was unconstitutional. The judge would need much greater certainty concerning the unreasonableness of the burden on infertile couples and surrogates who want to contract in order to rest the decision on constitutional grounds.

Balancing Surrogacy's Benefits against Its Harms

Whether we are looking at reasonableness under the due process clause or at what a lawmaking body should opt for as a matter of policy, it is necessary to inquire whether there are other elements as well that should be weighed in the harms-benefits balance. Besides the interests of the parties to the contract, the interests of the child might seem very important. In fact those interests would be dominant, if they were coherent and ascertainable. In a sense, the agreements are certainly in the child's interest because it is the agreement that produces the child; in a sense, it gives the particular child the opportunity for life. But this interest is not really relevant, because when the contract is entered, the child has yet to be conceived. From that perspective, there is no child's interest to protect.[18]

Some would take the position that it is necessarily harmful to children to be born through surrogacy arrangements and would use that view as a basis for prohibiting surrogacy. But although many people who are part of a conventional nuclear family are prone to lament the lot of children otherwise situated, much experience suggests that children can feel all right about their origins if their parents do, and that children produced through "unusual arrangements" can grow up feeling secure and loved, as can adopted children.

Mary Beth Whitehead said outside the New Jersey courthouse, "This is no way to bring children into this world,"[19] a sentiment much of the American public shares. But it is not the surrogacy that seems harmful to Baby M as much as the hard-fought custody battle, with its attendant publicity. Surrogacy arrangements in which all perform without incident would not seem inherently to carry any particular risk to the child so produced. True, the child may want to know her biological mother. Unlike the typical adoption, information about the mother will often be available to the adopting parents, and as she grows up the child may be angry with them if they do not share the information with her. But it does not seem that children born of surrogacy need experience greater feelings of rejection than those common to adopted children generally. Reactions vary, of course. Some children produced by artificial insemination with an anonymous sperm donor express great anger and grief at their inability to trace their biological origins.[20] On the other hand, one woman reported, "Knowing about my AID origin did nothing to alter my feelings for my family. Instead, I felt grateful for the trouble they had taken to give me life."[21] In sum, there is no good evidence that children produced through surrogacy will be harmed, or invariably harmed, or more harmed by surrogacy than by other procreative schemes. If we start generalizing about what kind of families or situations it is detrimental to children to be born into, and make rules accordingly, we start down a long road fraught with peril for our civil liberties.

If we consider not whether to prevent the child's birth but instead how to promote her "best interests" after birth, no particular rule emerges. Whether it would be better for the child to remain with the surrogate mother or to live with the couple who contracted for her will vary with the facts and circumstances of the case. Yet it is not in the child's interest for parents to litigate and resolve the issue of the preferable custodian. The rule best serving the child's interest is a rule that discourages custody contests. Probably the way best to achieve this objective is to adopt a clear rule stating a strong presumption for one parent or the other (see Chapter 9). Beyond the desirability of avoiding litigation, it is not possible to generalize which parents would best suit the child.

Besides the interests of the child and the parties, societal interests could play a role. But we in this country, now at least, are not suffering from inadequate population; as a society we do not need more babies. There are no affirmative reasons for the state to promote surrogacy arrangements other than to fulfill the wishes of individuals who wish to use them. Fulfilling their wishes could be a sufficient reason, of course, depending upon the strength of their interests and upon the balance with the other interests at issue.

As well as the considerations discussed in Chapters 2 and 3, another argument against allowing surrogate motherhood is that the availability of surrogacy would cut back on the adoption of existing babies. Perhaps if infertile couples were unable to employ a surrogate to have a child for them, they would go about getting a child in some other way, one that would be much more beneficial to society. They might decide to adopt a child already in existence, or a child who will be born in any event and who is in need of a home and family. Fulfilling their parental urges in that way, they would perform an important service to the child and to society.

One problem for many couples is that adoption seems unavailable to them. Many couples today are waiting longer before attempting to conceive and thus are older when they discover that they have a problem. Especially if they take time to undergo fertility treatments before turning to adoption, they may find they are too old to be acceptable to conventional adoption agencies, which prefer couples under age thirty-five.[22] Moreover, adoption is not as easy today as it has been in the past, and there is a definite shortage of healthy newborns available for adoption in this country—especially healthy white newborns.[23] This shortage results from the prevalence of contraception and abortion and from many unmarried mothers' decisions to raise their own children. Although some healthy black children apparently are available for adoption, many states do not make them available to white parents; and most would-be adoptive parents are white.[24]

Indeed, some agencies have gone so far as to remove a child from a home in which he is thriving in order to avoid an interracial family. In *Drummond v. Fulton County Department of Family and Children's Services,* the U.S. Court of Appeals for the Fifth Circuit sitting *en banc* rejected a constitutional attack on the removal of four-year-old Timmy, an interracial child, from Robert and Mildred Drummond, a white couple who had raised him since infancy.[25] The child was thriving in that placement and the Drummonds provided excellent care, but when they sought to adopt Timmy the agency chose instead to remove him so that his permanent placement would be with some yet-to-be-determined black family. In the interim Timmy would leave the only family he had known and be placed in foster care. With policies like this, babies suffer and would-be adopters who are white cannot obtain a healthy infant of any race.

But there are some babies who need to be adopted and who are available, both in this country and elsewhere. Many couples or would-be single parents who have not been successful with domestic adoption agencies have managed to obtain a newborn from abroad.[26] Moreover, there are available in this country children with special needs who could benefit enormously from being taken into a family, and who have been adopted in greater numbers as the supply of "normal" babies has dwindled.[27] Of course, many couples who would like to produce a child would not be prepared as an alternative to take on a special-needs child. Nonetheless, society might make a judgment that *some* such couples would make that choice, thereby benefiting both children in need and society. Accordingly, a state might decide that it is best that infertile couples not be permitted to create another baby by contract, when at least a few of them might otherwise decide to take on a child in need.

Surrogacy advocates injure their case when they brag that as surrogacy develops, it will come to replace adoption.[28] That would be a clear social harm. The interests of existing children in having families, and society's concern that children grow up in as secure and loving an environment as possible, should not be ignored in the decision whether to encourage surrogacy, in vitro fertilization, and ovum donation. The National Committee for Adoption has been a consistent and outspoken critic of surrogacy and wants it to be outlawed. Part of its reasoning is that "so called surrogate mothering entails legal and moral problems which affect children and parents adversely and divert attention from the need of children to have permanent, stable and secure homes and families."[29] It is also concerned that allowing surrogacy would result in the widespread selling of unwanted babies who would otherwise be available for adoption.[30]

Infertile couples would argue that the chance to have a "normal" child, and a child as biologically connected to them as possible, is not afforded by special-needs adoption or even adoption of healthy newborns, and that although it benefits society more for them to adopt an existing child than to conceive a new one, the same is true for fertile couples, who nonetheless are permitted to reproduce without any restriction by the state. Moreover, it is hypocritical to raise the needs of deprived children against surrogacy when we as a society in other respects follow policies so obviously contrary to their needs. Indeed if we provided minimally adequate welfare for poor families with children, subsidized respite care programs for families of children with special needs, a national daycare policy, a program to meet the housing needs of poor people, and support for battered women who would take care of their children if they could, just to name a few obvious examples, poor families would be able to stay together, and there would be many fewer children in need of families. If we provided free prenatal care to those who cannot afford it, there would be many fewer special-needs children. Society does have a responsibility toward existing children in need, and it should exercise that responsibility, but it is unfair for it to meet its obligation simply by transferring the responsibility to couples who need surrogacy to reproduce.

In response it might be said that even though society should invest resources to help poor families and to hold families together, its failure to do so should not be used to justify disregarding even further the needs of existing children, including their need for families. Existing policies do create needy children, but even if society were to spend its funds more wisely, there would still be some children in need. Moreover, society does not have available a broad range of solutions for those children who are searching for families; even generous spending cannot necessarily produce families for children, and that is what they need, not just social services. Even paying families generously to take these children does not seem an appropriate response in light of the concerns surrounding childselling. A ban on surrogacy would not really impose an obligation upon infertile couples to care for existing children, although it would increase the likelihood that some of them will do so and that would be part of its purpose. The serious issue is whether it is fair so to preclude infertile couples and women who want to be surrogates, and that turns on a value judgment: whether the needs of existing children should be given precedence or whether the needs of parties who would use surrogacy are more important.

And so we return to the same arguments and balancing judgments used already in both the policy and the constitutional debates. The state, if it wants to uphold the prohibition, must contend that pregnancy for hire is sufficiently distinct from other pregnancy that it need not be treated the same. The couple, in support of surrogacy arrangements, must argue that the state should not deprive them of their means of most closely approximating what others do without any limit or regulation: having a child or children biologically linked to them. In order for the state to prohibit surrogacy, it should have to involve some real and discernible evil, which they argue has not been demonstrated here.

Problems Limiting Any Constitutional
Right to Surrogacy

One difficulty with resolving newly developing issues concerning surrogacy on the basis of constitutional doctrine is that it is not apparent that any constitutional right to use a surrogate thereby created would have any natural limits. Seemingly any procreative right to employ a surrogate would extend as well to all the developing reproductive technologies; they would all be available as a matter of constitutional entitlement.

Of course as a practical matter they would be available primarily to the rich. Some would solve that inequity by having the state pay to provide persons with alternative reproductive methods.[31] Insurance is another possibility. In Massachusetts, Governor Michael Dukakis recently signed a bill requiring insurance companies to cover in vitro fertilization, which costs about $5,000 per attempt.[32] In the case of IVF, there still will probably not be sufficient facilities for all who want to use it. Therefore, the main effect of requiring coverage will probably be to create some system of selection other than wealth. In the case of surrogacy, however, the supply of services might be able to keep up with the demand.

But who would be permitted to take advantage of these new procreative opportunities? Precedent already suggests that single women have a constitutional right to decide whether to bear a child[33] and that the Constitution protects single parents against discrimination.[34] Seemingly a court that accepted the equal protection arguments supporting surrogacy put forth above would also find it necessary to extend the right to use alternative techniques to single people; otherwise singles who could reproduce naturally would be able to parent whereas infertile singles would not.[35] Because some single persons, men and women, would not be able to have their own biological child without surrogacy and modern technology, their need is the same as the need of infertile couples.

Some people would argue that the interests of the children to be born militate against letting single persons become parents by choice[36]—an argument that ignores the less-than-ideal quality of many marital households and also ignores that many of the married will themselves become single parents when their children are very small. If we were to start regulating who is or is not fit to parent, marital status is obviously not the only relevant factor. To legislate on the basis of that factor alone, especially in an area of such great importance to the individual, would violate equal protection of the laws.[37]

Some might welcome a requirement that before any reproductive technologies—including artificial insemination—are employed, there must be an assurance that the home that is contemplated is a suitable one for offspring. That requirement would avoid explicit discrimination on the basis of marital status while still protecting the child-to-be from an inadequate home. But that requirement also might be deemed to discriminate against couples who need to use the artificial technologies, since persons procreating on their own are not subject to a home study requirement.[38]

Indeed, once a right of access to alternative technologies is found for infertile couples, whether on equal protection or due process grounds, any proposed solution other than universal access becomes difficult to defend. It is not obvious which distinctions should be drawn and where, if anywhere, the right of access should stop. If, as seems likely, society is going to experiment with different solutions and try approaches that may be open to modification after a few years' experience with them, then it would be better to proceed on the basis of policy and the creation of statutes rather than on the basis of constitutional law.

Fertile married couples cannot claim that surrogacy is necessary to them in the same sense it is to infertile couples and to some single persons, but they can argue for access to surrogacy because it increases their options. Some may have very compelling reasons for needing a surrogate. Someone like Elizabeth Stern, for example, who feared that pregnancy would worsen her health, would consider it unfair that she be made to run a perceived medical risk when others are given the choice to hire a surrogate. And some women have medical conditions more clearly incompatible with pregnancy or carry genetic disease that could be harmful to a child. Such women and their husbands might consider their own cases as compelling as that of infertile couples. Indeed the term *infertility* might be defined to include at least some of those persons.[39] It would probably also encompass a sixty-year-old woman who wants to provide a child for her forty-year-old husband.[40]

Others, however, may choose surrogacy out of mere predilection or convenience—fear of pregnancy, a desire to stay thin, a desire to pursue career choices that seem incompatible with pregnancy, for example. Although convenience and predilection seem the least compelling of all the arguments for the right to use a surrogate,[41] there is a strong constitutional argument even for them. Women's option to decide whether or not to bear children could rest upon the same basis that the abortion right does—the due process clause of the Constitution; both would rely upon a woman's fundamental interest in making decisions that will affect her own destiny and that control her own body. Just as a woman need not give up sex in order to avoid having children now that technology has brought safe contraception and abortion, so she need not give up having children in order to avoid pregnancy and childbirth once technology develops to provide that possibility. With surrogacy and ovum donation available, women could acquire the option to have their own biological children in much the same way that men always have. Of course, as a practical matter, the option might be available only to the well-to-do.

It seems clear that the possibility of a constitutional right, enjoyed by all, to procreate by any technologically possible means has ramifications and raises concerns that transcend those of the parties to any particular contract. But when the technology for use of gestational surrogates is fully developed and available, the Constitution may support a right of general access to the service.

Are There Useful Ways to Regulate Surrogacy without Prohibiting It?

A final factor that could play a part in the benefits-harms balance concerns the effects of prohibition. The couple might argue that societal interests counsel against prohibiting surrogacy, because legalization and regulation would more effectively control abuses. Because any legislation prohibiting surrogacy would not altogether stamp out the practice, it might seem unwise to prohibit it and thereby drive it underground, where it could not be regulated.

On the other hand, it may be difficult to think of state regulations that would sufficiently cut back on the difficulties of the unregulated system. As one opponent of surrogate mothering explains, "We don't want to find a nice way to do this. There is no nice way to sell women or to sell babies."[42]

What provisions would legislatures adopt in regulating surrogacy, if legalization and regulation were the chosen course? First, they might take a position on the debate whether surrogacy and other alternative reproductive methods should be limited to the married, to the infertile, to people who can demonstrate they have suitable home environments, or to any other group. Predictably some state legislatures will decide that surrogacy—and perhaps artificial insemination and in vitro fertilization—should not be available to facilitate parenthood for lesbian couples or for single men or women determined to raise their offspring alone, and the constitutional issues will be raised. If the U.S. Supreme Court decides that access cannot be so limited, that rule will prevail in all the states.

Although this feature of surrogacy is much discussed, very few of the bills that have been introduced to regulate surrogacy have stated any restriction on who can use the procedure.[43] The problem with the absence of regulation, however, is that the medical establishment instead makes the rules. Physicians or even the go-betweens make the decision on the basis of their own ideas and prejudices about gay people or single people as parents. Noel Keane reports that he employs surrogates for single men but, at his wife's urging, has refused it to homosexuals who want to procreate.[44] It seems, then, if people believe that general access to reproductive technology is desirable, or even compelled by the Constitution, regulation which grants general access, or which raises the issues and gets them determined, would be preferable to the current situation.

Another possible subject for regulation is compensation. One problem with regulating compensation is that it is difficult to decide which is preferable—high compensation or low compensation. Some proposals have limited the amount that could be paid; others have set a floor but not a ceiling.[45] Even when proposals concerning compensation have been made, they have usually not contained sanctions for violations.[46]

Confidentiality could also be regulated. Parties could be required to remain anonymous; or they could be required to get to know each other. Here as well, it is not clear which rule is best—a fact that suggests, perhaps, that participants should be free to make their own choice. Some proposed bills have, however, regulated confidentiality. Most of those have provided for anonymity, but in California and Michigan advocates of open adoption, in which adoptees are permitted to know their biological parents, prevented proposals for anonymity. It seems natural for a state's position on confidentiality within surrogacy arrangements to fit with its rule on confidentiality within adoption, but not all bills would follow that course. A bill introduced in Kansas, for example, would have required more confidentiality for parentage records in surrogacy than for those in adoption.[47]

Some bills introduced to regulate surrogacy have contained a requirement for screening of the couple proposing to raise the child.[48] Although people using surrogacy might object that such provisions discriminate against them in comparison to couples procreating naturally,[49] a state might nonetheless decide to conduct home studies of couples who wish to enter a surrogacy arrangement, just as states already do for would-be adopters. A few proposed bills have contained such a provision.[50] Although such a provision seems desirable to protect the child who will be born, the intervention of the state almost always carries with it the imposition of middle class values. A home-study provision could be used to eliminate all but conventional families from surrogacy, even if as a formal matter the ability to use a surrogate were available regardless of marital status.

Required screening of the surrogate mother is an obvious subject for regulation and is provided for in virtually all legislative proposals. Unlike screening of the father and his wife, this screening frequently occurs even in the absence of regulation; couples entering a surrogacy arrangement want to satisfy themselves to the greatest extent possible about the health of the mother and the likelihood that she will ultimately go through with the arrangement, even if no legal requirement of screening exists. Regulations could also require counseling for the surrogate mother and her family, and some agencies make it available even in the absence of a legal requirement.

Screening can be done in very different ways, and legislatures could regulate screening procedures. Although all agencies today provide screening, they differ markedly in the amount.[51] Noel Keane's practice reportedly examines whether prospective surrogates are competent and know what they are getting into but does not try to predict how well they will adjust to the role—a prediction Keane says is unreliable. That practice rejects very few women who apply. On the other hand, the Surrogate Mother Program in New York City turns down many would-be surrogates after intensive screening and a battery of tests. One person that program turned down was Mary Beth Whitehead, when she applied to it before going to Keane; it found Whitehead "totally unacceptable" as a candidate for surrogacy.[52] A founder of Surrogates for Choice suggests that surrogates are the people best suited to interview and screen surrogates-to-be.[53]

One kind of regulation which a legislature could usefully adopt, and which adopting couples and agencies will not impose by themselves, is establishing a minimum age for surrogate motherhood. A state might allow surrogacy but prohibit teenage women from becoming surrogates—or even women under the age of twenty-five. Many proposed bills, however, have not provided any age limit.[54]

Another regulation once proposed in the District of Columbia is that a woman could be a surrogate only once.[55]

Some of the bills that have been put forth to regulate surrogacy would remove altogether the right of the pregnant surrogate to abort or would limit that right to medically indicated abortions or even to abortions necessary to save the mother's life.[56] More commonly, the proposals would transfer control over the abortion decision to the father who has contracted for the child.

Any such provisions, if enacted, would be unconstitutional. Despite many states' persistence since 1973 in enacting constitutionally questionable statutes concerning abortion, the Supreme Court has upheld its ruling in *Roe v. Wade* that during the first two trimesters of pregnancy the state cannot remove from a woman her right to decide whether to terminate her pregnancy.[57] That ruling seems clearly to cover the surrogacy situation as well as others; thus bills attempting to remove the abortion option for surrogacy, if enacted, would be held unconstitutional unless the Supreme Court alters its abortion stance generally.[58]

Indeed, even a state's enforcement of a provision in a surrogacy contract limiting the mother's right to make decisions concerning abortion would violate the U.S. Constitution. In *Planned Parenthood of Mo. v. Danforth,* the Supreme Court held that the constitutional right to obtain an abortion belonged to the pregnant woman alone (with the consent of her doctor) and that the state could not constitutionally condition it upon the woman obtaining the consent of her spouse.[59] That holding does not fit well with the notion that a woman can contractually waive her right to choose about abortion. If she can be bound by contract, then why doesn't her marriage contract with her husband constitute an agreement not to abort their fetus without his consent, at least when a state by statute so provides? Even an explicit antenuptial contract in which the wife-to-be agreed to share the abortion decision with her husband would probably not be enforced against her wishes.

A husband has at least as great a stake in the outcome of the abortion decision as does the man who has given his sperm for surrogacy. If a wife cannot contract or otherwise agree in any form that binds her that her husband will control the abortion decision, it would seem most peculiar for a woman to be able to bind herself by an agreement with a stranger. It would be most uncomfortable to allow the father in a surrogacy situation to obtain greater rights by contract and by the payment of money than a husband has, or would be permitted to acquire by agreement with his wife, even if he is prepared to raise the child himself.[60]

Nonetheless, it is quite common for surrogacy contracts to contain a provision either committing a woman *not* to obtain an abortion, or committing her *to* obtain an abortion in certain circumstances. In the *Baby M* case, for example, the contract provided that Mary Beth Whitehead would undergo amniocentesis, and that if the results indicated genetic abnormalities, an abortion would be performed at Stern's request.[61] It does not seem likely that a court would enforce any such restriction upon the woman's right to choose; and in fact the trial court in *Baby M* held the provision unenforceable: "After conception, only the surrogate shall have the right, to the exclusion of the sperm donor, to decide whether to abort the fetus."[62]

Bills requiring that the pregnant surrogate follow her doctor's orders raise similar issues. The proposals take many forms. Some try to fit within the *Roe v. Wade* framework by giving the sperm donor and his wife control over the medical management of the pregnancy after six months of pregnancy.[63] A host of problems could arise concerning those provisions. If, for example, a woman asks for pain medication during labor, can the father refuse it because the medicine also affects the baby? Or if a father believes that a caesarean would be safest for the baby but the surrogate prefers a natural birth, is the father's decision to control?

It is not at all clear that the state can impose on a mother duties of prenatal care even outside the surrogacy situation. The issue arises concerning imposing obligations on the mother-to-be to visit the doctor, to eat healthy food, and to refrain from consuming substances such as drugs, alcohol, and cigarettes that could harm the developing fetus. Although the state cannot prevent a mother from aborting the fetus, it has a much more tangible interest in assuring the health of a child who will be born than in preventing the fetus from being aborted. It is in no one's interest to cause unnecessary deformities or health problems in the child-to-be. The biggest problem with state regulation of prenatal care, however, is that any remedy that was effective to prevent "abuse of the fetus" would have to be very extreme. Holding the mother in detention seems the only feasible remedy if the problem is alcoholism, drug use, or cigarette smoking, for example.[64] The state's only effective remedy would be required incarceration. Despite the validity of the state's interest, that remedy would be unconstitutional because it is so intrusive.[65] In addition, a state might attempt to enforce its rule by using the criminal law to punish mothers who have caused fetal harm. A prosecutor in San Diego recently took that course, but the case was thrown out on grounds that maternal fetal abuse was not within the scope of the state statute under which the woman was charged.[66] That ruling does not speak to the constitutionality of the legislature's regulating the pregnant woman, however; it only said that the California legislature had not done so. Lawmakers as well as prosecutors have recently turned their attention to the treatment of the fetus, and in the next few years we can expect to see courts grappling with the issue, both outside and within the surrogacy context, of whether legislatures and courts can constitutionally impose penalties for prenatal abuse by the pregnant mother-to-be.

Just as the father's supposed power over the abortion decision stems from provisions in the surrogacy contract, regulation of the mother's conduct during pregnancy is currently accomplished by contractual provisions in the surrogacy agreement rather than by state law. In the *Baby M* contract Mary Beth Whitehead waived her right to manage her own medical treatment, as well as her right to abortion. She was also required to undergo amniocentesis, and Stern in fact insisted that she do so, contrary to the advice of Mrs. Whitehead's doctor.[67] Stern assumed all legal responsibility for the baby even if born with defects (another common provision in contracts and also in proposed regulatory bills, and a provision that is in part the basis for the father's claim that he should control the pregnancy).

Similar provisions that are common in surrogacy contracts require the mother to attend to her prenatal care and to obey the doctor's advice. But how could the father force the mother to comply with the contract in this regard? These contractual provisions, like those concerning abortion, probably are simply hortatory and amount only to a statement of intent.[68]

In one area, however, some courts have already imposed and enforced an obligation of prenatal care upon the pregnant woman and have done so on the basis of state law rather than contractual provisions. A few courts have forced women to submit to childbirth by caesarean section when the prognosis is that a caesarean will benefit the child (although many courts rule the other way).[69] If government is permitted to impose upon the woman an obligation to undergo a surgical operation which she does not want but which the court believes would benefit the child-to-be, it could also require the pregnant woman to submit to intrauterine therapy, which is becoming increasingly available and effective in treating some fetal abnormalities. It is extremely intrusive so to limit a woman's usual prerogative to submit to surgery only when she assents.

Regulations obviously can either promote or obstruct surrogacy. Proposed bills run the gamut from banning surrogacy to allowing and enforcing it. Some are extremely male-oriented, having no apparent purpose or effect other than to transfer to the father rights that would otherwise rest with the surrogate mother—bills with provisions making the contracts fully enforceable, purporting to restrict abortion and require the surrogate to follow doctor's orders, and giving the father control over medical management of the pregnancy, for example.

If there were no particular regulations that it seemed useful and important to enforce, then it might be worthwhile to criminalize (or otherwise prohibit) surrogacy, since it is clear that a prohibition of surrogacy would reduce its incidence. Criminalization on a nationwide scale—perhaps by federal statute—would be the most effective. The degree to which surrogacy would be reduced would vary, of course, with the stringency of sanctions and with the extent of efforts to detect the existence of persisting arrangements. But no matter how vigorous the enforcement, it seems likely that some surrogacy arrangements would remain. Another effect of prohibiting surrogacy would be to increase the price of the surrogacy arrangements that would remain.

In contrast, the current movement toward viewing surrogacy as the easy solution to the infertility-adoption problem encourages more and more people to try surrogacy rather than other possibilities. A state could reasonably find that even though it would be impossible totally to eradicate surrogacy arrangements, the interest in reducing them was strong enough to make the contracts illegal. I believe if such policy analysis led a legislature to prohibit surrogacy, the Constitution would not forbid that result. But constitutional issues concerning surrogacy have not been definitively resolved by courts; indeed, only a very few surrogacy cases have yet been decided. And until the issue is decided by the U.S. Supreme Court, some judges may be receptive to the arguments that surrogacy is constitutionally protected, just as Judge Sorkow was.

Arguments That Enforcement of Surrogacy Contracts Is Unconstitutional

There are constitutional precedents and plausible constitutional arguments on *both* sides of the surrogacy issue. The couple may argue that surrogacy contracts are constitutionally protected, but the mother can argue with equal force that it would be unconstitutional to enforce them and thereby place the state's policy of enforcing contracts above the fundamental right of a mother to be with her child. In another context, the Supreme Court has held that the Constitution can make contracts unenforceable even when they are not void *ab initio*. In 1948 in *Shelley v. Kraemer* the Court held that courts should refuse to enforce privately negotiated racially restrictive covenants. Even where state law did not forbid such covenants, they would have effect only when the property owner opted to abide by them, and they could not be enforced against parties who declined to comply.[70]

If either of the parties' positions were upheld under the Constitution, either all states would be required to honor surrogacy contracts on a par with other contracts, or all states would be prohibited from giving them any effect. And if neither position was adopted as a matter of federal constitutional law, a state court could construe its own constitution to impose a similar rule, thereby eliminating its legislature's power to adopt a contrary position.

The infertile couple may have a fundamental interest in having a child, but the surrogate mother has a fundamental interest in keeping and raising the child she has borne.[71] The argument that her deprivation is fundamental has particular force when the surrogacy contract calls for the mother to lose all contact with the child after transferring her to the father.

The mother would have to argue that her interest in parenting should not be subordinated to respect for contract, and that although she chose at one time to enter the arrangement, the choice was not a real one—or at least it was not sufficiently informed or voluntary to bind her to give up her child. It is a settled precedent of constitutional law that the waiver of constitutional rights must be knowing and intelligent.[72] In this case, the mother would rely upon a constitutional right to know and to raise one's child, an aspect of the right to privacy that has been found in the due process clause.

Some surrogate mothers may argue from facts peculiar to their individual cases that their waiver was not genuine. Indeed, some surrogates report that their spouse coerced them to enter a surrogacy contract as an easy way to make money for unpaid bills or to help provide for the needs of the husband or other children.[73] If coercion came to be recognized as a basis for not enforcing surrogacy contracts against birth mothers, interesting questions would arise—such as whether extreme financial need is sufficient to keep a contract from being regarded as voluntary.

Some surrogates—such as twenty-four-year-old Donna Regan, who has had three children as a surrogate—have no sympathy with the critics of surrogate motherhood. "I'm an adult, and I take responsibility for my actions. Being a surrogate mother never seemed strange or wrong to me. In fact, to not help somebody would have been wrong."[74] But a number of women who were enthusiastic about the practice when they performed as surrogate mothers have come to feel great regret and guilt as they have become older.[75]

Elizabeth Kane (a pseudonym) is an early champion of the cause who changed her mind. In 1980 she was a thirty-seven-year-old Pekin, Illinois, housewife and had a child for an infertile couple for a price of $10,000. At that time she granted interviews to *People* magazine and also to Phil Donahue. "It's true that I accepted a fee, but I thought of this as a pure gift of love, no strings attached . . . All of us—my husband, my children, and I—would do it again, though we won't. We fought for what we believe in, and we won . . . To think that I could alleviate the pain and unhappiness of one woman filled me with awe . . . She is his mother. My part is over."[76] But in the autumn of 1987 Elizabeth Kane appeared before Congress with Mary Beth Whitehead to ask that surrogacy be made a federal offense. Her current perspective is: "All you're doing is transferring the pain from one woman to another, from a woman who is in pain from her infertility to a woman who has to give up her baby."[77]

Individual surrogate mothers may also plead mistake and maintain that they could not know what they were doing until they felt the child grow inside them; they underestimated the attachment they would feel for the developing child. On this basis many believe that women who have been pregnant before are preferable candidates for surrogate motherhood, and some psychiatrists maintain that only they can give "informed consent."[78] One well-known surrogacy center reports it does not require that the surrogate be married, but it does require that she have at least one biological child living with her.[79] A bill introduced in the District of Columbia legislature in March 1987 would have required the surrogate to have had one normal pregnancy and a healthy child of her own.[80]

But even those who have been mothers are sometimes surprised by their reaction to surrogacy. One woman reports that she entered the arrangement believing that she would feel differently during the pregnancy and childbirth than she had with her two older children. "You think because the baby was not conceived out of love, things will be different. That's a bunch of bull. I feel sorry for people who can't have children. But this is wrong: It's against nature, and it's against God's law."[81] A northern California surrogate "started having doubts as soon as I was pregnant. They had these girls on TV saying how easy it was and how good it made them feel, but nobody warned me how strange it is to have a baby and not keep it." Because her couple had been so kind to her, she said, "I had to go through with it," but she would not do it again.[82] And an expert witness for Mary Beth Whitehead said that she "could not have anticipated her reactions until she became pregnant and was faced with the reality of being forced to give away her child."[83] Indeed, the same witness believes that surrogate mothers generally "are incapable of understanding the impact that surrendering a child will have upon them until they have a living, breathing baby and contemplate handing it over to a stranger. Most women are incapable of doing this and must not be compelled to do so merely because they believed they could or were told it was an easy thing to do by others."[84]

Some surrogates maintain that it *is* an easy thing. One surrogate reports: "It wasn't my baby. There was no attachment at all. I knew from the beginning that this was their baby, not mine."[85] And another woman reports that she is sure it will be easy for her: "There is no need to worry. Normally, it would be hard for a woman to give up a child she has carried. But I am getting pregnant with the plan of doing exactly that. No problem."[86] Perhaps the most that can be said is that the surrogate mother's reaction to her pregnancy is unpredictable.[87]

One could have a system in which the surrogate mother could argue in any particular case that her previous experience or her pregnancy was such that her agreement before conception was not sufficiently knowing and intelligent to bind her to give up her child. The outcome of each particular case in which the mother changed her mind would then be litigable. The outcome would be heavily influenced by the judge's reaction to the facts of the particular case and by her or his individual views on surrogacy. Perhaps over time there would develop a case law that could guide and produce consistency upon such questions as how desperate a woman's situation has to be for her "choice" to be nonvoluntary and insufficient to waive a constitutional right.

But it may make more sense to acknowledge that surrogacy arrangements are not voluntary in some systemic way,[88] and not to make each mother who has changed her mind litigate the reasonableness of that choice on the facts of the particular case. Perhaps the law should recognize that a decision to perform as a surrogate cannot be truly voluntary when social and economic conditions are such that surrogacy is the best way for some women to support themselves: given women's underpayment in the marketplace and their current responsibility for children, surrogacy for some seems the ideal job, allowing them to stay at home to raise their older children while still making money to support the family.

Such arguments suggest that even when a woman does "know what she is doing," there is no real choice that could adequately bind her to such a fundamental deprivation as giving up her child. One can, of course, conceptualize the surrogacy contract as the surrogate's choice and regard it as patronizing not to allow her to make a binding surrogacy arrangement. But it is equally valid to view enforcement of the contract as society's taking from the poor yet another basic dignity of life—this time, the right to raise one's own children. If society has created circumstances that coerce poor women to give away or sell their children, then rather than honor their choice as one of free will, it would be better to preserve for the poor the dignity—the basic right—of raising their own children. And on this type of rationale one can argue that it is unconstitutional for the state not to give more respect to the right of women to remain with their children than to freedom of contract in the form of surrogacy arrangements.

Research has shown that giving up children does cause permanent damage to the vast majority of birth mothers.[89] Phyllis Silverman, a professor and social worker who specializes in how women who have suffered a loss manage their grief, has studied many birth mothers who gave up a child for adoption. She reports that they perceive the experience as "having a protracted negative influence on their lives in the areas of marriage, fertility, and parenting"; in addition, she finds it clear that the women surveyed did not comprehend beforehand what surrendering a child would actually be like: "It is one thing to agree in the abstract to give up a child, quite another to actually hand over a living human being after it is born and in the mother's arms."[90] Many of those mothers felt that they had not wanted to surrender their child but had been pressured to do so by social workers who counseled that the child would be better off in a two-parent family.[91]

On the issue of surrogacy, Silverman concludes, "Surrogate agreements should not be enforced by the courts . . . These arrangements will cause grave psychological and social damage to the surrogate mother. The result will be depression, loss of self-worth, destruction of self-identity, difficulty in forming or continuing close interpersonal relationships, and a grieving process that will continue every day for the rest of the mother's life. The impact on these women will be enormous and it will be permanent."[92]

Constitutional arguments, like policy arguments, can, then, be framed on either side of the issue. At this time, when our society seems uncertain how it wants surrogacy to be treated, there seems little benefit in a constitutional approach. The same arguments that would be meaningful in arguing for or against the parties' various constitutional rights could also be used to argue that a particular position reflects preferable policy—or a preferable interpretation of existing contract, adoption, and family law. Even if one proceeds on grounds of policy and statutory enactments or common law instead of constitutional grounds, the spectrum of available decisions ranges from illegality to total enforceability.

Chapter Five

Making Surrogacy Contracts
Unenforceable under Contract Law

So far we have surveyed a range of positions concerning the effect of the surrogacy contract and how those positions could be supported under contract, criminal, and constitutional law. One possibility is to prohibit surrogacy, in which case criminal penalties might attach to parties who engaged in it. At any rate, if surrogacy were illegal a court would not respect the contract even when both parties were ready and willing to perform.[1] For example, a Kentucky court in *In re* Baby Girl denied a petition to allow a surrogate mother and her husband to terminate their parental rights, establish the alleged biological father's paternity, and transfer legal custody of a child to her biological father.[2] And in England, couples who have arranged for the pregnancy of a surrogate mother and agreed to adopt the child have had difficulty obtaining custody of the child from the English courts even when the surrogate mother has been ready and eager to complete the transaction. In one case, for example, London authorities interfered with the performance of a surrogacy contract by obtaining a "plan of safety order" a few hours after birth to assume state protective custody over a child born to a surrogate mother, before the child was handed over to the biological father. The biological father, an American who had arranged through an agency in the United States for the conception of the child, had to commence wardship proceedings. But the court did ultimately grant the biological father's motion for wardship, finding that the biological father and his wife "are devoted to each other . . . are both professional people, highly qualified . . . [with] a very nice home in the country and another in town . . . [and] are both excellently equipped to meet the baby's emotional needs."[3] After this case, and partly in reaction to Americans' arranging such contracts, commercial surrogacy was banned in the United Kingdom. Brokering surrogacy contracts is now a criminal offense, punishable by imprisonment.[4] A bill now pending in Congress is modeled on the British one, except that it also attempts to plug loopholes in its British counterpart by imposing criminal liability on commissioning parents and surrogates as well as on go-betweens, and by prohibiting private surrogacy agreements as well as those arranged through agencies.[5]

At the opposite extreme from finding surrogacy contracts illegal, a legislature or judge might believe that surrogacy contracts should be enforceable like any other contract. This is the view that the contracting couple would prefer and that the mother who changes her mind must argue against. It is also apparently the view most prevalent among lay people in the United States today. In a January 1987 Gallup poll for *Newsweek,* respondents were asked: "Who should get custody of Baby M—the natural mother or the couple who paid her to have the baby?" Of all women polled, 61 percent thought that custody should be granted to the couple who paid to have the baby, 22 percent thought that custody should be granted to the natural mother, and 17 percent did not know who should get custody. Of all men polled, 58 percent thought that custody should be granted to the couple, 28 percent thought that custody should be granted to the natural mother, and 14 percent did not know who should get custody.[6] Similarly, a survey of television viewers produced a 70 percent response that "a contract is a contract" and that the adopting couple, rather than a surrogate mother who changed her mind at birth, should receive custody.[7] Traditional contract law could support that view.[8] In many ways all the requisites of a valid contract are present in the typical contract for surrogacy.

Another option in contract law, however, is to adopt a position midway between illegality and enforceability—that the contracts are unenforceable over the surrogate mother's objection. It is important to distinguish between the possibility of criminalizing or otherwise prohibiting surrogate motherhood contracts and this suggestion of simply not making them enforceable. Under this middle position, if parties enter into a surrogacy arrangement and all parties remain willing to go through with the arrangement, then there is no legal barrier to its performance; the state will not interfere with this arrangement between willing parties. But if the mother changes her mind about parting with her child, the state will not put its force behind the agreement, and the baby will not be removed from her because of a document that she signed before the baby was conceived.

A nonlawyer might expect that the strongest case for unenforceability could be made by the women who had not been paid for their promise. Contract law does require "consideration" for any promise to be binding,[9] and in a real sense the contracting woman who is not to be paid expects no benefit from the contract. Even if her medical expenses are to be paid, and the father would thus incur a cost because of the contract, the mother does not receive a financial benefit, because she would not have had the expenses without the contract. (This argument would not apply if living expenses were paid, however.)

Despite the logic of this position, it is fairly clear under contract doctrine that even in the context of unpaid surrogacy there is sufficient consideration for the contract to be binding. Under traditional contract doctrine, giving sperm, paying or promising to pay medical expenses, and promising to adopt the child would all be consideration.[10] The father's promises, or detriment (payments made), or even reliance (purchase of the crib) could constitute consideration even if the mother received nothing of value. Moreover, women found to be performing as surrogates for their own satisfaction and not for valuable reward have received consideration as contract law defines it.[11] Any of those forms of consideration would be sufficient to make the contract binding.

The same kind of consideration would not support a charge of babyselling. A point of interest in each jurisdiction is how its definition of the consideration that makes a contract binding fits together with its babyselling laws. A conviction for babyselling most commonly requires that the perpetrator have received something of actual market value—not just payment of expenses that would not even have been incurred except in service of the contract, or the donation of sperm, which is of little value to the recipient. Much less is necessary, then, to constitute consideration that makes a contract binding than is necessary to constitute exchange in a typical babyselling offense.

It is in the gulf between the two standards—consideration and valuable exchange for purposes of babyselling—that surrogate contracts would still be enforceable, in a jurisdiction that decided to punish surrogacy arrangements under its babyselling laws. As discussed in Chapter 1, that would lead to the inappropriate result of making contracts enforceable against the unpaid surrogate, but not against the paid one. To avoid this anomaly, unpaid surrogacy contracts should be held unenforceable wherever paid surrogacy is illegal.[12]

But the proposed solution is broader and applies to both paid and volunteer surrogacy. If surrogacy arrangements are not to be illegal as a matter of public policy, then rather than treating surrogacy contracts just like any other contract, the law should make the arrangement performable or not at the option of the mother.

One attractive feature of this solution is that it helps avoid resolution of the debate, which is currently dividing feminists, about whether surrogacy exploits women or liberates them. It recognizes the truth of both positions. Surrogacy is still available when the surrogate mother desires ultimately to carry out the contract by giving the child to the father and his wife. But it avoids one of the most troubling features—a contract severing the maternal bond when the mother is unwilling to relinquish her child. This rule leaving options with the surrogate mother would not eliminate all the exploitative aspects of surrogacy, but it would reduce them. In a sense, then, the proposal is a compromise, because it does not force a choice between banning surrogacy and accepting surrogacy contracts as fully enforceable.

The justifications for such a resolution bear some similarity to the arguments for making surrogacy illegal, but in this context they are even stronger. The argument for unenforceability relies upon the same special sphere outside the marketplace for procreation and other personal and fundamental rights. Some aspects of living are so visceral and personal that a person's positions (or change of position) on them should not be judged by the same yardstick of rational agreement as bargains made in the workplace; and having a baby is one of those things.[13]

Our laws concerning prostitution and childselling show that we consider sex and the rearing of one's children also to be in the same realm where we as a society would like to maintain a line between the commercial and the personal: even if a state decriminalized prostitution, it would not enforce contracts to engage in prostitution when the prostitute had changed her mind. Nor would it enforce contracts to sell babies over the objections of the natural parents.

Indeed even contracts to marry are not specifically enforceable.[14] And marriage, unlike surrogacy, is an institution which society has traditionally promoted and which is deemed to represent important societal interests.[15] A promise to marry may be as certain and explicit as a promise to be a surrogate; there may exist at least as great expectations and disappointment if one of the parties has a change of mind. Yet it seems unimaginable today that the law would award specific performance, largely because this is an area society wishes to maintain as a personal one. Some states today apparently retain actions for breach of promise to marry, but they are never specifically enforceable. (Indeed even damage actions are rare in those few jurisdictions that still seemingly allow them.)[16]

Similarly, it seems unimaginable that the law would enforce a contract to undergo an abortion, an area in which the Constitution gives the mother a right to choose. Instead the right would be held to be inalienable,[17] and even if the mother signed a contract, she could not give up the right to make her own decision.[18]

Many of these examples of contracts concerning prostitution, marriage, and abortion are explainable under the standard contract doctrine that personal service contracts are not enforceable by specific performance.[19] That doctrine also appears to create difficulties for advocates of enforceable surrogacy contracts. Although they like to characterize surrogacy agreements as agreements for services and not for a child, in order to escape accusations of childselling,[20] the standard doctrine that personal service contracts are not enforceable by specific performance could be problematic. Even if the transaction is characterized as rent—for the use of the surrogate's womb—it would seem to be a contract for personal service.

But the rule that personal service contracts cannot be enforced by specific performance may not help the mother after she has completed her personal services of conceiving and giving birth to the child. Traditionally the rule could not be invoked to prevent transfer of a completed object, such as an art work that had been commissioned and has already been finished.[21] Describing the contract as one for personal services would, however, aid the mother who changed her mind *before conception,* and it would also aid the man who changed his mind before he gave the sperm for insemination. Moreover, it would aid a woman who changed her mind after conception and before birth and who wants to abort the fetus. Even apart from any stipulation in the contract, however, a pregnant woman would retain the right to abortion.[22] And despite the traditional rule that specific performance can be ordered after the personal service is complete, a mother might argue that turning over her child—severing her connection with her baby—is such a uniquely personal act that it cannot be forced upon her, under reasoning similar to that which prevents courts from enforcing personal service contracts.[23]

In sum, even if a jurisdiction does not decide to make surrogacy arrangements illegal in order to enforce society's sentiments on the commercialization of baby producing, it need not necessarily enforce surrogacy contracts. The possibility of such contracts' being held unenforceable is not limited to constitutional decisionmaking. That position can be adopted as a matter of policy that will govern the application of contract law, under well-established contract doctrine. Taking this position would not commit the state to strive for some absolute line between the personal and the commercial. One can marry for money. Or a couple may decide not to have an additional child because they cannot afford it. But the line between natural pregnancy and pregnancy for hire is sufficiently distinct and sufficiently reasonable for a state to make a judgment that it wants to use it in attempting to delineate a personal sphere that is separate from the commercial one.

Even in areas other than the personal, contract law recognizes the concept of contracts that are enforceable or not at the option of one of the parties. The *Restatement of Contracts* recognizes voidable contracts,[24] contracts that are unenforceable on the ground that they violate public policy,[25] and option contracts[26] as valid contracts in which one of the parties has the right to decide whether to proceed;[27] and unilateral contracts in traditional contract law may or may not be performed at the option of one party.[28] In traditional nomenclature, a contract is unilateral rather than bilateral if a promise is given in exchange for an actual performance by the other party instead of in exchange for a promise. Classic examples of unilateral contracts, which the second *Restatement of Contracts* calls "offers acceptable only by performance," are "If you walk across Brooklyn Bridge, I'll pay you $30" or "If you paint my house, I'll pay you $1,000."[29] The law's recognition of one party's power to decide whether or not to perform rests sometimes on the parties' intent to create such an option, as in the case of unilateral contracts, where an offer is acceptable only by performance and at the option of the offeree; accordingly they may not be directly helpful to the surrogacy case in which both parties promised to perform and seemingly expected those promises to be mutually binding.[30] On the other hand, there is substantial evidence that people entering into surrogacy arrangements today do not expect them to be enforceable if the surrogate changes her mind;[31] if this can be shown, the unilateral characterization would be appropriate.

With respect to voidable contracts and contracts that are unenforceable on the ground that they violate public policy, however, the option to avoid the agreement is imposed on grounds of policy independent of the agreement. Well-known categories of voidable contracts are those induced by fraud, mistake, or duress or those in which one party is an infant. But even apart from such categories, a contract can be unenforceable or voidable on grounds of public policy that the court derives either from relevant legislation or from "the need to protect some aspect of the public welfare." One example is "judicial policies against impairment of family relations."[32]

As discussed earlier, surrogacy contracts are sometimes voidable on grounds of mistake (because in the particular case the mother did not understand the extent of the attachment she would form to the child she carried) or duress (because of the particular mother's modest financial circumstances, for example). Fraud is another possibility. Mary Beth Whitehead attempted unsuccessfully to have her contract with the Sterns voided on the basis of fraud, because Dr. Stern had told Whitehead that she was infertile when in fact she was not. If a state were to void surrogacy contracts on such grounds, and if enough cases occurred, there would develop over time a case law that would answer questions such as what constitutes improper overreaching, how much overreaching there has to be to constitute fraud or duress, and how contrary to the mother's expectations a pregnancy, birth, or child has to be to satisfy the doctrine of mistake.

Even if courts defined mistake, duress, and fraud very liberally, the woman who wished to repudiate the contract would have to litigate the facts of her particular case. A better approach would avoid the need for such disputes by considering surrogacy contracts in general voidable for reasons of public policy such as those discussed above. Under this analysis public policy considerations would render all surrogacy contracts performable or not at the option of the mother. Only if the surrogate did perform—did turn the child over to the father—would the contract terms be given effect. The systemic factors that make surrogacy contracts inherently hard for some to resist would support this proposal of extending the ability to avoid the contract beyond women who have experienced some particular fraud, duress, or mistake.

In addition to a characterization of the contract that would allow it to be performed or not at the option of one party, doctrines associated with the remedy of specific performance could have the same effect. Specific performance is discretionary with the court.[33] It may not be ordered when it seems unfair or creates unreasonable hardship, when the bargain reflects an inadequate exchange,[34] or when it is in violation of public policy.[35] Specific performance is not of course the only remedy known to contract. Although that remedy would not be available to enforce surrogacy agreements by transferring the baby, sometimes other remedies would be suitable. Damages is the obvious example. In other contexts in which specific performance is not available, damages sometimes are. For example, the opera singer who has contracted to perform cannot be forced to do so, under the rules relating to personal service contracts, but when she breaks the contract, she can be held responsible in damages for expenses and lost profits. As we shall see in Chapter 7, damages for some breaches of surrogacy contracts may be appropriate in some circumstances, but under the suggested analysis they would not be appropriate for a failure to perform by turning over the child; unlike the opera singer, the surrogate has no duty to perform—she has an option to decide whether to perform or not.

Chapter Six

Integrating Surrogacy with Laws Governing Adoption

I n addition to law in arguably analogous areas where contracts are or would be considered unenforceable, or unenforceable by specific performance, the law of adoption could quite directly support an argument that the mother cannot commit herself to part with her baby before the baby is born (let alone before the baby is conceived!). Adoption differs from surrogacy arrangements in two obvious respects: (1) the mother has already become pregnant (usually unintentionally) by the time any issue of adoption presents itself, and (2) the baby as a rule does not have any biological connection to the father of the adopting couple.

The Analogy between the Contracting Couple and Couples Using Independent Adoption

In an adoption situation, no state in this country binds a mother to give up her child because of a consent to adoption or a contract with prospective adoptive parents that was executed before the child was born.[1] Different states pursue this policy of reserving the natural mother's rights in different ways. Many states have statutes expressly prohibiting a parent from executing enforceable prebirth consent to adoption.[2] Others have accomplished the same result by judicial decision. They may, for example, construe the act of adoption necessarily to imply the existence of a child to adopt.[3] The effect of the policy is the same whether it is imposed by the legislature or by the courts. If this policy were carried over to surrogacy arrangements, it would effectively support the surrogate mother's right to decide *after* the child is born whether or not to keep her child.

In *Surrogate Parenting Associates, Inc. v. Kentucky,*[4] the Kentucky Supreme Court held that paid surrogacy was not illegal babyselling, but the court applied to surrogacy the rule concerning adoption that prohibits enforcing prebirth consent. The result is a policy in Kentucky substantially the same as the one I have proposed—that surrogacy contracts even if legal are not enforceable. In several other states, bills were introduced in 1987 that would have allowed surrogacy but permitted the mother to change her mind.[5]

Surrogacy arrangements are sufficiently similar to other adoption arrangements that the same rule should apply. In the adoption context, allowing the mother to change her mind can result in great disappointment for the would-be adopters. Of course, if no couple has yet been selected as the parents who would adopt, there is no problem of shattered expectations. In the United States, however, fewer and fewer adoptions are being arranged through agencies, which typically keep waiting for four or five years even those who eventually succeed in obtaining a healthy newborn.[6] Instead, more people are turning to private placements.

Private placements or independent adoptions are illegal in many jurisdictions,[7] and other jurisdictions disfavor them.[8] Even so, private placements form a substantial percentage of all adoptions nationally.[9] In 1982 "gray market" adoption (adoption arranged independently by lawyers, doctors, and clergy) exceeded the number of adoptions through licensed private agencies for the first time since 1961.[10] In California, 80 percent of all adoptions are private.[11] And even where private placement is prohibited, it still is often allowed between relatives.[12] Fees can run high, and the total cost is sometimes comparable to that of surrogacy.[13]

States that allow independent adoption strive to maintain the distinction between it and black-market adoption. Most important, they do not allow the mother who gives up her child to receive any fee. Some statutes do provide for the birth mother's living and medical expenses. The Florida statute states, for example:

> If a child is being adopted by a relative within the third degree or by a stepparent, or is being adopted through the Department of Health and Rehabilitative Services, an agency, or an intermediary, nothing herein shall be construed as prohibiting the person who is contemplating adopting the child from paying the actual prenatal care and living expenses of the mother of the child to be adopted, nor from paying the actual living and medical expenses of such mother for a reasonable time, not to exceed 30 days, after the birth of the child.[14]

But some states allow only for the birth mother's medical expenses and hospital charges and prohibit payment of living expenses. In *In re Adoption of Anonymous,* a New York court held that adopting parents may *not* pay living expenses; in that case the adopters had paid expenses for thirteen weeks before and five weeks after birth, which totaled almost $8,000.[15]

Private placements can occur in a number of different ways, but a common pattern is for the couple who want to adopt to meet the birth mother before the child is born. A private adoption can be initiated by either the birth mother or the adopting couple themselves—through advertising, for example—or either of the parties may turn to a private adoption service that specializes in bringing together pregnant women unable to keep their babies and couples who want to adopt. Either way, the birth mother herself often selects the couple who will adopt—on the basis of photographs and write-ups or personal interviews. (Indeed, one of the attractions of the arrangement for the mother may be that she feels less guilt at abandoning her offspring when she participates in selecting a loving home.) And in a great many cases, the adopting couple get to know the woman who is to bear their child, eagerly await her due date, and even participate in the delivery as her labor coaches.

The couples who arrange for private adoption of a baby who has not yet been born are much like couples seeking a surrogacy arrangement. They have usually tried for some time to have a child of their own and then have tried to adopt by other means. After they are selected as the adopters-to-be, they become very emotionally invested in the offspring they are expecting. If the birth mother changes her mind and does not give them the baby after all, they experience severe disappointment and grief. And sometimes the private adopters, like those in a surrogacy situation, have also invested money because of the promise of a child. Especially in jurisdictions where it is permissible to underwrite the birth mother's living expenses, a substantial sum may be involved.

Yet all recognize the right of the birth mother to undergo a change of heart. The expectant adopters very much hope it will not occur, and in the vast majority of cases the birth mother carries through her plan to place her baby for adoption, just as the vast majority of surrogate mothers give up their child without resisting their agreement. But if the mother does change her mind, all the would-be adoptive couple can do is either give up on becoming parents or try again.

It is true that the sensible and self-protective way for the expectant adopters to behave throughout the pregnancy is to tell themselves that there is a chance that the adoption will not work out and that they should not be too confident. In fact, like other couples, they could lose the child if a mishap occurs during pregnancy or at birth, as well as if the mother changes her mind about keeping the child. Indeed the mother could also decide to have an abortion.

But many people are not good at acting in self-protective ways. It is quite understandable that couples become very excited about the prospect of their forthcoming child. If the birth mother does change her mind, the couple are disappointed in very much the same way that the couple in a surrogacy arrangement can be. And the position of the mother is very similar in the two situations. Each woman may have had her medical expenses paid; each made an agreement, oral or written, to give up her child to specific parties at birth; each one, when faced with the reality of a pregnancy or a baby, has found herself unable to go through with the agreement she made. Just as we recognize and respect her change of heart in the situation in which she arranged for adoption after becoming pregnant, so we should respect that same change of heart when she arranged before becoming pregnant to turn the baby over to a particular family.

The parallels in the plight of would-be adopters in the private adoption and surrogacy scenarios are obvious. In both situations the adopting couple's expectations are severely disappointed. In both they are left with the unhappy alternatives of trying a similar arrangement again or giving up their dreams of having a child. The unrelated adopters know from the outset that their arrangement will fall through if the mother changes her mind, and lawmakers should clearly place the adopters in the surrogacy situation in the same position as other adopters. Either legislators addressing the problem or judges interpreting public policy and existing provisions of adoption and contract law should announce a clear rule that surrogacy arrangements are not enforceable when the birth mother changes her mind.[16]

This represents a feasible and just solution to the surrogacy dilemma and assimilates surrogacy to other adoption. The contracting couple in a surrogacy arrangement would then have the same knowledge as adopters that their arrangement was dependent upon the continued acquiescence of the mother, and they would have the same incentives to guard emotionally against the mother's change of heart as well as other possible mishaps.

Is the dilemma of the would-be adoptive couple considerably worse because the husband donated his sperm to produce the child? The decisive question is whether the differences that exist between couples in surrogacy arrangements and typical private adopters make it inappropriate to look to adoption law in the surrogacy context. The basic differences, of course, are that the couple in the surrogacy arrangement have participated in the creation of the baby in question and that the baby is linked biologically to the husband-father as well as to the surrogate mother. If the father does not get custody, he is left with the knowledge that the child he will not get after all is his biological son or daughter. He will have the knowledge that there is such a child in the world whom he is prevented from bringing up (just as the biological mother will if the contract is enforced).[17]

Should these differences between would-be adopters in the surrogacy situation and those in a private adoption situation call for different results? I do not believe that the differences are sufficient to sustain radically different rules concerning whether a contract is enforceable against the mother. If it is inappropriate in the private adoption context to make binding an agreement to give up one's child for adoption that is made before the child is born, then it is inappropriate in the surrogacy context to make binding an agreement to give up one's child for adoption that is made before the child is born or conceived. This is not to say that the father's biological ties to the child are irrelevant. They may be relevant in other contexts—after he receives custody, for example, or after the surrogate contract is put aside and he seeks to gain custody on another basis. (See Chapters 8 and 9.)

When Should the Surrogate Lose the Right to Change Her Mind?

One sensible approach would allow the mother to change her mind while she was pregnant, at birth, or before she turned the baby over to the adopting couple. Once she turned over the baby, however, she would have performed her part of the bargain and the contract would be complete and binding.

A rule that the natural mother is bound once the adopting couple take custody of the child is advantageous both to the adopting couple and to the child. It is especially after the couple have received the newborn baby and have started to care for her that they bond with her and experience her as a real daughter and not simply as an idea. Whereas it is sensible to ask the adopting couple to be prepared for the possibility that the adoption will fall through before they receive the child, it would be destructive to ask them not to form a parent-child bond once the baby is in their household; after all, a paramount aim of all of this law is to provide for the child as loving and stable a home as possible, and the first year of the child's life is important to the formation of the parent-child bond.

Moreover, it is best that a baby's custody not be changed back and forth, whether she is to live with her natural parent(s) or with an adoptive family. It is in the best interests of the child to have a clear rule from the outset as to who her proper custodian is, to prevent her from being transferred back and forth between parties who are feuding over their parental rights.[18] If the mother had a right to change her mind concerning whether she wanted to be the parent after the adopting couple had taken custody of the baby, or if the rule for who was the appropriate custodian was less clear than a rule turning on whether the child had yet been surrendered for adoption, the resultant conflicts could cause frequent transferrals back and forth as a custody dispute made its way through the state's appellate system, a process that can take years. The resulting instability and uncertainty would be destructive to the child as well as difficult for all the parents concerned.

Accordingly, there is a need for a clear cutoff to the natural mother's right to claim her child, and there is much to be said for choosing as the line the moment when the mother surrenders the child to the physical custody of the adopting couple. Different rules of course would apply to involuntary surrenders—when, for example, a mother hands over her child under court order. Moreover, this rule would not control the *Baby M* case, because when Mary Beth Whitehead handed over her child three days after birth, the rule was not in existence. Hence she could not have been aware of the rule and would have had no way of knowing that the physical surrender was the event that would determine all of her legal rights. It is important to the rule that mothers surrendering their children know what the rule is. To this end, it would be appropriate to apply it to cut off the rights only of mothers surrendering their children after the rule becomes law.

For the same reason, it also would be appropriate to require representation of counsel at any voluntary surrender of parental rights. The mother should have an attorney other than the one representing the adopting couple. A clear definition of the natural mother's rights, coupled with an attorney to assure that she knows the decision is hers and that it will take place at the moment of transfer, would prevent some involuntary surrenders from occurring.

If a jurisdiction was concerned as well that the mother have a period after birth in which to reflect upon her decision and feel comfortable about it, then it could impose a waiting period after the child's birth during which the mother could not surrender the child for adoption. Many states have such a rule for adoption, with waiting periods ranging from three to ten days.[19] Kentucky, as we have seen, has held surrogacy subject to its five-day waiting period.

Whether with or without a waiting period, a rule making the physical surrender of the child to adopting parents the determinative event would give the mother time to assess how she feels about adoption—during pregnancy and for a short time thereafter. A lawyer could explain the legal situation to her and could help her understand the legal consequences of what she was doing. And a clear line might help her to accept that when she parts with the baby the parting is final, and that the intelligent thing for her to do if she does give up the baby is to direct her attention and energies elsewhere. Indeed many parents who are certain they want to place their child for adoption decide to make it easiest for themselves by never seeing the child who is born.

A rule that imposed a waiting period of a few days before the mother was permitted to hand over her child would not interfere with this choice. For a few days, the baby could stay in the hospital. If the natural mother felt confident she was going through with the adoption, she could agree to let the adopters spend time with the newborn without violating a prohibition of surrendering the child before the waiting period expired. But an *extended* waiting period would not be a wise policy. It would prevent even the mother who knows she is willing to give up her child from placing her, with the result that the child must be placed in foster care. When this solution is required, it is both expensive for the state and destructive to the child, who should be permitted to start her life with her permanent family.

The argument for the moment of physical surrender as the time for termination of the natural mother's rights to rescind the contract applies equally to surrogacy and to the context in which the mother has told a particular couple they can adopt because she cannot raise her child. It does not apply when the natural mother has turned her baby over to an agency but the baby has not yet been placed with a family for adoption; in that situation it makes sense for a natural mother to have much greater discretion to change her mind and herself provide a home for her baby; if she is not unfit, she should be able to reclaim her baby at any time. Yet the law often does not distinguish between these two different situations in assessing whether the mother has a right to change her mind. Moreover, in some states the effect of surrender differs between agency adoption and private placements; usually private placements are more revocable than placements with an agency.[20] Those states pursue that policy even though a child who has been turned over to an adoption agency may have been placed in foster care or in another temporary setting and is not yet with a family who plans to adopt.[21]

In any event, that particular injustice bears little relation to surrogacy. Surrogacy arrangements are like the more difficult situation in which the mother revokes her consent after placing the child with the couple who are to adopt, or after an agency has already turned the child over to the adoptive family. In that setting it is much more appropriate for the mother to be bound by her surrender of her child.

Nonetheless, it is likely in the surrogacy context that the governing rules would be those for private or independent adoption, not those for public agency adoption. Jurisdictions prohibiting adoption except through an agency could therefore prohibit surrogacy, although that issue is complicated by the fact that the natural father is married to the adopter. Likewise, the New Jersey Supreme Court in *Baby M,* noting that private adoption, though legal in New Jersey, is " 'very much disfavored,' "[22] held that the rules making surrender of custody and consent to adoption revocable in private adoptions were the rules that were relevant to a surrogate mother's surrender and consent. The surrogate mother would not be bound in the way a mother who surrendered her child to an agency might be.[23]

A problem with following the time-of-surrender line for surrogacy arrangements is that it may not fit comfortably with a particular jurisdiction's policy concerning the rights of natural mothers who place their child for adoption. Although few states have an explicit law concerning the rights of a mother to change her mind in a surrogacy arrangement, every jurisdiction has had to cope repeatedly with the issue within the more common adoption situation, and each jurisdiction has a rather explicit law—either statutory or judgemade—concerning the time at which the mother's consent to adoption becomes irrevocable. In some jurisdictions the cutoff line is similar to the one I have suggested: some have the rule that once a natural mother has surrendered her child for adoption, she retains no right to revoke her consent to adoption unless she can show that her consent was obtained by coercion, fraud, or duress.[24]

The issue of what constitutes coercion, fraud, or duress of course can greatly affect the meaning of this rule, just as it does in contract law (see Chapter 5).[25] Most parents surrendering their child for adoption are operating under some sort of coercive circumstances, so a broad interpretation of those terms could effectively undercut the import of the rule, which more than any other seems to make the moment of surrender a moment of finality. In *Sims v. Sims*, for example, the court held that duress existed as a matter of law when a sixteen-year-old mother had consented to the adoption of her child only after her parents had said they would not fulfill their legal obligation to support her during her minority unless she surrendered the baby.[26] In *Huebert v. Marshall*, a court found duress when a mother consented to give up her eight-day-old infant only after the father lost his job and told the mother he was going to leave her.[27] Other cases, however, suggest that a much more exceptional situation is necessary to avoid the finality of surrender.[28]

Other states, in contrast, do not make the time of surrender even prima facie a moment of finality. At the opposite extreme, some states adhere to the rule that the natural mother has an absolute right to demand the return of her child until the final adoption decree;[29] jurisdictions differ as to the length of time that must elapse before the decree can issue, but six months or a year is a common period. And, as a middle position, many jurisdictions place the right of the mother to regain custody after surrender but before final adoption in the discretion of the court, which will in each case decide upon the facts whether revocation of the surrender is warranted.[30]

New York follows the discretionary approach. In *Scarpetta v. Spence-Chapin Adoption Service*, for example, the court permitted Ms. Scarpetta to withdraw her consent to adoption.[31] Ms. Scarpetta had changed her mind about giving up her child five days after the child was placed with the DeMartino family for adoption. (The child had been surrendered to an agency for adoption when she was four days old, twenty-three days before Ms. Scarpetta attempted to revoke.) The agency did not even inform the adoptive parents that there was any problem. Not until five months later did Mr. DeMartino learn for the first time of the litigation and of the possibility that the adoption might not be finalized.

The judge based his ruling upon a presumption that it is best for a child to be with her natural mother unless the mother is unfit. He was influenced by the fact that the mother seemed an appropriate caretaker for the infant. She had changed her mind about the adoption after learning that her family, who were "well-to-do, and devout in their religion," would be supportive if she kept her child.[32]

Although in one sense it is appealing to assimilate adoption in the surrogacy context to a state's adoption laws generally, some of the rules concerning the mother's ability to change her mind are quite troublesome and seem calculated to produce extreme problems for the courts, for the child, and for the parties—particularly the adopting parents. One recent case in California, which involved a private adoption, dramatically illustrates the problem. The Catanzero family adopted an infant at birth and took her home from the hospital. It was a private adoption, arranged through a lawyer and an "adoption counselor," and the Catanzeros never met the birth mother. Under California law concerning private adoption, the adoption is final only when the birth mother signs the adoption papers six months after the birth. In this case at the end of the six-month period the birth mother was nowhere to be found, so the final papers were not signed. When the child was eleven months old the Catanzeros found themselves in court, defending their custody of their daughter, and in a fifteen-minute hearing losing custody to the birth mother, who had not informed them that she wanted the child until the child was more than eight months old.

The Catanzeros did eventually win back the child. The original court had held for the mother on the ground that she "did not know what she was doing" when she gave up the infant.[33] According to California law, the mother who has not signed the final consent papers has a right to reclaim the child unless it can be proved that she intentionally abandoned her. Needless to say, this standard is flexible,[34] and one factor that might influence the judge's finding concerning abandonment is the judge's impression of which of the parties would make the better parent.[35] But the rule does state a presumption for custody by the natural mother. A couple in the position of the Cantanzeros could not predict with any confidence that they could prove intentional abandonment and that they would retain custody.

Because a rule that a natural mother can change her mind about adoption after the adoptive family has been given physical custody of the child seems as inappropriate for agency adoption or private adoption as it is for surrogacy arrangements, one might argue that the rule should be changed for all categories of adoption. One might conclude that if a court lacks power to make that change for adoption generally, the proper course is to assimilate the rules for surrogacy to those that prevail for adoption. If only the legislature can change the rules governing adoption, then it should change the statute with respect to all categories of adoption at once. Although there is a certain logic to that argument, a court that was convinced of the potential for damage in a rule leaving continuing discretion with the natural mother might latch onto the differences between surrogacy and the other adoptive situations to create a strict rule governing termination of the surrogate's rights, even if it felt disabled from applying that rule more generally. Although it would be stretching, a court might reason that the father's genetic connection with the child is particularly relevant when the father and his wife take physical custody; it may possibly ease or speed the process of bonding when the child goes to live with the new parents. Either under some such rationale, or simply upon a preference for a rule that the natural mother's rights end when she gives up the child, the court might thereby make a rule for surrogacy different from the rule established in that jurisdiction for adoption generally.

Although the ideal rule is one that would terminate the mother's rights when she gives physical custody to the adoptive couple, a legislative rule that drew another clear line and created only a very short period of uncertainty after the adopters took custody would not be objectionable. Presumably, all could live with a period of uncertainty, dependent upon the birth mother's continuing resolution, for a period of a week or less. (But if the birth mother did not affirmatively assert her right during that period, it would have to be cut off in order to avoid problems like that in *Catanzero,* in which the mother could not be located.) The objection is to any period for the natural mother to revoke that would result in any lengthy uncertainty after the adoptive couple have physical custody of the child.

Chapter Seven

Giving the Mother the Right to Renounce the Contract

I f surrogacy contracts are to be legal at all, the analysis in the preceding chapters would support treating them as contracts that are voidable because of considerations of public policy. As discussed in Chapter 5, there are other occasions in contract law on which voidable or option contracts are recognized, and the developed case law with respect to such contracts could appropriately apply to surrogacy contracts. Under this approach, the father in a surrogacy arrangement would be bound at least by the time the mother became pregnant, but she would not be bound until she turned over the child.[1]

A possible criticism of this proposal is that it seriously undercuts surrogacy arrangements while purporting to allow them. If in practice giving the mother the option to change her mind made the contracts sufficiently unattractive that infertile couples no longer wanted to use them, then it would seem pointless to allow the contracts in this form. But although the couple would doubtless prefer a fully enforceable contract, making the contract depend upon the mother's continued agreement seems unlikely to undercut entirely the appeal of surrogacy arrangements.[2] This would be particularly true if the jurisdiction had a clear rule (such as the one proposed in Chapter 9) that the father would not be liable for support.

Under either a unilateral or a voidable contract approach, the surrogate "contract" in a sense amounts to a statement of intent by the mother that she is willing to have a baby for the contracting couple and to give it up after it is born. There is every reason to believe that when women enter into such arrangements they do and will intend to perform; what experience there is shows that the overwhelming majority of surrogates do perform the contract without any resistance. That does not mean that these mothers do not feel grief at parting with their offspring; they do. But they know when they enter the arrangement that giving up the baby is what is expected of them; they generally do not feel they have the means to take care of the baby themselves; and most of them, accordingly, are satisfied that the course they want when the child is born is to turn the child over to the couple for whom they bore her. If current experience is any guide, therefore, the rule that the surrogate has the right to change her mind will not produce a change of mind in many cases; but when it does occur, the legal rights—at least the rights under the contract[3]—will be clear.

Problems of Fraud

Will the overwhelming majority of surrogate mothers continue to offer in good faith to perform and be generally prepared to stick with their agreement under a regime that clearly gives them the right to change their minds? Or will their clear options give them power that they might misuse against contracting couples? In predicting whether many women might enter into surrogacy arrangements fraudulently, it is appropriate to ask: What would a woman have to gain by offering to perform as a surrogate when she knows she will change her mind and keep the baby for herself?

The most obvious possibility is a long-term allowance from the father in the form of child support. If that will be available to a woman who keeps her child contrary to a surrogacy arrangement, there will be every incentive for women who want a child to make a fraudulent agreement with a well-to-do would-be father. A rule (discussed in Chapter 9) that, in the case of a broken surrogacy agreement, the father should not automatically be obligated to assume the usual responsibilities of a natural father is warranted both because it alone makes the voidable contract approach workable and because it is independently the fair way to treat the disappointed father.

What else could a woman gain by fraudulently agreeing to surrogacy? One thing the woman would obtain by making the promise is the sperm of the husband in the adopting couple. She surely would not obtain that if there were no surrogacy arrangement, for the only reason he is willing to give it to her is so that he can have a child that is biologically his. But it is difficult to see this as a very powerful incentive on her part to defraud him. Although his sperm is very special to him (and maybe also to his wife) because it enables him to have a child with whom he is biologically connected, it seems unlikely it would be very special to her or any more desirable than sperm she might easily obtain without any surrogacy promise.

Nonetheless a woman who wants to be pregnant might find an offer of surrogacy the most feasible means. A woman may have personal or moral reasons for accepting only artificial insemination. She might want it from a doctor, because she wants the donor to be medically screened or because she does not know anyone whom she can ask to volunteer. And artificial insemination through a doctor can be expensive. The Sterns, for example, paid $1,500 for six months of inseminations of Mary Beth Whitehead—a fee that was nonrefundable whether she conceived immediately or never.[4]

One woman who entered a surrogacy arrangement because she wanted a child of her own was Laurie Yates. She frankly stated on her application to be a surrogate that she wanted to earn the $10,000 fee so that she could spend it to be inseminated artificially. Yates needed the insemination because her husband was sterile. Many agencies would have eliminated from consideration an applicant who so described herself, finding her inappropriate because she wanted more children of her own.[5] Women who want their own children and need artificial insemination do have something to gain by fraudulently entering a surrogacy arrangement, unless those agreements are specifically enforceable.

The other possible incentive for a woman to enter a surrogacy arrangement fraudulently, knowing that she intends to change her mind, is payment—payment of her fee and also of her medical and other expenses. Of course the only payment she will receive if she does revoke is whatever passes before her change of heart; if she has an absolute right to revoke before the delivery of the child to the adopting couple, it would be wise to reserve payment of the greater part of the fee until that time. Even today, the fee is usually held in escrow or paid to a trust until the baby is transferred. But medical and some living expenses would probably be paid as they accrued and before the completion of performance. If surrogacy contracts were treated as voidable, the surrogate would be liable to repay if she backed out of the agreement. She might, however, expect that the contracting couple would not pursue her for the expenses, particularly if her ability to repay is questionable and if the expenses have not been very high.

It seems unlikely, however, that many women will sign on as surrogates because they really want a baby for themselves but want some chump to pay for their insemination and other medical expenses. Although a woman might expect thus to get her bills paid, she probably could get insurance for less than the lawyers' fees she risks incurring, and the avenue of insuring herself—or accepting Medicaid for some of the childbirth expenses—is likely to involve her in much less pain and suffering. One can hypothesize a woman who profiteers from fraudulently entering a surrogacy agreement to obtain a baby for herself, but it does not seem likely that any significant number will undertake surrogacy as a means of cheating the contracting couple out of either medical expenses or sperm.

Even if surrogate mothers are given the right to revoke, a contracting couple setting up a surrogacy arrangement should be able to assure themselves that they are entering an arrangement in which they have a good chance of obtaining a baby, although they will not have a certainty of success. At the interview stage, they will want to discover not only whether the prospective surrogate mother is healthy, genetically acceptable to them, and a person whom they would want to conceive and bear their child, but also whether she is sincere and sufficiently comfortable with her choice that it seems likely she will go through with the agreement. Even without a rule allowing a mother to revoke, such an interview—and perhaps even a thorough psychological study—is already considered necessary, and is arranged either by the contracting couple or, more commonly, by a surrogacy agency.[6]

Even though it is unlikely that giving the mother the option to change her mind will lead a wave of women to enter into these contracts pretending that they are willing to be surrogates, nonetheless, giving the mother the option to revoke is not without problems. Even apart from the obvious problem of the hardship it can impose on the would-be adopters, there are other difficulties with giving the mother power to decide whether or not to abide by the contract, and there are also problems with having a period in which it is legally uncertain who will be the parents of the child.

Problems of Extortion

The first difficulty is that the provision of a period in which the mother can change her mind creates, or rather exacerbates, an opportunity for extortion. If the agreed price in the contract is $10,000, and the surrogate has a legal right to back out, what is to prevent her, after the couple have developed expectations that they are about to become parents, from tripling her price?

Although this is a genuine and to some degree insoluable problem, it is not entirely the result of giving the mother a legal right to revoke, nor is it entirely preventable by any rule that may be adopted. Even in the uncertain situation of the law today, the mother could still threaten to resist enforcement of the contract unless the price were raised. Or she could threaten abortion during pregnancy unless her demands were met. Indeed the same possibilities for extortion exist today in the private adoption situation; although one might say the would-be adopters are less committed because neither of them has any biological link to the child, in fact the emotional commitment and level of expectation may also be very great, and the couple who want to adopt might well be willing to make a substantial payment under the table in order to assure the success of their arrangement.

Noel Keane reports on two surrogates, both of whom had agreed to serve without payment of a fee, who used their position to make demands upon the contracting fathers. In the first case, when the unpaid surrogate heard that other women were getting paid, she asked for $7,500 to fulfill the contract. Keane reports that she also threatened to abort the fetus and to refuse to relinquish the child after birth.[7] The character he describes, however, is based upon Denise Thrane, who apparently genuinely did want to keep her child and in fact eventually received permanent custody of her.[8] The other surrogate repeatedly made financial demands upon the child's father while she was pregnant; the father paid the money out of a feeling of desperation even though he feared it was used for illegal drugs and alcohol.[9]

Perhaps the most effective way to prevent the possibility of extortion in the context of surrogacy would be to give absolute rights to the adopting couple once the contract was executed, or as soon as the child was conceived, and allow them specifically to enforce the contract exactly as written. But, for the reasons discussed above, a solution that treats the baby like any other chattel one sells in the marketplace is not worth its costs. Moreover, even this extreme approach would not eliminate the possibilities for extortion, although it would reduce them. The natural mother could still threaten abortion. Even in the unlikely event that the option to decide upon abortion were legally removed from her, she would in fact have power to obtain an abortion and inform the couple only later—so the threat of so acting could be the basis for extortion. And even apart from abortion, if there was anything that the mother had power to do that would make obtaining the baby difficult for the adopting couple, such as changing her residence and being difficult to locate, she could threaten so to act and use the threat as a basis for raising the price she would be paid.

There is, then, nothing that the law can do to prevent all possibilities of extortion. Even if surrogacy were outlawed and efforts were put into enforcing the prohibition, some women would be willing to enter a surrogacy arrangement; they could charge a great deal for their services initially, and after they became pregnant they could raise their price. Such possibilities are inherent when the mother has something that the would-be adopters want very much—fertility, and later, a fetus, then a child whom the infertile couple very much want to have turned over to them.

Perhaps the best that the law can do to prevent the mother from being able to use her power over the disposition of the baby to extort additional money would be to make clear that any demand for a greater amount than was specified in the contract would constitute extortion or an attempt to traffic in children contrary to state law and, if discovered, would be prosecuted vigorously. The mother making such a threat would run the risk that the couple, rather than agreeing to her demands, would report her to the authorities. But this deterrent would not work in all cases. Presumably some would still take the risk, gambling correctly on the likelihood that the adopting couple would rather pay the higher price than lose the baby.

Problems If Both Parents Were Permitted to Renounce the Baby

A second problem from treating the surrogacy contract as voidable arises in the somewhat unusual situation when no one wants the baby. Two rather different situations might plausibly arise. (1) The mother gives birth to the child and is prepared to go through with the arrangement, but the couple who agreed to adopt have changed their minds either because they have conceived a child; or because they have separated. (2) The mother, who has always fully intended to fulfill the agreement, gives birth to a child, but during the birth process the child suffers oxygen deprivation, and the prognosis is that she will be at least mildly retarded; the couple who had agreed to adopt conclude that they do not want to adopt a retarded child and would rather try again through another surrogacy arrangement.

The first case is the easier of the two because the interests of the child are not as strongly implicated. If the child is a healthy newborn and neither the birth mother nor the couple who had planned to adopt want to provide a home for her, someone else will accept the baby with enthusiasm. The contract problem must still be resolved, because the mother presumably will still want her fee. If it has not yet been paid, she might go to court saying that she wants to collect: she performed her part of the bargain, and it is not her fault that the couple changed their minds. Should the contract be enforced against them?

Some would find it inherently unfair for the couple to be bound by the surrogacy contract when the mother is not and for the surrogate alone to have the option to withdraw. Others would point out that the mother never indicated an intention to withdraw from the contract and did all that was expected of her, and would allow her by an offer to surrender the child to make the contract a binding one. They also would point out that this result fits with the traditional treatment of voidable, unenforceable, or option contracts and with the current treatment of unilateral contracts. A standard resolution of those contract situations is that one party has the option whether to perform (see Chapter 5), and it has not been considered troubling in these areas that only one party has the option to withdraw.

Of course, some contracts are unenforceable by *any* party;[10] policy considerations would determine whether that resolution applied to surrogacy. If the contracts were to be mutually unenforceable, they might be characterized as void rather than voidable. Contracts to adopt, at least those made before the child's birth, are sometimes void rather than voidable.

Some would argue as a matter of policy that the fairest course is to make the contracts either mutually binding or mutually void. Unless one is enthusiastic about surrogacy arrangements, it is difficult to get too upset about the unfairness that would be visited upon the surrogate mother in this hypothetical if neither party were permitted to insist upon the contract. Since the baby can be well cared for even without the surrogacy arrangement, there is no compelling case for enforcing it; the interest in enforcing it would be simply to allow the surrogate mother to get her $10,000 and to count absolutely upon an arrangement that the adopters are *not* allowed to rely on and that does not on balance advance social policy. Although contract doctrine is available to protect the surrogate mother in this situation, and although that is the course that would probably be chosen, the contrary resolution—making the surrogate take the risk that she will not be paid in the unlikely event that the adopters change their minds—would not seem seriously objectionable as a matter of policy. Moreover, such a remote contingency would be unlikely to deter many women from entering into surrogacy contracts, although it might deter some.

It is unacceptable to allow the contracting couple to withdraw, not because of the first situation, involving a healthy and adoptable baby, but because of the second example, involving a handicapped and presumably much less adoptable baby, for in that situation the child's needs are compelling. The *Stiver-Malahoff* controversy was one such case, in which all parties renounced the newborn. More recently, doctors in Washington, D.C., have reported the birth of a baby "with AIDS" under a surrogacy agreement.[11] Both the natural mother and the contracting couple have refused the baby. Arguably, the AIDS diagnosis alters the analysis slightly, because the strong likelihood is that the disease came from the mother and not from the donor of the sperm. (One might wonder why medical screening did not reveal that the mother carried the virus.) Similarly, the condition of a child born with fetal alcohol syndrome will certainly be the result of the mother's intake of alcohol. Nonetheless, for the sake of the child, it seems best in assigning the parental obligations not to rule upon the basis of "whose fault" caused the handicap.

After all, the interests of the child should be paramount. The child's interests are to have a home or at least a family. The child will suffer greatly from any uncertainty concerning who her legal parents are and who should at least take responsibility for her placement and her care. That uncertainty would inevitably arise if all parties to the contract were given an opportunity to renounce it after birth.

In this situation, there is a strong policy argument that the couple who promised to adopt should not be permitted to withdraw from the contract if the mother attempts to turn the child over to them. This suggestion is especially defensible if there was no indication before the baby was born that the mother herself had second thoughts about fulfilling the contract.[12] Except for the fact that the child was born with a handicap, there is every likelihood that the adoption would have taken place; in the vast majority of cases the surrogate mother complies with the contract without resistance, and there was nothing to indicate that would not be the case here.

No considerations of equity call for allowing the couple, who participated in the creation of this baby, to assure themselves of a perfectly healthy newborn and to be able to reject a newborn who does not meet their specifications—a privilege natural parents do not share. Since there was every likelihood that the adoptive couple would achieve their ends with the contract had there been no difficulty in the birth process, and since they are probably in the better position to cope with the problems of caring for a handicapped child, if only financially, it seems best from the point of view of social policy, and also from the point of view of the baby's best interests, to lay the problem at their door. After all, a surrogate mother who had every intention of going through with the contract may never have had the resources even to take care of a healthy child and did not make that part of her plans. The couple, on the other hand, had made the commitment to have a child, developed an expectation of receiving that child, and possess the financial resources to handle that responsibility; they should not be permitted to withdraw at the child's expense just because she is born with a handicap.[13]

The adoptive couple in a private placement adoption would also be vulnerable to much of this policy argument. They would probably be treated differently because (1) they did not participate in the creation of the child; and (2) they are unlikely to have an actual contract, and, if any exists, it plays much less of a role in their relationship with the birth mother. If they do get the baby from the mother, it will be because of an understanding they have with her but not because of a contract.[14] In many jurisdictions, there would be nothing to prevent her even from giving the baby to another couple. The adopting couple in a surrogacy arrangement, by contrast, are proceeding on the contract, though a voidable, option, or unilateral contract. Even though the surrogate mother is not bound to perform, the contract will define their mutual rights and obligations once she does turn the baby over. Moreover, if the surrogate mother decides to give the baby to anyone other than the couple with whom she contracted, they probably have a stronger claim to the baby. They probably have a right to the baby against anyone in the world except the natural mother, because of the father's biological connection,[15] and perhaps because of the contract as well.

Void Contracts, Voidable Contracts, and a Remedy of Damages

One consequence of conceptualizing the contract as voidable rather than as void or illegal is that it increases the possibility of damages for its breach. We have assumed that if the mother decides not to abide by the agreement, she will be liable to repay any money she has received under it. That is the rule in the context of adoption: if, after giving birth, the mother changes her mind about turning over the child, she is liable to repay any medical or living expenses that she has received.[16] Of course the rule may be of limited effectiveness: undoubtedly in some situations the mother's financial situation will make it unrealistic to expect that the repayment will ever be made.

When a contract is called "void," however, courts sometimes refuse to grant any relief, and they sometimes do so when the contract is "illegal."[17] One rule is that even when a party has profited by a contract, by maintaining that the contract is void or illegal as contrary to public policy he can prevent the contract from being enforced against him. A contract to kill a person, for example, is not only unenforceable but also cannot be the subject of an action by the person who has performed and wishes to collect his fee. If that approach were followed for surrogacy contracts, a surrogate who got paid and then changed her mind would *not* be liable to repay; and also, if a surrogate complied with the contract by delivering the child, she could not maintain a legal action to receive her fee. Accordingly, an early British case allowed the surrogate mother to repudiate the contract as violating public policy and to keep both the child and the money she had been paid.[18]

The difference between void and voidable contracts will also be relevant if the mother does perform the contract by turning over the infant to the contracting couple and by consenting to termination of her parental rights. If the contract is voidable rather than void, it will at that moment take full effect; if the mother performs it will define the rights and obligations of the parties. For example, the contract will govern the extent and form of payment of the fee to the mother, and whether or not she will retain any right to visit the child. One would also expect that at that point actions for damages as recompense for any contractual duties that were not performed would be permissible under the contract. Indeed, the possibility of damages is often the most important consequence of characterizing a contract as voidable rather than as void.[19]

Damages would be appropriate, however, only for valid contractual duties. A failure to deliver the child to the contracting couple would *not* render the surrogate liable for damages, if a jurisdiction had adopted the suggested approach under which the surrogate has no duty to deliver the child. Nor could she be liable in damages for deciding to abort, or for not aborting when the donor wanted her to, even if the contract purported to make her liable. Regardless of what the contract provided, it would be unconstitutional for a court to enforce a damage provision against her for exercising her constitutional right to choose. A more difficult question is whether the mother could be held liable in damages for violating contractual provisions concerning her conduct during pregnancy. Even if the courts agree with the suggestion above that the father has no right to supersede the mother in managing her pregnancy,[20] that rule does not foreclose holding the mother responsible in damages if her conduct during pregnancy endangers the child and causes permanent damage.

The reason it seems inappropriate to allow the father to coerce the mother during pregnancy does not necessarily carry over to prohibiting a damage action. The problem with the action for specific performance is not that there is no duty not to damage the fetus that will develop, but only that any obligation cannot be enforced through specific relief. Specific performance is prohibited because it would involve pervasive regulation of the mother and deprivation of her freedom. It is less clear that it would be inappropriate to hold the mother liable for damages when her child is born with fetal alcohol syndrome because of her excessive intake of alcohol, or when her child is hurt by her heroin use during pregnancy. Since contracting fathers should not have power to order mothers confined, and since it is important to the child's interests not to allow the father to revoke, damages may be more appropriate than any other legal remedy. If (as seems unlikely) a legal incentive were necessary to encourage surrogate mothers to act properly toward their unborn offspring and were effective in doing so, damages would be the preferable choice.

Even if damage actions are sometimes permissible for some breaches of surrogacy contracts, the occasions when they will be appropriate are very limited. Most significantly, damages should not be available when failure to receive custody of the child is the complaint.

PART II

CUSTODY CONTESTS INDEPENDENT OF THE SURROGACY CONTRACT

Even if the approach suggested in these chapters prevails, so that a contract is not enforceable when the mother changes her mind before surrendering the child, there is still some question what the rights and obligations of the parties are in the absence of the contract.

In the classic adoption context, in which the expectant parents have no biological relationship with the child, they clearly have no legal rights to enforce any understanding to acquire a child who in fact has never lived with them. In the surrogacy situation matters are considerably more complicated: if the adoption does fall through, the father may be able to claim a right to the child because of his biological connection. His inability to prevail on the contract (either because the mother is not bound by it or because surrogacy contracts generally are considered illegal in that jurisdiction) will not necessarily determine whether he has any rights to custody or visitation or, indeed, any obligation to support his offspring.

There are some specific rules that may affect which parent will get custody when the parents are not married to each other. Rules sometimes differ according to whether the insemination was natural or artificial and whether the mother has a husband or not. At least when conception results from sexual intercourse and the mother is unmarried, the prevalent rule is that both biological parents have equal rights to custody. Chapters 8 and 9 discuss how these rules should apply when a child has been produced through a surrogacy arrangement and the mother has decided to fight to keep her child.

Chapter Eight

Rules Affecting Biological Parents' Claims to Children

The Relevance of Artificial Insemination

One variable that may affect whether the contracting father has rights independent of the contract is whether or not the surrogate was inseminated artificially. Most states provide by statute either that sperm donors have no rights or obligations in the offspring produced by their sperm, or that legally they are not the natural father of the child so produced. In many states, however, these provisions do not apply when the insemination was accomplished privately rather than through a doctor.[1]

Seemingly sperm donors could have the same parental rights and obligations as unwed parents, in cases in which the insemination was privately performed. Such a rule would benefit the biological father in the surrogacy situation, if the insemination was private. Sperm donors have occasionally won parental rights, but the cases are bizarre. In *Jourdan C. v. Mary K.*, California declined to apply its provision that a sperm donor is not the natural father of offspring conceived by artificial insemination, when the sperm donor sought parental rights and the insemination had been accomplished, not in accordance with the statutory requirement of physician's supervision, but by the mother-to-be herself.[2] The parties in that case had not made any written agreement, and the testimony conflicted as to what their understanding had been. The mother, a lesbian, was raising the child with another woman and sought unsuccessfully to have her partner recognized as a de facto parent and given joint legal custody.[3]

Similarly, in *C. M. v. C. C.*, the sperm donor wanted to assume the responsibilities of a father, and the inseminated mother, who was not married, was not permitted to resist this overture.[4] In that case the mother and the donor did have a personal relationship. According to the father's testimony, which the court accepted as true, they "had been seeing each other for some time and were contemplating marriage. She wanted a child and she wanted him to be the father, but did not want to have intercourse with him before their marriage"; they had sought the aid of a doctor, but he had refused to participate in their scheme, so over a period of months the father would come to the mother's apartment and "would stay in one room while [the mother] went to another room to attempt to inseminate herself with semen provided by [him]." When the mother-to-be was three months pregnant, they broke off the relationship.

The court said that because the insemination was privately accomplished, the father had parental rights, even though the insemination was artificial. But the combination of circumstances rather than the mere fact of private insemination may explain the result. Some courts are especially protective of the rights of biological fathers when no other man is playing the role of father for the child, and this court laid great stress on the fact that the mother was not married: "It is in a child's best interests to have two parents whenever possible."

Although sperm donors have occasionally won parental rights and taken on concomitant obligations, it is not clear that a mother can force financial responsibility upon a semen donor who seeks to dissociate himself from the child. Clearly she cannot when the insemination has been performed by a doctor. As the California court said in *Jourdan C.*, the purpose of statutes governing insemination is to permit individuals to donate semen for artificial insemination without fear of liability for child support, and also to provide a way for women to be impregnated without fear that the donor may claim paternity.[5] The California statute limiting liability applied only when a doctor had performed the insemination, however. When insemination is performed privately, it is uncertain whether the mother can force financial responsibility upon the father.[6]

In any event that issue is relevant only to surrogacy arrangements in which insemination was accomplished by the parties themselves and the mother decided to keep the child and to sue the father for child support.[7] It does not affect the more usual problem in surrogacy arrangements of deciding whether the sperm donor can initiate a parent-child relationship and obtain custody or other parental rights.

Even when insemination has been accomplished through a doctor and not privately, some sperm donors who contracted for the child but cannot enforce the contract will seek to assert a right to custody as the child's father. They may be successful. Some states permit the nonpaternity statute to be avoided if the parties have agreed in writing to paternity, as they will have if they have a surrogacy contract. A New Jersey statute provides, for example, that, given written consent and a doctor's supervision, the semen donor is to be treated in law as if he were not the father of a child conceived "unless the donor of semen and the woman have entered into a written contract to the contrary."[8] And even without such a clear statutory provision, some state courts hold that existing statutory provisions blocking parental rights and parental obligations of sperm donors do not apply when the insemination purported to be part of a surrogacy arrangement, regardless of how the insemination was performed. They reason that the statutes were not intended to cover situations in which the parties intended the father to have parental responsibilities. These decisions protecting and enforcing contracting fathers' intent to acquire parental rights even where existing statutes appear to cut them off are at the opposite extreme from the cases discussed earlier that prohibit fathers in surrogacy arrangements from using existing laws to establish paternity, even when the surrogate mother does not oppose them.[9]

In situations in which the father is not barred by special provisions governing sperm donors—either because the insemination was natural or because no special provision applies—it would appear that the law concerning the rights of a biological father who is not married to the mother of their child would apply.[10]

The Relevance of the Surrogate Mother's
Marital Status

Under the law concerning the rights and obligations of parents who are not married to each other, the rights and obligations of the biological father can vary according to whether or not the mother has a husband. Traditionally a child born to a wife during a marriage was presumed to be the child of that marriage;[11] whether the presumption was rebuttable or conclusive varied by state.[12] The presumption persists to some extent. Often even when the presumption is only rebuttable, only the mother or the mother's husband is allowed to attack it; a putative father can challenge the presumption in only a minority of states. Consequently, in order for a putative father—including a biological father who is a party to a surrogacy arrangement—to establish his paternity, he must in many states have the cooperation of the surrogate mother or her spouse.[13]

In recent years, however, the rule has been subject to constitutional attack, and some of the challenges have been successful. One fact that may have influenced some courts' change of position is that paternity testing is much more accurate now than it was two decades ago. Earlier, challenges to the husband's paternity might simply have cast a shadow of doubt and destroyed family security, without actually resolving who the father was. But recent developments in blood testing, especially the use of human leukocyte antigen (HLA) tests in combination with the many other available blood tests, enable litigants to produce very persuasive proof in most cases.[14] Another reason courts are now more reluctant to accept a presumption preventing putative fathers from contesting paternity when the natural mother is married is that the law is increasingly recognizing the unwed father's parental interests generally, with the U.S. Supreme Court suggesting even that he must be treated equally with the unwed mother.

One argument that the presumption must fail is that the right to assert paternity of one's biological child is protected by the due process clause of the Constitution; Supreme Court cases suggest that there must be some avenue by which a putative father can establish his paternity. Due process claims often rely upon *Stanley v. Illinois,*[15] but they go much further than the Supreme Court did in that 1972 case. In *Stanley* the mother had died. The state was threatening to remove the children from Stanley to place them in the custody of the state. Stanley had lived with the children's mother for eighteen years, and had lived with and supported the three children all their lives.

The Supreme Court asserted in *Stanley* that the state statute eliminating him as a proper custodian was based upon a conclusive presumption that unwed fathers are unfit parents; it held that in these circumstances Stanley must be given a hearing concerning his actual fitness before he could be separated from his children. However, its holding requiring a hearing may be limited to natural fathers who have lived with their children. It also deals only with fathers' position vis-à-vis the state and does not suggest that they have any rights to act against the natural mother's wishes.[16]

Later cases, however, contain language supporting a procedural due process right, though a limited one, on the part of putative fathers.[17] Accordingly, courts probably would recognize a right on the part of the putative father to assert paternity when the mother is not married and in that situation would allow a father who has followed the state's procedures for asserting his paternity to insist upon blood tests to establish his paternity, even though the blood tests require that the mother and child also have their blood taken and analyzed. But despite the Supreme Court's language suggesting that each state must provide some avenue for asserting paternity,[18] some states have continued to apply even conclusive presumptions that a child born during a marriage is the offspring of that marriage, and the Supreme Court will soon review whether such holdings are constitutionally permissible.[19] It is easy to understand a reluctance to allow any person claiming paternity to insist upon blood tests to dispute the paternity of the mother's husband if neither the mother nor her husband want to submit to testing. A state legislature could reasonably make the judgment that, in cases in which the natural mother is married and her husband acts as father to the child, it is in the child's best interests to accept the mother and her husband as the child's nuclear family; accordingly a court should be able to prevent a third person from requiring blood tests to prove that he and not the husband is the biological father, without violating the Constitution.

Moreover, it is not altogether clear from the Supreme Court cases to date that even a man who has established he is the biological parent will necessarily gain parental rights to the child. The Constitution may not require that the biological father who has no relationship with his child be able to obtain parental rights, even if it does require that he have an opportunity to be heard when parental rights are determined.[20] It might be constitutional for a state to have a rule that a biological father may attend the hearing and speak to the issues but could disrupt a stepfather adoption only by showing the stepfather unfit or by showing that he himself had an established relationship with the child. In short, a putative father may have a right to be heard, or even to insist upon blood tests, without having an absolute right to establish a parental relationship with his offspring, even if he is fit.

Courts often do not distinguish between the procedural due process claims—rights to notice and hearing—and the substantive due process claims—rights to custody or visitation, and the right to block an adoption; courts often discuss them as if they were one. And not all courts and commentators interpret Supreme Court cases to require even a right to be heard in all circumstances. Courts also divide upon whether it remains constitutionally permissible for a putative father to be prohibited from proving paternity of a child born to a married woman whose husband acts as natural father. Some courts hold that it is constitutional to bar the unwed father in those circumstances;[21] some courts have found a due process right in putative fathers to procedures to establish parental rights;[22] others have construed their statutes to permit a putative father to try to establish rights, in order to avoid the constitutional issue.[23]

Accordingly, although there may be a presumption that the child is the child of the marriage when the surrogate is married, it may not apply today—or it may not apply conclusively—depending upon the jurisdiction. If the mother is not married, or if her jurisdiction has no conclusive presumption, or even if it does and the biological father mounts a successful constitutional attack on the conclusive presumption, then the problem will remain of how to determine the respective rights of the biological mother and father without regard to any contract between them.

The Rights of Unwed Fathers

At common law the father rather than the mother had the right to custody and all other rights over the children. A change in favor of the mother occurred around the middle of the nineteenth century.[24] Until recently the law was relatively clear that when an unwed mother had a child, the right to custody lay with her.[25] Of course she could be deprived of custody if she was unfit, as can any parent or set of parents, but unfitness is very strictly defined. Otherwise the unwed mother was the custodian of her child; the unwed father had no claim to custody against her.

In recent years this principle has undergone some change, and the law is much more uncertain now than it has been in the past. Today unwed parents who battle out in court their legal rights to their offspring encounter two major uncertainties: (1) what the law is, and (2) how whatever principle is accepted will apply to them, given their facts and circumstances, or given the facts and circumstances about themselves that they can establish in court.

In *Caban v. Mohammed,* the mother and father had lived together for more than five years and had had two children, who were two and four years old when the parents separated.[26] Caban was listed as the father on the children's birth certificates. During the period they lived together, both parents had been important caretakers for the children.

After the mother and father separated and each married, the mother consented to adoption of the children by her husband, and the father opposed the petition, asking that he be the custodial parent and that his wife be permitted to adopt.[27] New York law at the time gave the unwed mother the power to consent to or veto adoption but did not give the father either right. In New York, as in most jurisdictions, adoption altogether severed the parental tie with the other biological parent. In *Caban,* when the New York courts passed upon the adoption, the natural father found himself faced with the prospect of losing all ties with the two children he had fathered and raised until the separation only three years before. The U.S. Supreme Court, in a five-to-four decision,[28] held that it was a violation of the equal protection clause for a state to apply an absolute preference for the mother over the father of an illegitimate child.

Four years later, in *Lehr v. Robertson,* however, the Court made clear that equal protection does not require identical treatment of the mothers and fathers of illegitimate children; it held that fathers who have not participated in their children's upbringing do not share the right to equal treatment and have no constitutional right to prevent the mother's husband from adopting. The Court indicated that unwed fathers need not be treated on an equal plane with fathers who are married to the mother of their children, pointing out that "the institution of marriage has played a critical role . . . in defining the legal entitlements of family members" and that "state laws almost universally express an appropriate preference for the formal family."[29] The Court also pointed out that the father had not offered to marry the mother; this was not a case in which he was willing to formalize the relationship and legitimize the child but the mother stood in the way of that course.[30]

The Supreme Court in *Lehr* held that there is a "clear distinction between a mere biological relationship and an actual relationship of parental responsibility"; it said that an actual relationship, not a mere biological connection, explained its decision in *Caban.*[31] Although the potential to develop an actual relationship deserves some degree of constitutional protection, it is not on the same level as the protection due a developed parent-child relationship.[32] In *Lehr* the Court held that the Constitution was satisfied by the state's provision for putative fathers to register their claim to paternity, which would entitle them to receive notice and an opportunity to be heard if there was a proceeding to adopt the child. The existence of the procedure was adequate to bar Lehr, even though he had not known about it. There was no constitutional requirement that he be afforded notice of adoption proceedings or an opportunity to be heard even though both the child's mother and the judge who approved the adoption knew of his attempt to establish his paternity before adoption was ordered.[33]

Even in *Caban v. Mohammed* there had been clear signs that the

Court was not creating a model of pure equality, either between all unwed parents or between married and unmarried fathers. The Court explicitly left open the question of the unmarried father's rights at the time his offspring is born. The answer to that question would be very important to a surrogacy arrangement if the parties were litigating on a theory of the rights of the unwed father, instead of litigating as parties to a surrogacy contract.[34]

The unconstitutionality that the Court found in *Caban* was that New York law distinguished solely on the basis of gender between unmarried mothers and fathers. The state had defended this distinction on the ground that mothers generally have closer relationships with their children than fathers do. The Court pointed out that such differences do not invariably exist, and it contrasted this case, in which both parents had fully participated in the upbringing of their children,[35] with an earlier case in which it rejected an unwed father's constitutional claim when "he has never exercised actual or legal custody over his child, and thus has never shouldered any significant responsibility with respect to the daily supervision, education, protection, or care of the child."[36]

The most significant argument the Court had to contend with in *Caban* in holding this gender-based classification unconstitutional was the argument that the state's law fulfilled a state interest in promoting the adoption, and the consequent legitimation, of illegitimate children. Allowing both natural parents equally to veto an adoption would cause the children to remain illegitimate. Although the Court found that state interest "an important one"—serving the interests of the child because it would "remove the stigma under which illegitimate children suffer"[37]—the Court said the state could not accomplish that end by as irrational a distinction as that between natural mothers and fathers. Justice Stevens' powerful dissent in *Caban* focused on the importance of this state interest in promoting legitimation.[38]

Finally, to meet the objection that it can be difficult to identify and locate unwed fathers, the Court suggested that for *older* children the state *could* differentiate between unwed parents as long as the distinctions between them were not gender-based. For an obvious example, the state can distinguish between unwed parents who live with their child and those who do not, even if those who live with their child are much more likely to be unwed mothers than unwed fathers. Moreover, the Court said specifically that it expressed no view as to whether even a gender-based line could be drawn between the mothers and the fathers of *newborn* children, because the question was not before it.[39]

Justice Stevens in his dissent discussed primarily the situation surrounding newborns, saying that the overwhelming majority of adoptions involve infants, and claiming that the Court's own rule was limited to "adoptions of older children '. . . [in which] the father has established a substantial relationship with the child and is willing to admit paternity.' "[40] In his discussion he emphasized the differences that exist between mothers and fathers at the moment when a child is born.[41]

It is those differences that exist at birth that would be relevant in a custody contest between the natural parents after the mother repudiated a surrogacy contract and the father asserted rights as an unwed biological parent. What Justice Stevens suggested, and what much of the Court's language in *Caban* and *Lehr* would support, is that it would be permissible, perhaps even appropriate, for the state to have a rule favoring mothers as custodians at this stage. At the moment of birth the mother has a relationship with the child. She has borne the child for nine months, has given birth to her, and most probably is capable of breastfeeding her.[42] The father has yet to establish a relationship with the child, other than his own expectations and his biological connection.[43]

True, the father's comparative lack of relationship is not the father's *fault;* on the contrary, it seems to be beyond his control and biologically determined. Does that mean that he should not be treated the same as the fathers who failed to establish a relationship with their child, whom the Court discussed in *Caban;* or is the existence or nonexistence of the relationship the determinative factor rather than the presence or absence of fault? In *Lehr* also it appeared that it was not the father's fault that he had not established a relationship with his child; according to the dissenters, the mother had prevented him from seeing their son for the first two years of the child's life. Nonetheless, because the mother had had a continuous bond with her child, she was permitted to cut off the natural father's rights by consenting to the child's adoption by her husband.

There is certainly something to be said for equality between natural parents even when the parents are not in a de facto family relationship. The main thing to be said against it is that any rule emphasizing equality, at least equality between parents in the awarding of custody of newborns, seems to lead in the direction of custody contests over who is the better parent.

Chapter Nine

Custody Contests to Determine the Better Parent

I f parents do not constitute a family and each has an equal claim to custody of the child, one likely result is protracted and bitter litigation in which all the facts and circumstances relevant to each parent are examined and the court determines which one is the better custodian from the point of view of "the best interests of the child." But if it best accords with the child's interests to avoid the custody contest (as I shall suggest it does), the rule is destructive, because it affords no basis for predicting which of two fit parents will prevail and thereby diminishes any possibility that the parents can resolve the conflict out of court. A presumption for one parent or the other would reduce this problem. The rules I shall suggest for the awarding of custody of newborns whose parents do not constitute a family tend to favor the mother as custodian. This is not so much because mothers are particularly deserving or because fathers do not merit protection, as because the best interests of children require having a clear presumption as to who their caretaker will be.[1]

Presumptions Favoring the Mother as Custodian of a Newborn

Any presumption that is established as to who should be custodian need not necessarily be gender-based. Just as the Supreme Court struck down the gender-based presumption involved in *Caban v. Mohammed*, several states have invalidated a presumption that in custody suits historically preferred the mother to the father as the custodian of children "of tender years."[2] But rather than examine all the facts and circumstances of vying parents, several states have replaced the historical presumption for the mother with another presumption that is stated in gender-neutral terms. One of the most enthusiastically received of the proposed new presumptions would favor "the primary caretaker." That presumption usually will favor mothers, who more often than not are the primary caretakers of their children; but when custody disputes involve children other than newborns, it would favor a father who takes primary responsibility for childcare.

Garska v. McCoy is a leading case establishing the presumption of custody for the parent who attends to the daily needs of the children.[3] There the West Virginia Supreme Court of Appeals explained that "the loss of children is a terrifying specter to concerned and loving parents: however, it is particularly terrifying to the primary caretaker parent who, by virtue of the caretaking function, was closest to the child." The court went on to note that "the parent who is not the primary caretaker is usually in the superior financial position," and thus has better resources to fight a drawn-out custody battle if no presumption is to be operative; there is substantial risk either that the primary caretaker will lose custody through inability to litigate or that she may be tempted to trade the custody of the child for reduced child support or alimony payments—a trade that will not benefit the child.[4] According to the *Garska* court, "Since trial courts almost always award custody to the primary caretaker parent anyway, establishment of certainty in this regard permits the issues of alimony and support to stand upon their own legs and to be litigated or settled upon the merits of relevant financial criteria, without introducing into the equation the terrifying prospect of loss to the primary caretaker of the children."[5] The court also relied upon the propositions that "in the average [custody] proceeding intelligent determination of relative degrees of fitness requires a precision of measurement which is not possible given the tools available to judges" and that "there is an urgent need . . . for a legal structure upon which [parents] may rely in reaching a settlement."[6]

Another, and perhaps even more appealing, way in which the

court might have defended its presumption is that the child in all likelihood would be more upset and grieved by the loss of the primary caretaker than by the loss of the other parent, whom by hypothesis the child sees less and who does less for the child—at least less that the child is aware of. In asking who was the primary caretaker, the *Garska* court used the following criteria:

> (1) preparing and planning meals; (2) bathing, grooming, and dressing; (3) purchasing, cleaning, and care of clothes; (4) medical care, including nursing and trips to physician; (5) arranging for social interaction among peers after school, i.e., transporting to friends' houses or, for example, to girl or boy scout meetings; (6) arranging alternative care, i.e., babysitting, day-care, etc.; (7) putting child to bed at night, attending to child in the middle of the night, waking child in the morning; (8) disciplining, i.e., teaching general manners and toilet training; (9) educating, i.e., religious, cultural, social, etc.; and (10) teaching elementary skills, i.e., reading, writing and arithmetic.[7]

Custody is therefore to go to the person who serves as primary caretaker in the sense that she or he takes care of the child's daily needs.[8]

Such a presumption, of course, cannot solve all cases. The *Garska* court did say that of course its rule called for an exception if the primary caretaker fails to provide emotional support, routine cleanliness, or nourishing food[9]—the typical exception for unfitness. The court also recognized that its presumption would not provide any guidance in families when parents divide roles sufficiently that there is no primary parent who performs "the lion's share of the child raising."[10] On the other hand, in a great many cases the primary caretaker presumption will achieve a clear result that parties can take into account in settling their case or that a court can apply without protracted litigation: custody of the child will go to the primary caretaker parent as long as that parent is fit and as long as the child is not old enough to formulate and express a contrary desire.[11]

The primary caretaker presumption, which is followed in West Virginia and some other states, bears similarities to another suggested rule that many psychologists and experts in family law defend and that has been put forth most thoroughly by Goldstein,

Freud, and Solnit in a series of books:[12] the presumption for continuity of care. Usually that presumption arises when the issue is whether to transfer the child to a new placement, thereby severing the custodial relationships to which the child is accustomed. Goldstein, Freud, and Solnit warn against changing from a successful custodial relationship out of a desire to produce something "even better." They emphasize also that the "psychological parent"—the person who takes care of the child's needs on a daily basis—is the important figure to the child and that this relationship is more important to preserve than any biological connection.[13] The presumption for continuity of care usually arises when the contenders for custody do not live together, but if it were applied when both parents had been living together and with the child up until the moment of litigation, it would be equivalent to the presumption for a primary caretaker, and either presumption would lead to the same result.

These presumptions are often used in custody contests. How would they apply in a contest between parents who are not married to each other and who are arguing over custody of a newborn?[14]

If the tests are applicable at all to parents disputing over a newborn, it appears that the mother would at that moment in time be the primary caretaker and the person with whom the child has the greater relationship to continue. Not only has the mother given more of herself to the child (granted, not by choice but by biological necessity), but also the mother is far more familiar to the child than the father is. The infant has listened to her heartbeat, for example, for months before birth. Some psychologists believe that the child knows the mother from birth in a way the child knows no other person and that it is disruptive and even traumatic for the baby to part with her mother at that stage.[15] Moreover, the mother's ability to breastfeed the baby invites her to continue her close physical relationship with the child in a way that the father is unable to duplicate.

This analysis suggests that although presumptions for the primary caretaker or for the continuation of a successful ongoing relationship leave room for either parent to become custodian in many cases, in the case of a newborn they would apply invariably to award custody to a mother who herself had borne the child, as long as the mother was fit.

From the point of view of fairness to the father, the rule has obvious shortcomings, since there is nothing he could do or could have done (at least without continuing his relationship with the mother for a longer period) that would put him in a position of equality with the natural mother. But the rule should prevail unless the father has a more satisfactory presumption to suggest.[16] There is a compelling argument for using some presumption to resolve most custody contests rather than making courts decide on the basis of all the facts and circumstances which of two people would make the better parent. Indeed, deciding on the basis of all the facts and circumstances is likely to be equivalent in practice to a presumption in favor of the parent who is more affluent or more upper middle class.

The Problems with Custody Contests

One of the principal problems with custody contests, as the *Garska* court discussed, is the importance of any large monetary disparity between the parents. In litigation between divorcing parents, the parent with the most money available to spend on litigation can use that advantage either to obtain custody for himself or to negotiate a settlement that will leave child support unreasonably low. A second problem with custody contests is the difficulty of proving in court which parent would be better, when both meet the criterion of fitness. There are always problems in determining on the basis of a judicial hearing which of two fit parents would be the better custodian. A great deal depends not upon the reality outside the courtroom but upon the impression the parties make in court, the strength of the psychiatric testimony they produce, how well they prompt the child, and so on. For example, a person with less experience of the world or of having to present herself in a good light, or a person very nervous when coming to the forum where she may lose her child, may make a very bad impression even though she is impressive in her home and in her role as a mother. In addition, custody contests frequently involve difficult legal questions about how the law is to measure the attributes of one particular set of parents against another, and which factors a court can permissibly take into account.[17]

Several factors in the surrogacy situation exacerbate the usual problems and make even more troublesome the prospect of two biological parents' battling out the custody issue on the basis of who could be the better custodial parent. First, in the surrogacy situation there are likely to be significant disparities in wealth and class between the would-be adopters and the surrogate mother and her family. The class differences and the differences in style are likely to be much more numerous and much greater than in the case of conventional parents who have had a relationship with each other. The differences are not inevitable, of course; they usually would not exist in surrogacy between friends. But generally surrogacy is and has been a tool by which the wealthy and more powerful use the less fortunate. Even in biblical times, it was their handmaidens whom women used as childbearers for their husbands.[18]

Contested cases involving surrogacy arrangements are therefore especially likely to involve the troublesome question whether and how factors associated with wealth and influence—or the superior education of one of the parties—should properly be counted into the equation when a judge assesses the best interests of the child.[19] These are awkward questions in our system.

The Whitehead-Stern litigation is illustrative. The contracting parents were a professional two-career couple; the surrogate was a housewife who had not finished high school and had married when she was sixteen. Her husband Richard was currently a garbage collector; in the thirteen years before trial, he had held seven different jobs. Richard was also an acknowledged alcoholic (though never a violent or abusive one). The court noted that he had "not actively pursued assistance to control his alcohol abuse for some time."[20] According to the expert testimony, he was also "forthright, articulate, genuine, quiet and 'down to earth.' "[21] Moreover, "He does all the corny things kids love."[22]

Between them the Sterns made $90,000 annually from their jobs; Richard Whitehead made $28,000 and had two children to support besides his wife and himself.[23] Mary Beth Whitehead was a housewife and mother, with no income of her own. She had been on welfare for a period when she was separated from her husband. A warrant had been issued for Richard's arrest before he repaid the money owed the welfare board. When Mrs. Whitehead was twenty-one she had worked as a dancer in a bar for a few months because her husband's driver's license had been suspended and he was out of work. The court took note that "the Whiteheads moved at least 12 times, frequently living in the homes of other family members."[24] The Whiteheads had once filed for bankruptcy. At the time of the suit their mortgages were in default.

What is a judge to make of this evidence? In one sense the judge may believe that the child will be better off in the more stable, well-educated, and well-to-do household; but to take factors such as wealth into account raises an additional specter—that of the poor or uneducated being deprived of their children in order to benefit the wealthy and established. Both courts in *Baby M* clearly did rule that a family's financial ability was a factor in determining "the best interests of the child," the relevant standard in New Jersey and elsewhere.[25]

The New Jersey Supreme Court also noted the trial judge's "emphasis on the Sterns' interest in Melissa's education as compared to the Whiteheads'. That this difference is a legitimate factor to be considered we have no doubt." But, the court said, the purpose of the best interests inquiry is not "to create . . . a new member of the intelligentsia but rather a well-integrated person who might reasonably be expected to be happy with life. 'Best interests' does not contain within it any idealized lifestyle."[26]

Financial and educational factors will favor the more middle-class parent, and class differences also translate into different childrearing styles. One commentator points out that, because of the class bias inherent in our decision-making system, the inquiry into "the best interests of the child" will stack the deck against surrogate mothers who want to keep their child: "Given the elite backgrounds of most judges and their identification with the privileged, the chances of their deciding surrogacy disputes in favor of the natural mother are small. Their very definition of good childrearing is likely to differ from that of the mother."[27]

In other contexts, courts have sometimes noted the difficulties of introducing factors such as wealth and education into the analysis.[28] In *Garska,* for example, the court pointed out that although "the educational and economic position of the father is superior to that of the mother, nonetheless, those factors alone pale in comparison to love, affection, concern, tolerance, and the willingness to sacrifice," which the primary caretaker parent had shown.[29] And in *Scarpetta* (discussed in Chapter 6) the court refused to compare the competing families—a natural mother who had placed her child for adoption and changed her mind and the would-be adoptive family who had had custody of the child for a period. Parents who give up their children for adoption are generally less well-to-do than parents who seek to adopt, but the court said it was improper to compare the families; indeed it did not even allow the prospective adoptive parents to participate in the decision as either parties or witnesses.

> In no case . . . may a contest between a parent and nonparent resolve itself into a simple factual issue as to which affords the better surroundings, or as to which party is better equipped to raise the child. It may well be that the prospective adoptive parents would afford a child some material advantages over and beyond what the natural mother may be able to furnish, but these advantages, passing and transient as they are, cannot outweigh a mother's tender care and love unless it is clearly established that she is unfit to assume the duties and privileges of parenthood.[30]

But in order to avoid the comparative inquiry the court had to abandon a standard of best interests based on all the circumstances. It did so in favor of a rule that the best interests of the child *are* to be with her natural mother (rather than nonparents), essentially creating in the mother a right to custody (vis-à-vis nonparents) unless she is unfit.

It also is especially likely in situations involving newborns, as surrogacy does, that there will be little evidence besides the position, lifestyles, and personalities of the competing parents. At the outset, when the suit is brought, neither biological parent has had much experience parenting this newborn child; and indeed neither may have had experience parenting at all. We all know that it is not always predictable who will take to parenting and who will not. Even if the evidence shows that the surrogate mother is doing a fine job raising her other child, how is her mothering to be compared with the nonexisting parenting of the father and his wife?

In custody contests involving newborns, then, the inquiry would be even more speculative than usual, and the judge would have very few direct facts on which to rely.[31] In such situations, courts often look to experts to fill the void. But the *Baby M* litigation shows that this solution does not eradicate the possibility of class and personal bias, and indeed may tend to exacerbate it. *Baby M* provides ample evidence of bias from the experts. Mrs. Whitehead was called "narcissistic" in seeking custody of her daughter, for example, because the cost of the suit might lead to foreclosure on her house and long-term indebtedness for her family.[32] She also was called narcissistic because she wanted "to give the gift of life," whereas "for Mr. Stern the goal of maintaining the genetic family line was a chance to ward off existential loneliness."[33] This tendency to interpret everything to disfavor Mrs. Whitehead while remaining uncritical of Dr. and Mr. Stern is apparent throughout the testimony.

Dr. Michelle Harrison has written a thorough and devastating account of the bias reflected in the experts' testimony in the *Baby M* litigation. She documents in detail the pattern of bias in the experts' descriptions of the interaction between the parents and Baby M. She demonstrates that a pervasive theme in the experts' testimony was that the Sterns believed in and used the mental health system, whereas Mrs. Whitehead did not use family therapy or professional mental health counseling. The experts thought Whitehead should undergo psychotherapy. The experts admired the Sterns for their good judgment in this regard and were angered by Mrs. Whitehead, who was too certain of her own reactions.[34]

Just as criticizing a mother because her quest to keep her daughter undermines her family's financial security weights the balance against the less well-to-do, so does criticizing her for failure to use professional mental health counseling impose on her middle-class values that she may not share and may not desire to share. The less affluent as a group are less likely than the upper middle class to conceive of psychotherapy as the solution to their needs. And even if they desire it, they may find it difficult to pay for.

The failure to use professionals harmed Mary Beth Whitehead in another way as well, and it illustrates that the reduced access to professionals of the less affluent in our society is a real disadvantage in a custody (or other legal) battle. If, instead of fleeing the jurisdiction when the Sterns first obtained an *ex parte* order granting them custody of Baby M, Whitehead had appeared in court to contest the award of custody and had presented her position that a child cannot be taken from her mother on the basis of contract, she would have had a good chance of reversing the *ex parte* order at that time and retaining custody of Baby M during the litigation. Her illegal flight from New Jersey and her various actions over the next few months in her attempt to keep her baby—frequent changes of residence, living in motel rooms, threats and false accusations against Mr. Stern—were important in shaping the trial judge's and the guardian *ad litem*'s attitudes that Whitehead was impulsive, unstable, and untrustworthy. Her life as a housewife at her home in Brick Township would have yielded much less damaging evidence against her. And yet the flight from the police who had appeared with the Sterns to remove her daughter was an understandable reaction from a mother who was uncounseled, and who did not understand that an order issued in a hearing of which she had not received notice and at which she did not appear could be altered in a later hearing at which she appeared with a lawyer and presented her side of the case. The paramount reason Mrs. Whitehead was not counseled at the time was that she did not have money. She had tried and failed to obtain a lawyer, and she continued to try and fail during her flight from New Jersey; but, finding herself in an unprecedented legal situation without financial resources, it was a long time before she was able to obtain competent professional help.[35]

Whatever the source of the bias of the mental health experts involved in the *Baby M* trial, it is clear from the reports. As Dr. Harrison demonstrates, "If Mary Beth does poorly on a test it is a sign of psychopathology; if the Sterns do poorly it is either irrelevant or a sign of anxiety."[36] "When the baby crawls after Mr. Stern it is indicative of her attachment to him. Not so for her mother. The baby did crawl to Mrs. Whitehead, but the experts say that 'the baby shows "awareness" but "demonstrates no anticipatory behaviors" toward Mrs. Whitehead.' "[37] Mrs. Whitehead was faulted for failing "Pattycake" by saying "hooray" rather than "pattycake" when Sara-Melissa responded correctly. (Dr. Stern got it right; Mr. Stern did not play; Mr. Whitehead got it right too, but apparently that did not count.)[38]

Whereas Mrs. Whitehead was called impulsive, controlling, narcissistic, schizoid, and possessed of "borderline personality trait," the Sterns were given the benefit of the doubt when they revealed weakness.[39] Mr. Stern's perceived need to continue his family line and Dr. Stern's perceptions about the risks to herself in bearing children were treated sympathetically. The experts did not question their failure to investigate either whether adoption was available or whether there actually were risks to Dr. Stern should she become pregnant. Nor did they question the reasons the Sterns gave for avoiding adoption—fear of AIDS, fear of a child who "looks different," fear of having to convince a woman to give up her baby—exactly the situation their litigation actually produced.

Part of the explanation for the bias shown by the experts in *Baby M* may be that they were acting as "hired guns," taking any position that would support the party that continued to employ them.[40] But the experts described above were chosen by the guardian *ad litem* appointed by the court to represent Baby M. Their biases apparently resulted from their own personalities and positions.[41]

One problem with judging which of two fit parents would make the better custodian is that the quirks and prejudices of the individual decision maker—whether expert witness or judge—become too important. Moreover, the trial judge's decision on these matters is not effectively reviewable, since it depends not so much upon the rule of law as upon the trial judge's impression of the parties, whom the reviewing court does not meet. The New Jersey Supreme Court in *Baby M* said that the proper standard of review was whether the trial court's factual findings "could reasonably have been reached on sufficient credible evidence present in this record."[42] Rules of law that are more explicit than the best interests standard—the presumptions discussed above, for example—could cut back on the importance of the individual decision maker's personal reaction to the parties, although they would not eliminate the discretion altogether.[43]

One difficulty with custody contests generally is that when there is no evidence that would disqualify anyone, courts pass judgment on different styles, as though there was one right way to be and one right way to live. Why should it matter that Mary Beth Whitehead is the dominant one in her family, and her husband is comparatively passive? Why should it be a question for judgment and analysis that she selects the clothes her children wear and blow-dries their hair?[44] One problem may be personal or class bias, but the problem of bias is also inherent when decision makers have to make a judgment which party is the "better" parent even when both are fit.

Of course there is not a total absence of relevant evidence, even when the battle is over a newborn. During the litigation at least one parent will have custody of the child, and that parent will be building a relationship upon which a judgment could pass. Indeed that parent (and that parent's family) will be building with the child the kind of psychological relationship that it arguably will be harmful to the child to disturb if the judge's finding goes for the other parent. It is this fact that lays the foundation for the most compelling reason not to set up a system in which the custody of newborns will turn on the comparative fitness of the child's biological parents.

Under a system turning upon the general comparative qualities of the parties as parents, a temporary disposition usually is necessary at the outset of the dispute, in order to settle the child's residence pending the final decision. That temporary order is made on the basis of less than a full hearing. When the judge makes the final disposition, should the judge take into account events that transpired and relationships that formed during the period when the temporary order was in effect? There are serious problems either way this question is decided. If the judge does take into account that the "temporary custodians" have become the child's psychological parents, and that it would be detrimental to her to alter the placement to which she has adjusted, then the temporary disposition will in effect have determined the ultimate outcome. That does not seem fair to the parent who was denied temporary custody on the basis of less than a full hearing concerning the factors the law says are determinative. If, on the other hand, the judge decides not to let the permanent disposition be influenced by the temporary one, because that gives too great an advantage to the winner of the temporary order, the child runs the risk of having to sever a parental relationship that is important to her and to start over with another parent or parents. It is this loss of the psychological parent that many believe is seriously detrimental to the child's psychological development.

One solution to the dilemma was devised by a judge in Michigan. Laurie Yates, a Michigan surrogate, had twins for a couple in September 1987 and has refused to give them up. The judge has issued a temporary order of joint physical custody, with the babies alternating between the households every two weeks. The contracting couple, who live in Arkansas, have rented a house in Michigan in order to comply with this arrangement. It is not at all clear that such alternation is good for children. (Perhaps the judge is employing this creative decision making in an attempt to accustom the parents to sharing. Since twins are involved, the happiest solution might be for each family to keep one child and for them all to become the best of friends.)

Although a temporary order of equal joint custody is one way to prevent the child's bonding during litigation from controlling the outcome, the problem remains if the temporary custody is other than equal: in entering the final order, should the decision makers take into account bonding that has occurred during the temporary disposition? This issue presented itself at all stages of the *Baby M* litigation. When Judge Sorkow determined temporary custody in August 1986, should he have presumed in favor of Mrs. Whitehead because she had taken care of Sara during her first four and a half months? It seems inappropriate to stress the need for continuity of care when the custodian has obtained the child by kidnapping—as the Whiteheads did by fleeing New Jersey after the court ruled against them.[45] When the New Jersey Supreme Court ultimately decided the case, ruling upon a "best interests" rationale, should it have taken into account that Melissa had by then spent the preceding eighteen months with the Sterns and had bonded with them, and that by then it would be disruptive to her to return to her natural mother? Would it be fair to take that into account if the temporary order was erroneous and if the appropriate rule of law would have left custody with the natural mother?

The best solution for the future is to have a clear rule governing who will be the custodial parent. Such a rule would serve best by encouraging parents not to litigate at all. If it is clear under the law who will win any custody battle, it seems likely that many of those battles will not come to court. Furthermore, if a judge knows what the law is and it is clear how it applies on the facts of any particular case, the judge can apply that rule and have it govern an initial, temporary disposition, as well as a later one.

That would solve the dilemma of whether to allow the temporary order to control the final disposition, whichever way that question is resolved. If one believes that the events that occur during the temporary disposition *should* be taken into account in a final custody decree, the fact that the rule is clear and easy to apply and can be applied correctly at the outset makes it unobjectionable that the temporary disposition in fact controls the whole case. Only when the temporary disposition is different from what a full hearing would decide does any problem arise from making the temporary disposition controlling. And if one believes that the events occurring during the temporary custody should *not* play a part in the final disposition, a clear and easy-to-apply rule is also helpful, because it is important to the child that the final disposition come out the same way as the initial one.

It is important, then, to have a clear rule—or at least a presumption—as to who the custodian should be.[46] One possible rule would be to award custody to mothers, as long as they are fit. That rule, however, if made in those terms, is probably unconstitutional gender-based discrimination. Although arguments could be framed for many possible presumptions, the presumption for the primary caretaker and the presumption for the continuation of a successful placement seem most beneficial to the child. And in the context of disputes involving newborns, these presumptions would appear invariably to favor the woman who has borne the child. (They differ from a simple preference for mothers of newborns, however, in the limited sense that under this test a couple who together conceived a child that was incubated outside of the mother would be on an equal footing. On those facts there would be no preference for the egg-donor mother over the sperm-donor father even at the moment of birth.)

At any rate, some such preference may be necessary if the objection to surrogacy is that it exploits women in order to provide children for the wealthy. The suggestion is frequently made that courts should avoid the surrogacy contract in case of dispute and decide custody instead according to "the best interests of the child," just as courts generally would in contests between unmarried parents. It is likely, however, not only that such an approach would be destructive of security for the child and all the parents, but also that the ultimate outcome of the custody battle would very often be the same as if the contract terms had been followed—with custody being awarded to the better-situated contracting father and his wife. Those who believe that a surrogate mother should usually be able to retain custody of the child she has borne should not be content with leaving resolution of custody disputes to a general best interests standard, without some principles that clearly govern how the inquiry should be resolved.

Today a father can argue not only that he is the better parent but also that the mother is unfit, if he is in a position to sustain that argument; and all the presumptions discussed above make an exception for the unfit caretaker. Unfitness, however, is very strictly defined. It is the standard by which the state deprives a parent or both parents of custody against their will even if there is no other family to adopt them. Currently, a father who does not have compelling evidence that the mother should not be allowed to raise her children is best advised not to press the issue of unfitness but to use the same evidence instead to establish that he is the better parent. But if unfitness were the only way to deprive a parent of custody, there is some danger that fathers would argue unfitness too readily and make the mother defend herself in an expensive and emotionally draining courtroom battle. The Sterns, for example, might have attempted to use the evidence they assembled about Mrs. Whitehead and her family in an attempt to prove she was un fit parent, even though much evidence showed that she was not and even though she had done a more than adequate job of raising her other two children. If it developed that fathers tended so to abuse the unfitness standard, or if courts became prone to relax it so that it amounted in effect to a comparative, best-interests approach, then the claim of unfitness should be permitted only in a proceeding brought by the state to remove the children from the custodial parent.

In its opinion in *Baby M,* the New Jersey Supreme Court discussed many of the problems considered here. For example, it ruled clearly that the best interests of the child must be considered as of the time of the final court's decision, not as they were at the outset of the litigation; therefore, the temporary disposition of the custody issue can control the ultimate outcome, even if the temporary order was rendered on less than full evidence and indeed even if it was clearly erroneous as a matter of law. To rule otherwise, according to the court, would be to punish the child for judicial errors.[47]

Several of the New Jersey Supreme Court's positions seem to be at variance with those proposed here. Most notably, it stressed that New Jersey's statutes make "the claims of the natural father and the natural mother . . . entitled to equal weight" and "that it would be inappropriate 'to establish a presumption . . . in favor of any particular custody determination,' as any such presumption may 'serve as a disincentive for the meticulous fact-finding required in custody cases' "[48]—the very fact-finding that I have argued should be eliminated because it is both destructive and unreliable. The New Jersey court also accepted without critical scrutiny the testimony the experts had given at the *Baby M* trial.

In combination, the New Jersey court's approaches seem to call for the worst of custody contests. But in fact the rule that the court announced for the future, though stressing equality between parents and the necessity of examining all facts and circumstances at the time of final disposition, is very close to the one proposed here—to award custody to the mother unless she is unfit. The New Jersey court arrived at a very similar result, though by a quite different route.

Although the rule had no effect on the disposition of the Whitehead-Stern conflict, the New Jersey court announced a new rule to govern temporary custody in disputes involving newborns:

> When father and mother are separated and disagree, at birth, on custody, only in an extreme, truly rare, case should the child be taken from its mother *pendente lite, i.e.,* only in the most unusual case should the child be taken from its mother before the dispute is finally determined by the court on the merits. The probable bond between mother and child, and the child's need, not just the mother's, to strengthen that bond, along with the likelihood, in most cases, of a significantly lesser, if any, bond with the father—all counsel against temporary custody in the father. A substantial showing that the mother's continued custody would threaten the child's health or welfare would seem to be required.
>
> . . . Any application by the natural father in a surrogacy dispute for custody pending the outcome of the litigation will henceforth require proof of unfitness, of danger to the child, or the like, of so high a quality and persuasiveness as to make it unlikely that such application will succeed. Absent the showing required, all that a court should do is list the matter for argument on notice to the mother.[49]

In New Jersey, therefore, the mother has a right to temporary custody of any newborn who is the subject of dispute, unless the mother is unfit.

Although the presumption for the mother covers only temporary custody, the rule sharply diminishes the father's chances of receiving permanent custody as well. Even though the court will judge the award of permanent custody on the basis of all the facts and circumstances, with the mother's and the father's claims being treated equally, the bond that the mother and the child have established during the period of temporary custody and the disruption that removal at that point would cause to the child will be important factors in determining the child's best interests at that point in time. The court recognized as much when it said that no presumption was appropriate for the awarding of permanent custody and that equality between parents was New Jersey policy: "This does not mean that a mother who has had custody of her child for three, four, or five months does not have a particularly strong claim arising out of the unquestionable bond that exists at that point between the child and its mother; in other words, equality does not mean that all of the considerations underlying the 'tender years' doctrine have been abolished."[50] As a practical matter, therefore, it appears that in New Jersey the mother seeking to retain her newborn will almost invariably receive permanent as well as temporary custody unless she is an unfit parent.

This rule favoring the mother as custodian—somewhat surprisingly, stated in gender-based terms—applies not only to surrogacy but to all parental disputes over the custody of newborns; it would apply in conflicts between divorcing parents as well as to parents who have never been married to each other. If this presumption for the mother is picked up and followed by courts in other states, it will amount to a very important development in the law, affecting many cases.

Given the New Jersey Supreme Court's holding that paid surrogacy is illegal—not simply unenforceable, as the Kentucky courts hold and as I have recommended—it was essential that the New Jersey court devise a rule favoring mothers as custodians when parents in a failed surrogacy arrangement are disputing over custody of the resulting child. The court's holding of illegality would have little effect unless supplemented by some deterrent to would-be fathers seeking to employ a surrogate. It is not at all clear from the *Baby M* opinion that criminal sanctions would be employed against people hiring a surrogate in violation of the ruling.[51] If there were no sanctions and if the father could participate in a custody battle on a basis of equality with the surrogate mother, it is easy to imagine that a would-be father might enter a surrogacy arrangement even after they were ruled illegal, expecting that the surrogate would not change her mind about performing the contract but knowing that even if she did, he was likely to prevail in any custody contest with the surrogate on the basis that he was the preferable custodian for the child. Of course, if no criminal sanctions are leveled, a would-be father in New Jersey can still enter a surrogacy contract expecting that the surrogate will perform as promised, or he can go to another jurisdiction where the contract has not been declared illegal. But announcing to the would-be father that in New Jersey the surrogate mother is likely to be awarded permanent custody if she decides she wants it could substantially deter surrogacy arrangements in that state.[52] It would be especially likely to have that effect if the father in that circumstance will be liable to support the child throughout the child's minority.

Problems concerning Visitation and Child Support

When the Father Receives Custody

One important difference between proceeding upon a theory of contract or adoption and proceeding through the model of a custody dispute between unwed parents is that visitation and child support are concomitants of custody disputes, but would not typically arise under surrogacy arrangements or under the laws of adoption.[53] There are therefore significant differences in the result, even if the natural father could succeed in obtaining custody under a custody-battle approach. For one thing, his wife would not be permitted to adopt the child without the natural mother's consent; instead the surrogate would remain the mother, and the father's wife would become a stepmother. Moreover, the natural mother would have rights of visitation, which the court would arrange and order if the parties could not reach agreement concerning them and which might be either minimal or considerable, amounting in effect to a sharing of custody. And in several jurisdictions the natural grandparents also would have rights of visitation.

Even if an amorphous best interests approach were followed and the surrogate mother did lose custody in that inquiry, the standard rules concerning visitation would place the mother who has changed her mind about parting with her child in a much more comfortable position than the usual surrogacy contract. She would be allowed to see the child and spend some time with her, and the child would visit at her mother's home. Professor Julia Wrigley has suggested that this approach would minimize surrogacy because contracting couples would not want the child to continue to have a relationship with her mother: the "prospect of being connected with a woman they barely knew, a woman moreover who is almost certainly of a different social class and who has a different lifestyle," would deter many.[54] Couples might, however, expect that the surrogate would adhere to the contract terms, and that a dispute over custody and visitation would never arise, just as couples might continue to attempt surrogacy arrangements even if the mother had an absolute right to change her mind and keep the child. But even if the prospect of sharing responsibility when the mother changes her mind does not sharply deter surrogacy arrangements, it would produce a result that may seem more humane: the loser of the custody contest would not have to lose contact with her or his child, but instead would be in much the same position as other parents who lose custody but retain visitation rights. One important difference between a custody-contest approach and the typical surrogacy contract is, therefore, that in a custody battle courts are more likely to recognize a right on the part of both parents to participate in bringing up the child.

Professor Wrigley's suggested probable reaction of the contracting couple is borne out by the conflict between the Whiteheads and the Sterns. At one point Mrs. Whitehead offered to settle the dispute if she were permitted to know the child as she was growing up; she asked for visitation rights of one weekend a month and two weeks in the summer. Dr. and Mr. Stern refused, insisting that Mrs. Whitehead's rights be terminated. Bill Stern made clear that he wanted "complete termination . . . no contact, no visits."[55] They continued this theme when interviewed by the expert witnesses, claiming there was no value in having Baby M continue a relationship with her mother. Indeed Betsy Stern went so far as to say that she would "not entertain any participation in the child's life if Mary Beth Whitehead also participates."[56] Bill Stern also said that if Mary Beth Whitehead was given custody he would not want visitation rights, claiming that it would not be in the child's best interests to maintain contact with the noncustodial parent.[57] Mrs. Whitehead, in contrast, claimed that "if she were given custody of the baby, she would encourage the Sterns to have visitation and participate in the major decisions of the baby's life."[58]

It may or may not be good for the child to maintain a relationship with both parents. This is a question upon which experts disagree, even in the case of an older child who has already formed a relationship with both of her parents.[59] Obviously, the case for having two homes and two sets of parents is less compelling when a newborn is the subject of the dispute. However one feels about that issue, all agree that if there is to be real visitation, and not simply minimal supervised visits like those allowed to Mrs. Whitehead during the litigation,[60] it will be much more beneficial for the child if the adults are willing to cooperate and to show consideration for each other.

Indeed, if Sara-Melissa (who may now be called Elizabeth, the middle name given her by both families and a name that both of her mothers share)[61] is to thrive, Mary Beth Whitehead and the Sterns must start getting along with each other. It would be bad for the child to have two sets of parents who battle with each other. But if the parents can get along, allowing both parents contact with the child is far preferable to the alternative of having the child grow up with the knowledge that her mother fought for her and was prevented, by the parents she knows and by the law, from having any contact with her.

Once a mother resists a surrogacy contract, therefore, the preferable solution is to permit both parents to maintain contact with the child. And although it may remain relatively rare for a well-paid surrogate to change her mind and seek custody of her child, a large percentage of surrogates may change their minds about disappearing altogether from the lives of their offspring. A good many surrogates may decide they want to maintain contact with the baby they bear and to exercise rights to visitation. Hopefully, commercialization will not extend to allowing annual payoffs to persuade them not to exercise this right; and hopefully surrogates will not use the threat of refusing to terminate parental rights (one of which is visitation) to extort additional money from would-be adopters. If the surrogate is permitted to change her mind concerning surrender of the child, she necessarily will also have the right to change her mind concerning visitation and termination of her parental rights. Some mothers who want continued contact with their child will agree to terminate their parental rights, but only upon condition of an open adoption, in which they are permitted to know their biological child and are given rights of visitation.

Although such adoption arrangements are not the norm, they do not transgress the public policy of most states.

Not only could surrogate mothers opt for visitation; in situations in which parents truly are able to cooperate and also live near each other, joint physical and legal custody may be a possibility.[62] That solution was adopted in February 1987, when a San Diego judge awarded joint custody to Alejandra Muñoz, of the daughter she had borne for Natty and Mario Haro.[63]

If parents in surrogacy arrangements are unable to cooperate, however, a child may be better off having one set of parents rather than two. Such circumstances would seem to support either a contract-and-adoption approach or a rule of absolute rights for the mother rather than a custody-and-visitation approach. But the child growing up cannot be limited to one biological parent if the other biological parent resists. Only when a biological parent formally terminates parental rights sometime after the birth of the child does that parent lose the right to insist on maintaining contact with the child. It is extremely rare for courts to find that the best interests of the child preclude any contact, and in the vast majority of cases a biological parent can insist upon some visitation.

To the extent that a judge believes that it is easier on a child psychologically to have one principal home, the visitation may not involve a substantial percentage of the child's time. It is not necessary for a child to be split down the middle, especially when the custody and visitation schedule is to be decided at the outset, when the child is newborn. A child who has already lived with two parents when they separate, and who has had a close relationship with both of them, may need to spend a substantial amount of time with each parent. But usually a newborn child whose future is to be decided should start the world with a principal home, even though that resolution places the best interests of the child over any principle of equality between the parents.

When the Mother Receives Custody

Current family law would grant visitation to the father (unless he is cut off by sperm donor provisions or by the mother's marital status) if the natural mother receives custody as the result of a custody dispute, as she almost always would both under the presumption recommended above and under the New Jersey approach. The father (and perhaps his parents) would be entitled to visitation, which might or might not involve substantial time with the child. Moreover, the law concerning the obligations of unwed fathers would seem to render him liable for child support, if the natural mother chose to enforce this obligation against him.[64]

In states in which surrogacy is illegal and the aim is to prevent it, it would be entirely appropriate to place upon the father the obligation of supporting the child. But a state with a more neutral stance on surrogacy—one that made surrogacy contracts legal but unenforceable—should not routinely hold such fathers liable for support. If the father who has legally contracted for a baby and hoped to receive custody of the child conceived with his sperm is not permitted to enforce the contract and obtain custody, and also cannot prevail as the better parent for the child because the mother is not unfit and at the time of litigation has a closer relationship with the child than he does, it seems harsh to hold him to support the child for eighteen years. Indeed the best course for the father to take, if surrogacy arrangements are to remain legal though not specifically enforceable, is to pick the surrogate carefully, to hope that she goes through with the arrangement, but if she does not, to give up and try again through another surrogate or through adoption.[65] This course is obstructed if the father incurs a large and long-standing liability with the failed surrogacy arrangement.

Although it may seem fair to exempt from support obligations the father who wants to put the unfortunate transaction behind him, existing law may prove problematic. In other situations in which the unmarried father could claim that the equities required not holding him responsible—when the mother deceived him into impregnating her, for example—courts have held that the father remains liable. Two rationales seem most important to this rule. First, child support is for the benefit of the child and not of the mother; it would be wrong to make the child suffer and to deprive her of the support of the other parent because of the conduct of the mother, even if it is questionable. Second, it would not be satisfactory to have a rule that turned upon whether the woman caused the pregnancy by acting unfairly, because there is rarely hard and convincing evidence upon which a court could confidently decide this question, and efforts to do so would involve the court in many private details of the parties' lives that it would best avoid.[66]

In *Pamela P. v. Frank S.*—the best-known case involving deception—the reviewing court, for these reasons, overturned a ruling by the family court that had attempted to protect the child's needs and also to pay some heed to the equities between the parties.[67] The lower court had ruled that the father should be liable for support only if the mother was not able to shoulder that burden herself and would otherwise be dependent upon welfare benefits to support the child. The reviewing court held that Frank Serpico should remain liable as the father even if the mother had "tricked" him into impregnating her by falsely claiming that she was on the Pill.

Although that court was correct to apply the usual child support rules despite testimony that the mother deceived the father into impregnating her[68]—an approach that ideally would encourage potential fathers to take some responsibility for birth control rather than making it solely the responsibility of their partners— the usual child support rules should not apply in the situation of the broken surrogacy contract, in jurisdictions in which surrogacy is legal. In some states they may not apply because sperm donors are shielded from child support suits, or because the child is conclusively presumed to be the offspring of the mother's marriage. (In those states fathers would also usually lose any right to litigate against a fit mother for custody.) But even where there is no such rule, the balance of equities, together with the possibility that the wisest course for all concerned is for the father to accept the disappointment and turn his attentions elsewhere, would suggest an exception to the usual support requirements imposed on unwed fathers, or a modification such as the one imposed by the lower court in *Pamela P.*, making the father liable only if otherwise the child must live in poverty. Although the ruling of the reviewing court in *Pamela P.*—that it is not worth having court battles over how and why someone became pregnant in order to weed out a few cases in which the mother consciously deceived the father—is sympathetic, the same sort of issue would not arise in surrogacy cases. In surrogacy cases, it is clear how the pregnancy occurred; the facts and the plan are set out between the parties in a contract that the mother decided not to perform. If the mother, who has decided to keep the child after all, is able adequately to support the child without the father's assistance, and if the father wishes to cut his ties with the biological child who is the product of the broken agreement, then the mother and her family should provide the sole support, even though the child might be better off with additional money coming from the natural father.

This suggestion that the contracting father need not be liable for child support reveals a need to do more than simply fit surrogacy arrangements into existing laws.[69] Even if in general lawmakers try to address issues concerning surrogacy by applying contract, adoption, and family law that is already developed, on the issue of the father's liability for support there is need for some special law specific to surrogacy contracts.[70] If the mother is to have power to avoid the contract and is favored in the custody dispute, it is necessary to relieve the father from liability for child support, both because that approach best comports with the equities and because it states the most workable rule. A rule that treated the contracting father like other unwed fathers, imposing support on him even when he cannot have custody and wants nothing to do with the child, would probably render it unworkable to allow surrogacy contracts but let the mother decide whether to comply. A clear opportunity to impose support upon the father would create a powerful incentive for some women to enter a surrogacy arrangement with the real intent of pulling out when the time came to surrender the child. Allowing the mother to impose child support upon the father is appropriate if surrogacy is banned, but not if it is considered legal.

The father's option to avoid support should apply only when the father has decided that the course he should take is to put behind him the situation that produced his biological child. That decision is understandable, but a father might react differently: he might feel that he wants to maintain contact with his offspring and know her as she grows up, even though he is not permitted to be her custodian. If the father does choose to take this course, he should be entitled to visitation rights on the same terms as other fathers who are not married to the mother of their child. And a father who opts to take that course should be liable for support on the same basis that other unwed fathers are.

Conclusion

Good arguments can be made that surrogacy contracts should be altogether prohibited; but if they are not, they should not be subjected to specific performance. Instead, the natural mother should have the right to renounce the contract (and pay back any money she has received under it) up until the time she turns the child over to the couple who arranged for the conception. Once the child moves into the home of the natural father and his wife, however, the contract takes full effect, and the rights of the mother to claim the child terminate.

If the mother rejects the contract, the biological father should not be able to prevail in a custody dispute with her as long as she is a fit parent, which will almost always be the case. Instead of disputing with the mother, the father should accept that the adoption did not go through and turn his attentions to arranging another adoption, through a surrogacy arrangement or otherwise. If he elects to develop and maintain a relationship with the biological child that he produced through his agreement, he has the right to do so, and the relationship he then develops will receive even constitutional protection, equivalent to that afforded other noncustodial fathers. If he does opt to develop such a relationship, he also becomes liable for child support. Moreover, the father should not have the right to change back and forth. Once he takes on the responsibility to act as a natural father toward the child, he should be bound to continue that responsibility, as other natural fathers are, until the child reaches majority. The child should not be subject to the father's taking on and then renouncing responsibilities as other things in the father's life make the child more or less convenient to him.

These rules avoid having child taken from mother and the maternal bond severed because of a contract. Moreover, they are clear and specific, enabling all the parties to know their rights and to avoid litigation as much as possible and enabling any litigation to be swiftly and easily resolved. Under this approach surrogate motherhood contracts will continue to be executed and performed. The possibility that women might decide to retain custody would probably not substantially deter surrogacy. But the likelihood that surrogates will choose to retain visiting rights is substantially greater than any likelihood that they will choose to retain custody. That would reduce the appeal of surrogacy for couples reluctant to share parenting or to have an open adoption.[1] Even if surrogacy contracts are deterred, however, that is not sufficient reason for abandoning these rules.

There is no reason for society to *encourage* surrogacy contracts. Given society's interests in discouraging commercialization of sex and childbearing, preventing exploitation of women, and encouraging adoption of existing children, appropriate positions for jurisdictions to take toward surrogacy range anywhere between prohibition of surrogacy contracts and tolerance of them. As jurisdictions adopt provisions concerning surrogacy, most will divide in various ways between these strategies but not deliberately promote surrogacy. Nor need they be concerned if some of the regulations they adopt from a balancing of the various needs result in discouraging some people from entering into surrogacy arrangements. Surrogacy for hire is probably with us for the long term, but society can afford to move slowly in evolving toward the new era of options in childbearing.

Appendix

Notes

Selected Bibliography

Index

The Current Legal Status of Surrogacy Arrangements

Few jurisdictions have any specific rules concerning surrogacy, although many are considering them and debating which rules to adopt. Efforts to reach some nationwide consensus have been few and have not led to the proposal of any usable standards. For example, the Ethics Committee of the American Fertility Society expressed "serious reservations" about surrogacy but reached no firm conclusions. One member of the committee, in dissent, believed that surrogacy should be made illegal forthwith.[1]

United States

State Legislatures

To date, only three of the many bills that have been introduced in state legislatures have become law. Louisiana (in July 1987), Nebraska (in February 1988), and Michigan (in June 1988) all have made surrogacy contracts void and unenforceable. Only Michigan's statute also makes it criminal to enter or arrange a surrogacy contract and imposes substantial penalties of fines and imprisonment.[2] In Arkansas, the legislature adopted the opposite position, passing a bill that would have made surrogacy contracts enforceable, but the governor vetoed the bill.

Bills that are still under consideration in many states take a wide variety of positions. Some would ban surrogacy altogether. See, for example, Nebraska's L 674 (introduced by Chambers), which parallels the British enactment described below; New Jersey's A 4138 (introduced by Kavanaugh); Iowa's S 358 (introduced by Hannon); and Maryland's S 613 (introduced by Mitchell). At the other extreme are bills that would make surrogacy paid and enforceable, such as New Jersey's A 956 (introduced by Kern).

Some bills effect a compromise. For example, New York's A 2403 (proposed by Halpin) would make the contracts unenforceable if the mother objects within twenty days after birth. The position is similar to the one advocated in this book. Connecticut's H 5398 (introduced by Tulisano) falls somewhere between unenforceability and illegality. That bill defines any child born as a result of artificial insemination as belonging to the mother and her husband. Even if the mother is willing to give the child to the contracting father and his wife after the birth, she cannot surrender the child directly to them; instead she has to place the child for adoption, and it is not certain that the sperm donor will be chosen to adopt. Thus, rather than making the contracts illegal, this bill tries to discourage them by creating a complex of rules that could prevent them from accomplishing their intended purpose. The Tulisano bill, however, was defeated in committee in May 1987.

Many legislators remain undecided. For example, John Dunne of New York originally proposed a bill that would have both allowed payments to surrogates and removed all option for the surrogate to change her mind. When it failed for lack of support, Dunne withdrew it and introduced instead a bill (S 1429) that places restrictions on surrogacy.[3]

Many of the bills decline to take any position but simply recommend the establishment of study commissions. Examples include Rhode Island's S 386 (introduced by Carlin and recently signed into law), Delaware's SJR 4 (introduced by Holloway), and Louisiana's HCR 2 (introduced by Fernandez).

State Courts

The only states other than Louisiana, Michigan, and Nebraska that now have clear law concerning the legality of surrogacy arrangements are Kentucky and New Jersey. There the rules have been announced in decisions of the state supreme court. In *Surro-*

gate Parenting Associates, Inc. v. Kentucky, the Kentucky Supreme Court held that the operation of surrogacy clinics does not violate the state's statute prohibiting babyselling, but that the surrogate has an absolute right to withdraw from the contract for five days after the baby's birth.[4] In New Jersey, the supreme court held paid surrogacy contracts illegal and unpaid ones unenforceable.[5] It also devised rules that for the future would favor the mother in a dispute with the father over the custody of a newborn child.[6]

In other states, lower courts have rendered a variety of decisions, but because the highest state court has not spoken, state law remains unclear.[7] Michigan has had the most activity. In *Doe v. Kelley* the intermediate state court held that payment is prohibited in connection with adoption and that it is constitutionally permissible to prohibit paid surrogacy.[8] The case was brought by a married couple who wished to enter a paid surrogacy arrangement and who sought a declaration as to its validity. In *Styrkowski v. Appleyard* the Michigan Supreme Court overturned lower court decisions prohibiting the use of the Paternity Act to transfer parental responsibilities to a father in a surrogacy arrangement that all parties wished to perform.[9] Although that was a decision of the state's highest court, it does not definitively control whether surrogacy, or paid surrogacy, is permissible. And those decisions give no guidance concerning the effect in Michigan of the surrogate mother's change of heart. In *Yates v. Keane,* a Michigan trial court held surrogacy contracts void and unenforceable because they exploit women and children. It was never clear that the trial court's position represented state law,[10] and in June 1988 all these judicial decisions were displaced by the new state statute.

Federal Government

On the federal level, three bills have been introduced in Congress. On May 14, 1987, Democrat Tom Luken of Ohio introduced a bill in the House that would amend 18 U.S.C. §89 to prohibit making, engaging in, or brokering a surrogacy arrangement on a "commercial basis," that is, "under circumstances in which a person who makes, engages in, or brokers the surrogacy arrangement receives or expects to receive, directly or indirectly, any payment for that conduct." The bill would also prohibit advertising for surrogacy. The bill is much like the one in effect in the United Kingdom, discussed below, except that it imposes criminal liability on commissioning parents and surrogates as well as on go-betweens, and it also prohibits private paid arrangements.

Another proposed federal enactment would forbid federal enforcement of surrogacy contracts (but would leave them enforceable in state courts that allowed them); and the third proposed enactment would prohibit the use of federal funds to pay for veterans to hire surrogates.

Europe

The status of surrogacy contracts is clearer in the United Kingdom than in the United States. An early case in Britain permitted a surrogate mother to repudiate the contract as being against public policy.[11] A 1984 report by the United Kingdom's Committee of Inquiry into Human Fertilization and Embryology had suggested that "legislation should be introduced to render criminal the creation or the operation in the United Kingdom of agencies whose purposes include the recruitment of women for surrogate pregnancy or making arrangements for individuals or couples who wish to utilize the services of a carrying mother; such legislation should be wide enough to include both profit and non-profit making organizations."[12] Subsequently, in 1985, commercial surrogacy arrangements were banned in the United Kingdom, but the ban does not extend to private arrangements, and only agencies and go-betweens are criminally responsible, not those who use their services.[13]

It is less clear what the rules are in other countries, although there are indications. In France it appears that surrogacy contracts are deemed illegal babyselling, and both agencies and individuals who use their services are subject to prosecution. In Germany, two recent court decisions have addressed issues raised in surrogacy agreements. The Berlin Court of Appeal ruled in a case that was factually similar to *Baby M* that the surrogate mother and her husband—who was presumed the father—had the right to custody of the resulting child and that their interests could not be waived by any prebirth agreement to give the child up. In another case, the Regional Appeal Court of Hamm ruled a surrogacy contract void as being *contra bonos mores* because the child was treated as merchandise. The court returned the surrogacy fee to the sperm donor. Strangely, that suit had been initiated by the donor, who had discovered that the surrogate mother's husband was in fact the child's father.[14]

Notes

Introduction

1. Noyes v. Thrane, No. CF7614 (L.A. Cty. Super. Ct. 1981). See Lois Timnick, "Surrogate Mother Wants to Keep Her Unborn Baby," *Los Angeles Times,* March 21, 1981, p. I-1; Michele Galen, "Surrogate Law: Court Ruling," *National Law Journal,* September 29, 1986, p. 1.

2. Ellen Goodman, "Wombs for Rent: New Era on the Reproduction Line," *Los Angeles Times,* February 8, 1983, p. II-5.

3. "Surrogate's Baby Born with Deformity Rejected by All," *Los Angeles Times,* January 22, 1983, p. I-17.

4. "Man Who Hired 'Surrogate Mother' Isn't Child's Father," *Los Angeles Times,* February 3, 1983, p. I-17.

5. See Lori Andrews, "Stork Market: The Law of the New Reproductive Technologies," *American Bar Association Journal,* 70 (1984), 50.

6. Report of Dr. Harold Koplewicz for use in *Baby M* litigation, 1987, p. 4. Koplewicz was chosen as an expert witness by the Whiteheads.

7. Report of social worker Judith Brown Greif for use in *Baby M* litigation, 1987, p. 11. Greif was chosen as an expert witness by the guardian *ad litem.*

8. Barbara Kantrowitz, "Who Keeps Baby M?" *Newsweek,* January 19, 1987, pp. 44–49.

9. Galen, "Surrogate Law," p. 8.

10. Report of Phyllis R. Silverman for use in *Baby M* litigation, October 23, 1986, p. 3.

11. See In re Baby M, *Family Law Reporter,* 14 (1988), 2010 (N.J. Sup. Ct. 1988). Indeed the judge performed an adoption ceremony immediately after announcing his decision, with the aim of solidifying the Sterns' parental rights and terminating Mrs. Whitehead's.

12. See ibid., pp. 2012, 2024.

13. Quoted in Report of Dr. Allwyn Levine for use in *Baby M* litigation, 1987, p. 16. Levine was an expert witness selected by the Sterns.

Even before the New Jersey Supreme Court decision, Whitehead may have had some success in discouraging surrogate motherhood. The response of legislators to surrogacy was much more negative after the *Baby M* trial than before. New York state senator John Dunne explains: "After Baby M there clearly was a shift . . . I think it opened up the eyes of people and made a lot of them so turned off by the practice, and really so bitter toward it, that there's more and more of a broad public feeling that says, 'Let's not encourage this.' " Legislators from other states confirm that the *Baby M* trial led to a broad reassessment of surrogate motherhood; Iver Peterson, "States Assess Surrogate Motherhood," *New York Times,* December 13, 1987, p. I42. By the end of 1987, even before the New Jersey Supreme Court decision, seventy bills seeking to regulate, ban, or study surrogacy had been introduced in twenty-seven states; twenty-one of them would have either banned surrogacy or prohibited payment of a fee. One such bill passed in July 1987, when the Louisiana legislature made surrogacy contracts "null and void and unenforceable"; the bill did not, however, impose penalties for violation; William L. Pierce, "Surrogate Parenthood: A Legislative Update," *Family Law Reporter,* 13 (1987), 1442. See Appendix, page 155.

14. The gestational surrogate, who carries the developing fetus but provides neither egg nor sperm, is considered further in Chapter 3.

15. See generally Richard Lacayo, "Whose Child Is This?" *Time,* January 19, 1987, pp. 56–58. Although there are no serious empirical studies concerning surrogacy, the voluminous writing available on the subject (see the Bibliography) provides a fairly consistent picture of what practices are.

16. Of these 500 contracts, 495 have been fulfilled without incident. See Charles Krauthammer, "The Ethics of Human Manufacture," *New Republic,* May 4, 1987, pp. 17–19.

17. In a Gallup telephone survey of 766 adults on January 7 and 8, 1987, 35 percent answered yes to the question: "If you wanted a child but could not have one because of fertility or other health problems, would you consider having a child by a surrogate mother?" "Surrogate Mothers: A *Newsweek* Poll," *Newsweek,* January 19, 1987, p. 48.

18. Ibid.

19. In 1982, the year for which the best statistics are available, there were 141,861 adoptions. Of these, 91, 141 were adoptions by relatives. Of the remaining 50,720, 17,602 were adoptions of healthy infants, 5,707 were adoptions of children from other countries, 14,005 were adoptions of children with special needs, and 9,591 were adoptions of children by foster parents. (These four categories are not mutually exclusive.) See National Committee on Adoption, *Adoption Factbook* (Washington, D.C., 1985), p. 102. In 1984, 2 million couples competed for the 58,000 children placed for adoption (a 35-to-1 ratio). See Andrew B. Wilson, "Adoption, It's Not Impossible," *Business Week,* July 8, 1985, p. 112.

20. See Kantrowitz, "Who Keeps Baby M?" p. 47. The statistically typical candidate is a twenty-five-year-old Christian married woman with a high school education and at least one child.

21. At this time the only jurisdictions in this country besides New Jersey

whose rules are settled are Kentucky, where the state supreme court has issued a definitive ruling—see Surrogate Parenting Associates, Inc. v. Kentucky, 704 S.W.2d 209 (1986)—and Michigan, Louisiana, and Nebraska, where statutes have been passed making surrogacy contracts void. See La. Rev. Stat. Ann. 9:2713 (codifying Act 583, 1987 Regular Session); "Surrogate Motherhood Voted Down," *Washington Post,* February 6, 1988, p. A5. Other jurisdictions are considering a broad spectrum of proposals. For a summary of the existing law on surrogacy and some proposed legislative enactments, see the Appendix.

22. The Supreme Court rather than Congress would decide whether federal law was controlling only if it based a decision upon the Constitution—if it were to decide that the due process or equal protection clauses required a particular result in the surrogacy area, for example, or if it were to find that a federal enactment exceeded Congress's power in some other respect. It seems clear, however, that Congress can constitutionally legislate in the area of commercial surrogacy—see Hoke v. United States, 227 U.S. 308 (1913) (upholding the Mann Act, which prohibited the transportation of women in interstate commerce for immoral purposes)—and Congress can also act to protect any individual liberty interests it finds in surrogacy arrangements, under section 5 of the Fourteenth Amendment. It is unlikely that the Supreme Court would decide surrogacy issues on constitutional grounds, at least at this time (see Chapter 4).

23. See Ill. ch. 89, § 1; Or. Rev. Stat. § 106.020.

24. Hawaii Rev. Stat. ch. 572, § 1; Md. Code Ann. Fam. Law § 2-202; S.C. Code Ann. § 20-1-10.

25. More states prohibit than allow first-cousin marriages, but there are a substantial number of states on each side of this issue. Indiana has the most unusual provision, allowing marriage between first cousins, but only if both parties are age sixty-five or older; Ind. Code Ann. § 31-7-1-3.

26. See Sosna v. Iowa, 419 U.S. 393 (1975); Williams v. North Carolina, 325 U.S. 226 (1945).

27. For example, adoption is fully available to out-of-staters in Colorado, Delaware, Florida, Indiana, Louisiana, Michigan, Minnesota, Ohio, Oregon, Pennsylvania, Rhode Island, and Virginia.

28. For example, Alabama, Alaska, Arizona, Georgia, Idaho, Illinois, Iowa, Massachusetts, Mississippi, Missouri, Montana, Nebraska, North Carolina, Wisconsin, and Wyoming permit only residents to adopt.

29. For example, West Virginia, Washington state, and South Carolina permit nonresidents to adopt independently but not through agencies (for other than special needs children); New Mexico has the opposite rule, allowing out-of-staters to adopt only with licensed agencies, whereas independent adoption is available to residents.

30. For example, Arkansas, California, Kentucky, New Jersey, South Carolina, and Utah allow nonresidents to adopt only children with special needs. For a complete survey, conducted in 1982, see National Committee on Adoption, *Adoption Factbook,* pp. 76–85.

31. See Noel Keane and Dennis Breo, *The Surrogate Mother* (New York: Everest House, 1981), pp. 16, 183, 210, 217, 274.

32. Some require prior state permission or even follow-up reports for exportation, but the regulations usually do not apply when the natural mother takes the child out of state. More troublesome for the nonresident adopter are importation rules in most states, which regulate in various ways, such as requiring prior approval by the state welfare department and the posting of a bond. See generally Morton L. Leavy and Roy D. Weinberg, *Law of Adoption*, 4th ed. (Dobbs Ferry, N.Y.: Oceana, 1979), pp. 8–13.

1. Are the Contracts Illegal?

1. See *Juvenile Delinquency (Interstate Adoption Practices): Hearings before the U.S. Senate Subcommittee to Investigate Juvenile Delinquency,* pursuant to S. Res. 62, July 15–16, 1955, p. 11.

2. William L. Pierce, "Survey of State Activity regarding Surrogate Motherhood," *Family Law Reporter,* 11 (1985), 3001.

3. Cynthia A. Rushevsky, "Legal Recognition of Surrogate Gestation," *Women's Rights Law Reporter,* 7 (Winter 1982), 115.

4. See, e.g., Mary Joe Frug, "The Baby M Contract," *New Jersey Law Journal,* 119 (1987), 337–338 (February 26, 1987, pp. 33–34): "If she actually gives up her child at birth, [the surrogate mother] . . . is not selling a child but selling the use of her womb."

5. E.g., Karen Marie Sly, "Baby-Sitting Consideration: Surrogate Mother's Right to "Rent Her Womb" for a Fee," *Gonzaga Law Review,* 18 (November 1983), 539; American Fertility Society, Ethics Committee, *Ethical Considerations of the New Reproductive Technologies* (Birmingham, Ala., 1986) p. 67S. Most contracts and proposed regulations, however, provide for no payment to the mother if she miscarries, even after many months of pregnancy; instead they condition payment upon the handing over of a live child. Clearly, such restrictions are incompatible with the characterization of payment for "services" or "rent".

6. In re Baby M, *Family Law Reporter,* 14 (1988), 2012.

7. N.J. Stat. Ann. ch. 9, § 3-54.

8. Surrogate Parenting Associates, Inc. v. Kentucky, 704 S.W.2d 209 (1986). There were two forceful dissents.

9. Cf. Arthur L. Corbin, *Contracts,* 12 vols. (St. Paul: West, 1950–64), I, § 130, pp. 557–560; III, § 586, pp. 489–501.

10. See, e.g., *Los Angeles Times,* April 17, 1986, p. I-2; Doris Sue Wong, "Mass. Couple Ask for Va. Ruling in Surrogate Case," *Boston Globe,* January 14, 1988, p. II-23.

11. See generally Eileen Markoutsas, "Women Who Have Babies for Other Women," *Good Housekeeping,* April 1981, p. 96; Kantrowitz, "Who Keeps Baby M?" p. 47 (quoting Michigan psychiatrist Philip J. Parker, who interviews prospective surrogates for Noel Keane).

12. Daniel Goleman, "Motivations of Surrogate Mothers," *New York Times,* January 20, 1987, p. C1. See also Kantrowitz, "Who Keeps Baby M?"

p. 47; Iver Peterson, "Baby M Case: Surrogate Mothers Vent Feelings," *New York Times,* March 2, 1987, p. B4.

13. Keane and Breo, *The Surrogate Mother,* p. 197. One woman who served without pay explained that surrogacy was "her own private protest against abortion"; ibid., p. 187. See also Goleman, "Motivations of Surrogate Mothers."

14. Keane and Breo, *The Surrogate Mother,* p. 179. For another story of a woman who wanted "a perfect birth," see ibid., p. 223. That woman was a midwife. She was also adopted, believed in adoptees' rights to know their birthparents, and was a feminist who believed "in helping my sisters, even to the extent of donating my body, if necessary." See also Moira K. Griffin, "Womb for Rent," *Student Lawyer,* 9 (April 1981), 30.

15. Keane and Breo, *The Surrogate Mother,* p. 36. See ibid., pp. 141–142, 216, for another story of a woman who wanted "the selfish experience of giving birth without having to be responsible for raising a child." See also ibid., pp. 230, 254.

16. Ibid., p. 187.

17. See Krauthammer, "The Ethics of Human Manufacture," p. 19.

18. Kantrowitz, "Who Keeps Baby M?" p. 48 (quoting Lisa Walters, a thirty-two-year-old Grantsburg, Wisconsin, housewife and mother of two).

19. Ibid., pp. 46–47 (quoting Becky McKnight, a thirty-five-year-old Los Angeles mother of three).

20. Ruth Bayard Smith, "Choosing Sides," *Boston Globe Magazine,* January 3, 1988, p. 30 (quoting thirty-four-year-old Karen Battjes).

21. See Goleman, "Motivations of Surrogate Mothers"; Peter Bowal, "Surrogate Procreation: A Motherhood Issue in Legal Obscurity," *Queens Law Journal,* 9 (Fall 1983), 8–9; and Mary Ruth Mellown, "An Incomplete Picture: The Debate about Surrogate Motherhood," *Harvard Women's Law Journal,* 8 (Spring 1985), 234, 237–238.

22. In re Baby M, 217 N.J. Super. 313, 343, 525 A.2d 1128, 1142 (1987).

23. Dame Mary Warnock, Chairman, *Report of the Committee of Inquiry into Human Fertilization and Embryology* (London: United Kingdom Department of Health and Social Security, 1984), p. 47 (hereafter cited as Warnock Report).

24. Surrogacy Arrangements Act, 1985, ch. 49.

25. *Topeka Capital-Journal,* February 26, 1984.

26. See, e.g., Keane and Breo, *The Surrogate Mother,* pp. 264–267; Elizabeth Mehren, "A Capital Site for a Surrogate Parent Center," *Los Angeles Times,* April 19, 1983, p. V-1 (reporting on Harriett Blankfield and her National Center for Surrogate Parenting, located in Chevy Chase, Maryland); Beth Ann Krier, "Surrogate Motherhood: Looking at It as Business Proposition," *Los Angeles Times,* March 30, 1981, p. V-1 (reporting on Bill Handel and his Surrogate Parent Foundation, Inc., which operates in North Hollywood, California).

27. Doe v. Kelley, 307 N.W.2d 438 (Mich. Super. Ct. 1981), cert. denied 459 U.S. 1183 (1983).

28. The Luken bill (H.R. 2243), introduced on May 14, 1987, and pending

in Congress, would also prohibit paid surrogacy. Several bills have been introduced in state legislatures that would allow surrogacy but prohibit payment; for example, Democratic assemblyman Patrick Halpin introduced such a bill in New York. The Indiana Superior Court has reached the same result, ruling that payment in excess of hospital and medical expenses and counsel fees is not allowed; Miroff v. Surrogate Mother (Ind. Super. Ct., Marion Cty. Oct. 2, 1987); see *Family Law Reporter,* 13 (1987), 1260. The *Miroff* decision also took the position that the mother could not be bound by the contract, which is in violation of public policy. The American Fertility Society's Ethics Committee preferred that surrogates not receive payment "beyond compensation for expenses and their inconvenience" but "recognize[d] that in some cases payment will be necessary for surrogacy to occur"; American Fertility Society, *Ethical Considerations,* p. 67S.

29. In another recently proposed bill prohibiting payment, Florida's state senate approved a prohibition on fees for surrogacy by a five-to-one margin and appended that ban to the state law forbidding the sale of human organs. The Florida house, however, took no action. A bill was introduced in Wisconsin similarly prohibiting payment and allowing reimbursement only for medical expenses; Peterson, "States Assess Surrogate Motherhood."

30. In re Baby M, *Family Law Reporter,* 14 (1988), 2012; N.J. Stat. Ann. ch. 9, § 3-54b. (Supp. 1987); Michigan's S. 228, enacted June, 1988.

31. The possibility that the contracts should not be enforced because the mother received nothing of value is discussed in Chapter 5.

32. See " 'Baby M' Decision Creates Flurry of Legislative Activity," *Family Law Reporter,* 13 (1987), 1296.

33. In re Baby M, *Family Law Reporter,* 14 (1988), 2027.

2. Exploiting Women and Commercializing Childbearing

1. See Kantrowitz, "Who Keeps Baby M?" p. 46.

2. See Keane and Breo, *The Surrogate Mother,* pp. 31, 181. The book also tries to portray the surrogate mother as a person with sufficient financial resources to have real choices. For example, it describes the typical surrogate in another program as "a married woman who has two or three children, has a minimum twelfth-grade education with some college, is from middle- to upper-class, and may have a profession" (p. 219). Pointing out that he could not at that time offer surrogates any fee, Keane goes on to say that he was not so "elitist and exclusive" in picking his own surrogates.

3. *Boston Magazine,* August 1985, p. 285.

4. E. R. Shipp, "Death Draws Public's Eye to Adoption," *New York Times,* November 29, 1987, p. B1, mentioned $75,000 as an amount that might be paid in connection with black-market adoption.

5. See Janny Scott, "Pair Duped Her on Surrogate Mother Pact, Woman Tells Court," *Los Angeles Times,* February 20, 1987, p. I-22. In that case the contracting couple, Mario and Natty Haro, reportedly had brought the surrogate

into the United States illegally. The surrogate also claimed they had promised that if she carried the embryo for only three weeks, it would be transplanted to Mrs. Haro's womb. Instead at that time they tricked her into signing a surrogate motherhood contract.

6. See Amicus Brief (Rutger's Women's Rights Litigation Clinic) at p. 19, 217 N.J. Super. 313, 525 A.2d 1128 (1987).

7. See Iver Peterson, "Baby M Trial Splits Ranks of Feminists: Surrogate Motherhood Stirs Exploitation Issue," *New York Times,* February 24, 1987, p. B1.

8. Mellown, "An Incomplete Picture" (p. 236, n. 33), and Peterson, "Baby M Case: Surrogate Mothers Vent Feelings," describe three-time surrogates.

9. Margaret Jane Radin, "Market-Inalienability," *Harvard Law Review,* 100 (June 1987), 1930.

10. Compare a report that a Florida couple sold their three-month-old for a 1971 Chevrolet (*Long Island Press,* January 16, 1976, p. 1) and a report that a New Jersey woman sold her eighteen-month-old in Florida for $1,208 (*New York Post,* September 21, 1972, p. 5).

11. At least in theory, our society has made the same judgment about prostitution—that it should not be allowed; but it is largely theoretical: enforcement is substantially unsuccessful, and prostitution remains very common. Whereas proposals to legalize prostitution have been presented to many legislatures, laws against childselling have not been the subject of decriminalization attempts. See generally Avi Katz, "Surrogate Motherhood and the Baby-Selling Laws," *Columbia Journal of Law and Social Problems,* 20 (1986), 1–53; and Nancy Erbe, "Prostitutes: Victims of Men's Exploitation and Abuse," *Law and Inequality,* 2 (August 1984), 624–625.

12. Kantrowitz, "Who Keeps Baby M?" p. 46.

13. See Rushevsky, "Legal Recognition of Surrogate Gestation," p. 112, n. 39.

14. Sandy Rovner, "Ethical Choices in Reproductive Technology," *Washington Post Weekly of Medicine, Health and Fitness,* September 9, 1986, p. 15.

15. Barbara Katz Rothman, *The Tentative Pregnancy* (New York: Viking, 1986), p. 2.

16. Most contracts include no such provision. But see Daniel Shapiro, "No Other Hope for Having a Child," *Newsweek,* January 19, 1987, p. 50; "60 Minutes," CBS, September 20, 1987, both reporting a policy of partial payment for a miscarriage, with the amount to be determined by length of pregnancy. Whitehead's contract with the Sterns provided that if she miscarried or if the child was born dead, the fee would be $1,000 instead of the $10,000 she would receive if she performed in full. Although most proposals to regulate surrogacy have contained no provision for partial payment, a South Carolina bill provided for partial payment in the event of miscarriage after the fifth month of pregnancy; Pierce, "Survey of State Activity."

17. Mary Kay Blakely, "Surrogate Mothers: For Whom Are They Working?" *Ms.,* March 1983, p. 18.

18. Report of Lee Salk, Ph.D., for use in *Baby M* litigation, 1987, p. 2; Robert Hanley, "Reporter's Notebook: Mother Plans to Tread Softly in the Baby M Trial," *New York Times,* February 9, 1987, p. B3.

19. Salk testified in this fashion without ever having met Mrs. Whitehead.

20. American Fertility Society, *Ethical Considerations,* p. 67S. That position does not govern paid surrogacy, even though the egg is sold, on the theory that eggs are more like blood, sperm, bone marrow, and other self-renewing substances, which we recognize as different from vital organs. Eggs, however, are not self-renewing.

21. Moira K. Griffin, "Wives, Hookers, and the Law," *Student Lawyer,* 10 (January 1982), 18 (quoting Priscilla Alexander).

22. A major goal of the group is to have legislation passed that will "protect not prohibit" the practice. See Ruth Bayard Smith, "Choosing Sides"; "Group to Guard Rights of Surrogate Mothers," *New York Times,* November 13, 1986, p. C11; and "Surrogate Mothers Form Lobby Group," *Los Angeles Times,* November 12, 1986, p. II-6 (reporting on an earlier group, the National Association of Surrogate Mothers, formed by three surrogates from southern California "to ensure that women will continue to have the right to bear babies for childless couples"). For another defense of the right to be a surrogate see Lori Andrews, *New Conceptions* (New York: Ballantine, 1985), pp. 179–219.

23. The lack of consensus is not surprising, since people also disagree about whether prostitution should be illegal. Marian Swerdlow would combine legalization of surrogacy with disdain for it: "Women's right to control their bodies cannot exclude the right to sell their bodies. However, for working-class and poor women, the conditions of this sale are inevitably exploitative. We therefore must support this right but without ever supporting the right of the exploiters or the exploitative practice itself"; "Class Politics and Baby M," *Against the Current,* 2 (September–October 1987), 53.

24. See, e.g., Keane and Breo, *The Surrogate Mother,* pp. 15, 18–20, 24, 62, 114; and Krier, "Surrogate Motherhood: Looking at It as Business Proposition" (discussing Bill Handel and his surrogacy agency in southern California). The American Fertility Society, however, believes that "barring heavy-handed commercialization, frequency will remain low"; *Ethical Considerations,* p. 68S.

25. See Pierce, "Survey of State Activity"; idem, "Baby M Decision Creates Flurry of Legislative Activity," *Family Law Reporter,* 13 (1987), 1295; idem, "Surrogate Parenthood."

26. See Ellen S. George and Stephen M. Snyder, "A Reconsideration of the Religious Element in Adoption," *Cornell Law Review,* 56 (May 1971), 782, n. 13 (reporting that in New York applicants are required to submit information about infertility, and that in Kansas regulations explicitly prefer sterile couples); and Richard Frank, "What the Adoption Worker Should Know about Infertility," in *A Study of Adoption Practice,* ed. Michael Schapiro, vol. II (New York: Child Welfare League of America, 1956), 113.

27. For example, North Carolina specifically rejected a preference for childless couples because that policy was illogical; see George and Snyder, "A Reconsideration," p. 782, n. 15.

28. John Stehura of the Bionetics Foundation, a surrogate agency, suggests that in poverty-stricken parts of this country surrogates could be found for half the standard fee ($5,000) and that in the Third World one-tenth of the current fee ($1,000) would suffice; Gene Corea, *The Mother Machine: Reproductive Technologies from Artificial Insemination to Artificial Wombs* (New York: Harper & Row, 1986), pp. 214–215.

29. A lawyer in 1976 suggested finding a surrogate in Lebanon and inseminating her with frozen sperm; Keane and Breo, *The Surrogate Mother*, p. 31.

3. Do New Reproductive Techniques Threaten the Family?

1. See Peterson, "Baby M Case: Surrogate Mothers Vent Feelings," pp. B1, B4 (recounting the story of surrogate Donna Regan's five-year-old son, Steffyn, who asked, "You're not going to give them me, are you?"); and Kathy Pollitt, "The Strange Case of Baby M," *The Nation*, May 23, 1987, pp. 667, 682–688.

2. Richard Whitehead reported that " 'the thought of taking $10,000 for Ryan and Tuesday by selling their sister' " worried him; Kantrowitz, "Who Keeps Baby M?" p. 49.

3. Ibid., p. 48. See also Keane and Breo, *The Surrogate Mother*, pp. 77–79.

4. See generally Brent J. Jensen, "Artificial Insemination and the Law," *Brigham Young University Law Review*, 4 (1982), 935.

5. Keane and Breo, *The Surrogate Mother*, pp. 17, 68, 86.

6. Gordon Reginald Dunstan, "Moral and Social Issues Arising from A.I.D., Law and Ethics of A.I.D. and Embryo Transfer," *CIBA Foundation Symposium*, 17 (1973), p. 52.

7. Martin Curie-Cohen, Lesleigh Luttrell, and Sander Shapiro, "Current Practice of AID in the United States," *New England Journal of Medicine*, 300 (1979), 585, reported that only 9.5 percent of the physicians they surveyed said they had inseminated single women.

8. John A. Robertson, "Extracorporeal Embryos and the Abortion Debate," *Journal of Contemporary Health Law and Policy*, 2 (1985), 54. For a general discussion see Clifford Grobstein, "External Human Fertilization: An Evaluation of Policy," *Science*, October 14, 1983, p. 127.

9. See Penelope McMillan, "Natural Parents' Embryo Living in Surrogate Mother," *Los Angeles Times*, November 29, 1986, p. II-1 (describing "the West Coast's first surrogate mother for a 'test-tube' baby"); Wong, "Mass. Couple Ask for Va. Ruling in Surrogate Case" (describing an "ovum implantation" that the surrogate did out of friendship); also "Non-Surgical Transfer of In Vitro Fertilization Donated to Five Infertile Women: Report of Two Pregnancies," *Lancet*, July 23, 1983, p. 223; Richard D. Lyons, "2 Women Become Pregnant with Transferred Embryos," *New York Times*, July 22, 1983, p. A1; Phillip J. Hilts, "Two Embryos Transplanted in Human," *Washington Post*, July 22, 1983, p. A12; Harold M. Schmeck, " 'Pre-Natal Adoption' Is the Objective of New Technique," *New York Times*, June 14, 1983, p. C1.

10. Jay Mathews, "Boy's Birth Is First from Embryo Transfer," *Washington Post*, February 4, 1984, p. A14.

11. Kevin Jacobs, "Surrogate Mother Gives Birth to Triplets for Her Daughter," *Boston Globe,* October 2, 1987, p. 1; Dan Rather, "CBS Evening News," October 1, 1987.

12. Krauthammer, "The Ethics of Human Manufacture," p. 19, discusses the contradiction in reasoning. A response, of course, is that adoption is not in fact analogous to surrogacy, because it addresses the needs of children already in existence. Adoption arrangements raise very different questions from the issues of what society's norms and sanctions should be for the *creation* of children.

13. Much recent criticism centers on the family structure's historic economic disempowerment of women. See, e.g., Sylvia Law, "Women, Work, Welfare, and the Preservation of Patriarchy," *University of Pennsylvania Law Review,* 131 (May 1984), 1249; and Diana Adlam, "The Case against Capitalist Patriarchy," a review of Mary McIntosh's *The State and the Oppression of Women,* in *Feminism and Materialism: Women and Modes of Production,* ed. Annette Kuhn and Ann Marie Wolpe (London: Routledge and Kegan Paul, 1978).

14. For a thoughtful look at both alternatives, which also evaluates previous scholarship on the subject, see Michèle Barrett and Mary McIntosh, *The Anti-Social Family* (London: NLB, 1982). The authors are members of the editorial collective of the *Feminist Review.*

15. The world's first "test-tube" quintuplets were five boys born in London in March 1986. See "Quintuplets Artificially Conceived Are Born," *New York Times,* January 13, 1988, p. A14.

16. Ibid.

17. Tom Brokaw, "NBC Evening News," January 12, 1988. See generally Gina Kolata, "Multiple Fetuses Raise New Issues Tied to Abortion," *New York Times,* January 25, 1988, p. 1.

18. See Richard Saltus, "Guidelines Urged for Fetal Tissue Transplants," *Boston Globe,* July 22, 1987, p. 9.

19. Warnock Report, p. 66; American Fertility Society, *Ethical Considerations,* p. 57S; Committee to Consider the Social, Ethical and Legal Issues Arising from In Vitro Fertilization, *Report on the Disposition of Embryos Produced by In Vitro Fertilization* (Melbourne, Australia: State of Victoria, 1984) (hereafter cited as the Waller Report), p. 47.

20. See John Fletcher and Kenneth Ryan, "Federal Regulations for Fetal Research: A Case for Reform," *Law, Medicine & Health Care,* 13 (Fall 1987), 130.

21. See the excellent discussion in Robertson, "Extracorporeal Embryos and the Abortion Debate," pp. 57–59 (the facts of early development of the pre-implantation embryo). Professor Robertson concludes (pp. 58–59): "To summarize, the extracorporeal embryo is a living human entity of a few nondifferentiated cells that has the potential, if transferred to a uterus, to attach and eventually produce a live birth. Unlike a fetus, however, the extracorporeal embryo has no organs, no neuromuscular structure or spinal column. Indeed, it will first develop a trophoblastic or placental layer before the embryo proper that could develop into an individual is formed. Not until ten to fourteen days after fertilization will the most rudimentary of all embryo structures emerge—the

embryonic disc out of which the embryonic axis and spinal column will eventually, if development continues, emerge. Only later will an organ, neuromuscular and nervous system develop. At some later point the capacity for sentience will also emerge. Wherever we place the point of sentience in the fetus, it is clear that the external, preimplantation embryo (or pre-embryo, to be accurate) has no differentiated organ structure, and has not even developed the rudimentary structure of the embryo itself, which develops after implantation in the uterine wall occurs."

22. It is unclear exactly when this stage begins; somewhere between six and eighteen weeks is likely. See Peter Singer and Helga Kuhse, "The Ethics of Embryo Research," *Law, Medicine and Health Care,* 14 (September 1986), 133–137: "The minimal characteristic needed to give the embryo a claim to consideration is sentience, or the capacity to feel pain and pleasure. Until the embryo reaches that point, nothing we can do to the embryo can harm *it.*" For a suggestion that the fourteen-day period is adequate but that it should be flexible to allow for the developing needs of medical research, see Robertson, "Extracorporeal Embryos," p. 68.

23. One proposed solution is that a moral duty is owed the fertilized ovum only when there is an intent to transfer; Robertson, "Extracorporeal Embryos," pp. 59–60.

24. See Bowen v. American Hospital Ass'n, 106 U.S. 2101 (1986). It is the author's belief that failure to treat or to feed "Baby Does" who are handicapped is a discrimination against the handicapped that violates both the Constitution and Congress's prohibition of discrimination; Rehabilitation Act of 1973, sec. § 504, 29 U.S.C.A. § 794 (1982).

25. Otto Friedrich, " 'A Legal, Moral, Social Nightmare': Society Seeks to Define the Problems of the Birth Revolution," *Time,* September 10, 1984, p. 55.

26. As of September 1985 the Rios' "orphan embryos" were stored, frozen, at the Queen Victoria Medical Center in Melbourne, with their legal status still uncertain. For a discussion of the broader legal and ethical views, see George P. Smith II, "Australia's Frozen Orphan Embryos: A Medical, Legal, and Ethical Dilemma," *Journal of Family Law,* 24 (1985–86), 27.

27. Cf. W. Barton Leach, "Perpetuities in the Atomic Age: The Sperm Bank and the Fertile Decedent," *American Bar Association Journal,* 48 (October 1962), 942.

28. The discussion in Chapter 9 suggests other reasons supporting the claim of the gestational mother over the claims of gene donors, in the event of a custody dispute.

29. See Rita Arditti, "Surrogate Mothering Exploits Women," *Science for the People,* May–June 1987, pp. 22–23.

30. An indication either that times are changing or that people become more conservative concerning this topic as they age is the response to a January 1987 Gallup poll question for *Newsweek:* "Do you approve or disapprove of surrogate mothers bearing children for women who cannot bear children themselves?" Among the 48 percent who approved, there were marked differences by age

group: 68 percent of the respondents from 18 to 29 were positive, compared with 49 percent of those from 30 to 49, and only 30 percent of those 50 or older; "Surrogate Mothers: A *Newsweek* Poll."

31. Marjorie Schultz, comments to Women in Legal Education Section, American Association of Law Schools Convention, Miami Beach, Florida, January 8, 1988. See also Clifford Grobstein, *From Chance to Purpose: An Appraisal of External Human Fertilization* (Reading, Mass.: Addison-Wesley, 1981).

4. Constitutional Arguments—For and Against

1. In Sherwyn & Handel v. California State Department of Social Services, 218 Cal. Rptr. 778 (Cal. Ct. App. 1985), the plaintiffs claimed there was a constitutional right to surrogacy. The court refused to decide the issue, however, because any right to surrogacy would not have belonged to the plaintiffs, who were lawyers who broker surrogacy but were not themselves parties to surrogacy arrangements. Accordingly the plaintiffs lacked standing to bring the lawsuit.

2. Eisenstadt v. Baird, 405 U.S. 438 (1972); Griswold v. Connecticut, 381 U.S. 479, 496–97 (Goldberg, J., concurring) (1965).

3. Krier, "Surrogate Motherhood: Looking at It as Business Proposition" (quoting Bill Handel, a lawyer who arranges surrogacy agreements).

4. A closer comparison would be between a male sperm donor and a female egg donor, although that comparison is also tenuous, as the process of donating an egg is much more intrusive than the giving of sperm. Egg donation involves a surgical technique in which the immature eggs are drawn out through a hollow needle inserted into the patient's abdomen. See Joseph J. Saltarelli, "Genesis Retold: Legal Issues Raised by the Cryopreservation of Preimplantation Human Embryos," *Syracuse Law Review,* 36 (1985), 1021, 1026–27.

5. Of course, there are some analogies between sperm donation and surrogate motherhood, and some of the same arguments can be made against them. For example, payment for sperm arguably also constitutes commercialization of procreation. One sperm donor who learned that conception was accomplished by his sperm refused to take a fee because to do so would make him feel like a prostitute; Wilfred J. Finegold, *Artificial Insemination,* 2d ed. (Springfield, Ill.: Charles C. Thomas, 1976), p. 34.

6. In re Baby M, 217 N.J. Super. 313, 387–389 (1987), 525 A.2d 1128, 1165–66 (1987). Professor John Robertson also believes it is unconstitutional for the state to distinguish between artificial insemination and surrogate motherhood; Robertson, "Embryos, Families, and Procreative Liberty: The Legal Structure of the New Reproduction," *Southern California Law Review,* 59 (July 1986), 939; see also Sly, "Baby-Sitting Consideration."

7. In re Baby M, *Family Law Reporter,* 14 (1988), 2021.

8. Although one might question whether the due process clause is properly interpreted as conferring substantive (as opposed to procedural) rights, it is likely that the Fourteenth Amendment was intended to confer some such rights through its privileges and immunities clause. That provision of the Fourteenth Amendment was rendered meaningless when the Supreme Court, which was hostile to

the new amendment, first construed that provision in the *Slaughter-House Cases,* 83 U.S. (16 Wall.) 36 (1873); the subsequent interpretation of the due process clause, and later of the equal protection clause, to perform the function originally intended for the privileges and immunities clause may be justified on the basis that it respects the original understanding of the amendment, if not of the particular clause.

In any event, the Ninth Amendment might be deemed to protect the right to procreate. It is likely that having children is a right that the framers considered important and basic and one that they supposed would not be taken from the people by government.

9. In re Baby M, *Family Law Reporter,* 14 (1988), 2021.

10. The American Fertility Society's Ethics Committee believed, however, that prohibiting surrogacy would "violat[e] the couple's right to privacy in making procreative decisions"; *Ethical Considerations,* p. 66S. The trial judge in *Baby M* also accepted this constitutional argument. He held for the contracting couple on this due process ground as well as on the equal protection one, finding them constitutionally entitled to access to technologies such as surrogacy that would enable them to have a child to whom they have a genetic connection: "[i]t must be reasoned that if one has a right to procreate coitally, then one has the right to reproduce non-coitally. If it is the reproduction that is protected, then the means of reproduction are also to be protected . . . This court holds that the protected means extends to the use of surrogates . . . While a state could regulate, indeed should and must regulate, the circumstances under which parties enter into reproductive contracts, it could not ban or refuse to enforce such transactions altogether without compelling reason. It might even be argued that refusal to enforce these contracts and prohibition of money payments would constitute an unconstitutional interference with procreative liberty since it would prevent childless couples from obtaining the means with which to have families."

"A woman with her husband have the right to procreate and rear a family. The means to do so can be withheld from them only in the showing of a compelling state interest . . . Legislation or court action that denies that surrogate contract impedes a couple's liberty that is otherwise constitutionally protected. The surrogate who voluntarily chooses to enter such a contract is deprived of a constitutionally protected right to perform services"; In re Baby M, 217 N.J. Super. 313, 386–387 (1987); 525 A.2d 1128, 1164–65 (1987).

The New Jersey Supreme Court, however, reversed on this point.

11. Robert Hanley, "Reporter's Notebook: Grief over Baby M," *New York Times,* January 12, 1987, p. B1; In re Baby M, 217 N.J. Super., p. 338, 525 A.2d, p. 1139.

12. Keane and Breo, *The Surrogate Mother,* p. 170.

13. Michelle Harrison, "Bias Predominates in Baby 'M' Expert Testimony" (Manuscript draft, March 18, 1987, provided by the author). A revised version of this paper was published as "Social Construction of Mary Beth Whitehead," *Gender and Society,* 1 (September 1987), 300–311.

14. Harrison comments: "People take more care and more time in choosing

a sofa"; "Bias Predominates," p. 5. Surrogates also sometimes complain that the contracting couple are interested in using them but do not care about them as a person. Keane and Breo, *The Surrogate Mother,* pp. 195–96, tell of a surrogate who stopped trying to get pregnant for a couple she felt was using her and explained that she wanted to help a couple who cared about her as a person.

15. Radin, "Market-Inalienability," pp. 1929–30.

16. Sly, "Baby-Sitting Consideration," pp. 539, 549.

17. The proposal would be harmful, however, from the point of view of meeting the needs of existing children, just as other surrogacy arrangements are. It also would probably be subject to the same commercialization objections.

18. On the same analysis, I disagree with the suggestion of the California court in Curlender v. Bio-Science Laboratories, 106 Cal. App. 3d 811, 829, 165 Cal. Rptr. 477, 488 (1980), that genetically deformed children could sue their parents for knowingly proceeding with the birth. It usually is difficult to credit a child's complaint that she was born, even if she has a serious handicap to cope with. Even if we understand her claim, it is difficult to evaluate legally a right to be aborted or to put a money amount on a violation of that right. The California legislature overturned the court's ruling by enacting: "No cause of action arises against a parent of a child based upon the claim that the child should not have been conceived or, if conceived, should not have been allowed to have been born alive"; Cal. Civ. Code § 43.6 (West 1981).

19. Hanley, "Reporter's Notebook: Grief over Baby M," p. B3.

20. "Phil Donahue Show," August 3, 1983, interview transcript no. 08033. Donahue interviewed two women in their mid-thirties who had been so conceived. The comment of one of them summed up their reaction: "I want to know who I am. I want to know my name. I want to know my medical history."

21. Lillian Atallah, "Report from a Test-Tube Baby," *New York Times Magazine,* April 18, 1976, p. 48.

22. See Kathryn V. Lorio, "Alternative Means of Reproduction: Virgin Territory for Legislation," *Louisiana Law Review,* 44 (July 1984), 1642, n. 4; and Kantrowitz, "Who Keeps Baby M?" p. 47.

23. National Committee on Adoption, *Adoption Factbook,* p. 102.

24. See ibid., pp. 11, 32–40 (transracial adoption), 54–61 (who adopts).

25. Drummond v. Fulton County Department of Family and Children's Services, 563 F.2d 1200 (5th Cir. 1977) (en banc), cert. denied, 437 U.S. 910 (1978).

26. National Committee on Adoption, *Adoption Factbook,* pp. 14, 28 (intercountry adoption is rapidly increasing; it rose 45.5 percent nationally from 1982 to 1984; in 1984 over 8,000 foreign-born children were placed in this country); *New York Times,* June 26, 1986, p. C1 (from 1981 to 1984 adoptions of foreign-born children nearly doubled); Jane Truesdell Ellis, "The Law and Procedure of International Adoption: An Overview," *Suffolk Transnational Law Journal,* 7 (Fall 1983), 361, n. 1 (since 1976 an average of 5,000 children per year have entered the United States as immigrant orphans). See also Nancy O'Keefe Bolick, "The New Faces of Adoption," *Boston Magazine,* October 1986, p. 152.

27. According to a "conservative" estimate based on statistics from 1982,

healthy infants represent about one-third of all unrelated adoptions, including adoptions from other countries; National Committee on Adoption, *Adoption Factbook,* pp. 102, 103.

28. See, e.g., Keane and Breo, *The Surrogate Mother,* pp. 12, 15, 20, 24, 114.

29. 1984 Policy Statement of the National Committee for Adoption, quoted in Pierce, "Survey of State Activity," p. 3002.

30. See Peterson, "Baby M Trial Splits Ranks of Feminists" (quoting National Committee for Adoption).

31. Keane and Breo, *The Surrogate Mother,* p. 264, suggest that the state pay for surrogacy.

32. The enactment also covers other fertility treatments, but surrogacy is excluded. It does not restrict coverage to married couples. Maryland is the only other state requiring insurers to cover IVF, and its statute does not cover any other medical procedures for infertility. See Kevin Cullen, "Law Orders Coverage for Infertility," *Boston Globe,* October 9, 1987, p. 1.

33. Eisenstadt v. Baird, 405 U.S. 438, 453 (1972): "If the right of privacy means anything, it is the right of the *individual,* married or single, to be free from unwarranted governmental intrusion into matters so fundamentally affecting a person as the decision whether to bear or beget a child" (emphasis in original).

34. Cord v. Gibb, 219 Va. 1019, 254 S.E.2d 711 (1979); Andrews v. Drew Municipal Separate School Dist., 507 F.2d 611 (5th Cir. 1975), cert. dismissed as improvidently granted, 425 U.S. 559 (1976). But see Hollenbaugh v. Carnegie Free Library, 578 F.2d 1374 (3d Cir. 1978), cert. denied (with dissenting opinions), 439 U.S. 1052 (1978).

35. See Note, "Reproductive Technology and the Procreation Rights of the Unmarried," *Harvard Law Review,* 98 (January 1985), 669. Cf. John A. Robertson, "Procreative Liberty and the Control of Conception, Pregnancy, and Childbirth," *Virginia Law Review,* 69 (April 1983), 405; and Harry D. Krause, "Artificial Conception: Legislative Approaches," *Family Law Quarterly,* 19 (Fall 1985), 185.

36. This argument is similar to the argument that it harms the child to have parents who hired a surrogate.

37. Los Angeles v. Manhart, 435 U.S. 702 (1978), held that classification on the one factor of gender, when other factors are also relevant, constitutes gender-based discrimination. Stanley v. Illinois, 405 U.S. 645 (1972), and Caban v. Mohammed, 441 U.S. 380 (1979), which are discussed at length in Chapter 8, demonstrate that when fundamental interests in bearing and rearing a child are involved, imprecise classifications will not be tolerated. Whereas it is acceptable to remove a child from a person on the basis that *he or she* is not a fit custodian, it is not acceptable to do so on the ground that he or she belongs to a *group* many of whose members would not be fit custodians. That rule applies to childbearing as much as to childrearing. In constitutional law parlance, overbroad classifications are not permitted to deprive individuals of fundamental liberties, including the liberty interest in having and raising one's own children. See also "Single Factor Based on Petitioner's Marital Status Cannot Determine the Best Interests of the

Child: In re W. E. R., 663 S.W.2d 887 (Tex.)," *Texas Tech Law Review,* 16 (1985), 573.

38. Compare John J. Mandler, "Developing a Concept of the Modern 'Family': A Proposed Uniform Surrogate Parenthood Act," *Georgetown Law Journal,* 73 (1985), 1304 (suggesting requirements of bonding, insurance, and annuities for the adoptive parents), with Joan Hollinger, "From Coitus to Commerce: Legal and Social Consequences of Noncoital Reproduction," *University of Michigan Journal of Law Reform,* 18 (Summer 1985), 911, n. 274 (suggesting that financial requirements for the adopting parents in a surrogacy arrangement would not be warranted because the state does not require them for "children generated by coital means").

39. " 'Infertility,' as applied in this case, shall mean the inability to conceive and carry to term without serious threat of harm to one's physical well-being"; In re Baby M, 217 N.J. Super. 313, 380 (1987).

40. See Keane and Breo, *The Surrogate Mother,* p. 139.

41. Ruth Bayard Smith, "The Baby Broker," *Boston Globe Magazine,* January 3, 1988, p. 28. The American Fertility Society regards it as unethical to use surrogacy for nonmedical reasons—reasons of career or the convenience of not carrying the fetus to term; *Ethical Considerations,* p. 67S.

42. Gene Corea, quoted in Ruth Bayard Smith, "The Baby Broker," p. 31.

43. See Pierce, "Survey of State Activity," p. 3003.

44. Ruth Bayard Smith, "The Baby Broker," p. 31.

45. Pierce, "Survey of State Activity," p. 3003, reports that a bill proposed in New Jersey would have limited compensation to $10,000; bills proposed in several other states would have made $10,000 a *minimum* fee.

46. Ibid.

47. Ibid., p. 3004.

48. Ibid., p. 3003.

49. See note 38 above.

50. Pierce, "Survey of State Activity," p. 3003.

51. Ruth Bayard Smith, "The Baby Broker," p. 28.

52. Ibid.

53. Ibid.

54. Pierce, "Survey of State Activity," p. 3003.

55. Ibid.

56. Ibid.

57. 410 U.S. 113 (1973).

58. Phyllis Coleman, "Surrogate Motherhood: Analysis of the Problems and Suggestions for Solutions," *Tennessee Law Review,* 50 (Fall 1982), 85–86, supports this analysis of the abortion issue.

59. 428 U.S. 52 (1976). See also Jones v. Smith, 278 So.2d 339 (Fla. 1973), cert. denied, 415 U.S. 958 (1973) (denying the right of the potential father of an illegitimate child to restrain the mother from seeking an abortion); Ponter v. Ponter, 135 N.J. Super. 50, 342 A.2d 574 (Ch. Div. 1975) (denying a husband's right to veto his wife's decision to undergo sterilization).

60. One Indiana court has not been tolerant of attempts in surrogacy con-

tracts to change other aspects of the preexisting legal order. In Miroff v. Surrogate Mother (Ind. Super. Ct. Marion Cty. October 2, 1986) it rebuffed a provision in a contract on the ground that it was a "blatant attempt to void the court's authority to enter a support order should custody be awarded to the biological mother"; *Family Law Reporter,* 13 (1987), p. 1260.

61. In re Baby M, 217 N.J. Super. 313, 345 (1987).

62. Ibid., p. 375.

63. Pierce, "Survey of State Activity," pp. 3003, 3004.

64. Detention was ordered in one case because the mother "tended to be on the run"; Ethan Bronner, "Advances Elevate Status of Fetus," *Boston Globe,* July 21, 1987, p. 1.

65. For example, anyone successfully holding a job would lose the job because of incarceration; and there are numerous other ways in which enforced detention could totally disrupt one's life on a long-term basis. It would stand up best if a state did require a pregnant woman who had an alcohol or drug abuse problem—or who smoked cigarettes—to submit to a good treatment program offered at state expense; then, even if incarceration were involved, the constitutional issue would become a closer one. In one sense, any such regulation would have the best chance of standing up to constitutional challenge if it were applied only to people in truly desperate substance abuse situations—people with very little left in life to disrupt. But in constitutional law it is troubling when a regulation that deprives persons of freedom itself is tailored so that it applies to a very unfortunate group. In sum, it seems likely that there is no way to tailor a regulation to prevent fetal abuse so that it would be both effective and constitutionally valid.

66. See Marcia Chambers, "Woman Facing Criminal Charges over Her Conduct in Pregnancy," *New York Times,* October 9, 1986, p. A22; idem, "Charges against Mother in Death of Baby Are Thrown Out," *New York Times,* April 27, 1987, p. A25. See also Reyes v. Superior Ct., 75 Cal. App. 3d 214, 141 Cal. Rptr. 912 (1977).

67. Kantrowitz, "Who Keeps Baby M?" p. 49.

68. A damage remedy is conceivable (see end of Chapter 7).

69. See Jefferson v. Griffin Spalding County Hospital Authority, 247 Ga. 86, 274 S.E.2d 457 (1981); In re A. C., slip. op. (D.C. Ct. App. June 16, 1987). For a decision declining to order the mother to submit to surgery for the benefit of the fetus, see Taft v. Taft, 388 Mass. 331, 446 N.E.2d 395 (1983).

70. 334 U.S. 1 (1948).

71. Santosky v. Kramer, 455 U.S. 745 (1982).

72. Johnson v. Zerbst, 304 U.S. 458 (1938).

73. See Pollitt, "The Strange Case of Baby M." Marta Dotterer, a machinist's wife from near Traverse City, Michigan, let her husband handle the $10,000 fee: "It was hard for me to take the money. I rationalized that we'd use it to get something for the kids and pay some bills and get a used car we need, because if the money was just for me I'd feel as if I'd sold her, and it would be dirty money, and I didn't want anything to do with it"; Peterson, "Baby M Case: Surrogate Mothers Vent Feelings," p. B4.

74. Quoted in Ruth Bayard Smith, "Choosing Sides."

75. See Peterson, "Baby M Case: Surrogate Mothers Vent Feelings," p. B1.

76. Quoted in Keane and Breo, *The Surrogate Mother,* pp. 222–223. See Sarah Moore Hall, "An Illinois Woman Decides to Bear a Stranger's Child as Surrogate for His Infertile Wife," *People,* April 21, 1980, pp. 38–42.

77. Quoted in Kantrowitz, "Who Keeps Baby M?" p. 46.

78. See Ralph Slovenko, "Obstetric Science and the Developing Role of the Psychiatrist in Surrogate Motherhood," *Journal of Psychiatry & Law,* 13 (1985), 503. Noel Keane reports that when he started arranging surrogacy contracts his view was that single surrogates were preferable. He not only foresaw fewer legal problems if the surrogate was not married, but he also believed it would be psychologically easier for the woman to turn over the baby if she had no other children; Keane and Breo, *The Surrogate Mother,* pp. 43, 49, 54. Another reason to favor women who do not have other children is the potential for harm to children who see their mother have a baby and give it away or sell it.

79. Mellown, "An Incomplete Picture," p. 238.

80. The bill was introduced by Democratic council member John Ray; Pierce, "Baby M Decision Creates Flurry of Legislative Activity," p. 1296.

81. Ruth Bayard Smith, "Choosing Sides," quoting Patricia Foster, thirty-two, of Monroe, Michigan. Foster is fighting to obtain the right to visit her son.

82. Quoted in Peterson, "Baby M Case: Surrogate Mothers Vent Feelings," p. B4.

83. Phyllis R. Silverman to Harold Cassidy (one of Mary Beth Whitehead's lawyers), October 23, 1986, included in Report of Phyllis R. Silverman for use in the Baby M litigation, October 23, 1986. See also Beth Ann Krier, "The Psychological Effects Are Still a Question Mark," *Los Angeles Times,* March 30, 1981, p. V-1, quoting psychotherapist Annette Baran, an expert on adoption.

84. Report of Phyllis R. Silverman, p. 5.

85. Kantrowitz, "Who Keeps Baby M?" p. 48.

86. Keane and Breo, *The Surrogate Mother,* p. 191.

87. Mary Beth Whitehead said in her application to be a surrogate that she would not have trouble giving up the baby because she has two healthy and happy children. Similarly, birth mothers generally greatly underestimate the degree of grief they will experience from giving up a child: "In a study currently underway, 246 birthmothers have responded to a questionnaire about their experience in effecting a reunion with their child . . . We asked them how they had expected to feel after the surrender. 40% said they had thought they would always grieve, 30% had thought that grief was finite, they would grieve and then stop, and 25% said they had expected to simply forget. In response to how they actually did feel, 95% of them felt that it was worse than they ever imagined"; Report of Phyllis R. Silverman for use in *Baby M* litigation, October 23, 1986, p. 4.

88. Elizabeth Kane says: "We birth mothers call it the big sleep, and eventually they will all wake up from this denial and realize what they've done. It just took Mary Beth Whitehead less time than most of us"; quoted in Peterson, "Baby M Case: Surrogate Mothers Vent Feelings," p. B4.

89. See generally Robin Winkler and Margaret van Keppel, *Relinquishing Mothers in Adoption* (Melbourne, Australia: Institute of Family Studies, 1984); and Suzanne Arms, *To Love and Let Go* (New York: Alfred Knopf, 1986).

90. Report of Phyllis R. Silverman, p. 4.

91. Ibid. The following quotations from the Silverman report provide a typical sample of the feelings of the birth mothers surveyed: "I was always aware, always looking for him in people I saw"; "I wondered how a loving God could do such a thing"; "Separation from my child has been a constant source of pain, worse than torture, because it never stopped, not even for a moment."

92. Ibid., p. 5.

5. Making Surrogacy Contracts Unenforceable under Contract Law

1. Corbin, *Contracts,* makes clear that contracts can be "illegal," as that term is used in contract law, without the attachment of criminal penalties—for example, when they are contrary to public policy or *contra bonos mores* (treated as illegal by prevailing community standards); VIA, §§ 1373–75, pp. 1–19. Sometimes contracts that are void are called illegal even though there are no criminal penalties for making them, and even though there are differences between void and illegal contracts; William M. Fletcher, *Cyclopedia of the Law of Private Corporations,* rev. ed., vol. VIIA (Wilmette, Ill.: Callaghan, 1978), §§ 3580, 3581, 3583; Corbin, *Contracts,* I, § 7 (pp. 15–17); V, §§ 993 (pp. 8–9); VIA, § 1373 (pp. 1–4). For a discussion of some differences between void and voidable contracts, see Chapter 7.

2. In re Baby Girl, *Family Law Reporter,* 9 (1983), 2348 (Ky. Cir. Ct. 1983). The court denied the motion to terminate rights and to declare the biological father the child's father, to award him custody, and to have his name entered on the birth certificate. The court held that the statute pertaining to termination of parental rights had been enacted to facilitate adoptions through licensed agencies, not through surrogacy. Moreover, state law recognized a woman's husband as her children's father. Accordingly, the court said it lacked power to terminate the parental rights of the mother and her husband in a surrogacy situation. Similarly, in Syrkowski v. Appleyard, 122 Mich. App. 506, 333 N.W.2d 90 (1983), rev'd 420 Mich. 367, 362 N.W.2d 211 (1985), the trial court and the appeals court were prepared to use existing laws to prevent execution of surrogacy arrangements that all parties were ready to perform, but the Michigan Supreme Court reversed. Finally, Wong, "Mass. Couple Ask for Va. Ruling," describes the case of a Massachusetts couple who supplied both egg and sperm and a Virginia surrogate; all parties were ready to fulfill the surrogacy arrangement, but Virginia's law presumes that the woman who gives birth is the legal mother.

3. See In re C. B. (1981) 1 All E.R. 16 (C.A.).

4. Surrogacy Arrangements Act, 1985, ch. 49. See Krauthammer, "The Ethics of Human Manufacture," p. 19.

5. See H.R. 2243, introduced by Congressman Tom Luken (D–Ohio) on May 14, 1987. This bill is currently being reviewed by the House Judiciary

Committee, Subcommittee on Transportation, Tourism and Hazardous Materials.

6. "Surrogate Motherhood: A *Newsweek* Poll."

7. "Miller's Court," television broadcast on Channel 5, Boston, February 22, 1987. See also "Majority in Poll Say Father Should Have Baby M," *Boston Globe,* April 13, 1987, p. 18.

8. It could be put forward on constitutional grounds as well; see Chapter 4.

9. Corbin, *Contracts,* I, § 110, pp. 490–494.

10. See American Law Institute, *Restatement (Second) of Contracts* (St. Paul, 1981), § 79 and comments. See also §§ 71(2), 72, 75, 78.

11. Ibid., § 32, comment b(4).

12. See the end of Chapter 1.

13. Similarly, one author has said: "a court will decline . . . to direct specific performance when an order to perform—to deliver over the child to the contracting couple—would introduce compulsion into close personal relationships"; Shari O'Brien, "Commercial Conceptions: A Breeding Ground for Surrogacy," *North Carolina Law Review,* 65 (November 1986), 150.

14. At times actions for breach of promise to marry have been enforceable, first as a tort and then as a contract, but they have been enforceable only by actions for damages and not by specific performance. See generally Samuel Green and John V. Long, *Marriage and Family Law Agreements* (New York: McGraw-Hill, 1984), §§ 2.02–.03.

15. Specific performance was not available, even though the breach of promise action was seen as vindicating an important social policy and not simply the private interests of the parties. "A basic argument in support of the [breach of promise] action is related to society's interest in the preservation of marriage, that the law is justified in enforcing performance of the contract because on its faithful performance the interest of society depends more than upon the faithful performance of any other type of contract"; ibid. It is difficult to sustain any similar argument of societal need concerning the preservation of the right to hire a surrogate.

16. By the 1930s most states had abolished or sharply limited breach of promise actions, but Illinois still retains a statute allowing the action; Ill. Ann. Stat. ch. 40, §§ 1801–10 (Smith-Hurd 1980) (limiting damages to actual damages and eliminating recompense for mental or emotional distress); and at least seven states (Georgia, Hawaii, Kansas, Nebraska, North Carolina, Texas, and Washington) retain a common-law action for breach of the promise to marry; see Green and Long, *Marriage and Family Law Agreements,* § 2.03, nn. 29–39. Therefore, "Although the breach of promise action is an ancient one, not frequently filed today and probably overlooked, the theory that every wrong deserves a remedy and the ingenuity of lawyers in fashioning new and recycled causes of action and defenses" explain the fact that, especially in the cohabitation context, the breach of the promise to marry action has not completely disappeared; ibid., § 2.03.

17. See Radin, "Market-Inalienability," p. 934; idem, "Property and Per-

sonhood," *Stanford Law Review,* 34 (May 1982), 957, 986, n. 101, notes the distinction between "inalienability rules" and "property rules."

18. Nor should courts enforce contractual promises about how the mother is to conduct herself during pregnancy, at least by specific performance. It is true that damage to the father—and, more pointedly, to the child—may be irreparable if the mother does not comply; that prerequisite to specific performance is met. But how can the father force the mother to comply without having her forcibly detained? For the possibility of a damage remedy, see Chapter 7, "Void Contracts, Voidable Contracts, and a Remedy of Damages."

19. See Corbin, *Contracts,* VA, §§ 1184 (pp. 341–347), 1204–10 (pp. 398–425). The childselling example cannot be so explained.

20. See Chapter 1.

21. Corbin, *Contracts,* VA, § 1204, pp. 398–404.

22. See Chapter 4, "Are There Useful Ways to Regulate Surrogacy without Prohibiting It?"

23. American Law Institute, *Restatement (Second) of Contracts,* § 367, describes the rationale behind personal service contracts and states that specific performance will not be ordered when compulsion is against public policy. The explanation in the text would also apply to childselling.

24. Ibid., § 7.

25. Ibid., §§ 8, 178–79.

26. Ibid., §§ 25, 45, 87.

27. Ibid., §§ 78, 79.

28. Corbin, *Contracts,* I, § 21, pp. 52–60; IA, §§ 152 (pp. 2–17), 157 (pp. 40–51).

29. American Law Institute, *Restatement (Second) of Contracts,* §§ 30, 32.

30. If the approach I suggest were followed, however, and surrogacy contracts were made voidable, parties would come to know that surrogacy contracts were not mutually enforceable, and the option would more frequently reflect the contracting parties' intent. In those circumstances the unilateral contract characterization—the characterization as an offer intended to be acceptable only by performance—would become more appropriate. See also Chapter 7, note 1.

31. See, e.g., Kantrowitz, "Who Keeps Baby M?" p. 45; and Keane and Breo, *The Surrogate Mother,* pp. 53–54, 64, 119, 144–145, 183, 190, 218, 235, 269, 275.

32. American Law Institute, *Restatement (Second) of Contracts,* § 179(b).

33. Ibid., § 357.

34. Ibid., § 364.

35. Ibid., § 365.

6. Integrating Surrogacy with Laws Governing Adoption

1. National Adoption Committee, *Adoption Factbook,* pp. 76–85. That source, which represents the best available empirical survey of actual adoption practices and policies, lists the state of Washington as an exception (p. 85).

Washington, however, does not bind a birth mother to a consent given before birth. It does sometimes allow prebirth consents to be operative, but it gives the mother a chance to renounce them after birth. Under Wash. Rev. Code § 26.33.160(2) (1985), "Consent to adoption is revocable by the consenting party at any time before the consent is approved by the court." In addition, a mother can revoke because of fraud or duress *or by written revocation "delivered or mailed within forty-eight hours after a prior notice of revocation that was given within forty-eight hours after the birth of the child"*; ibid., 2(b) (emphasis added). In other words, the mother can revoke within forty-eight hours after birth, if she follows up promptly with a revocation in writing, and she can do so even if a court approved her consent before the birth.

2. See, e.g., Ariz. Rev. Stat. Ann. §§ 8-107B (1987) ("a consent given before seventy-two hours after the birth of the child is invalid"); Fla. Stat. Ann. § 63.082(4) (West 1985) ("the consent shall be executed only after the birth of the child"); Ky. Rev. State. § 199.500(5) (1986) (no consent for adoption shall be held valid if given before the fifth day after the birth of the child); Mass. Gen. Laws ch. 210, § 2 (1986) ("written consent shall be executed no sooner than the fourth calendar day after the date of birth of the child to be adopted"); Nev. Rev. Stat. § 127.070.1 (1986) ("all releases for and consents to adoption executed by the mother before the birth of a child are invalid"); Va. Code § 63.1-225A (1986) ("the consent of a parent for the adoption of his or her child placed directly by the parent shall not be valid unless the child is at least ten days old at the time the parental consent is signed").

3. See, e.g., Anonymous v. Anonymous, 439 N.Y.S.2d 255, 260 (1981); In re Adoption of R. A. B., 426 So.2d 1203, 1205 (Fla. App. 1983); Korbin v. Ginsberg, 232 So.2d 417, 418 (Fla. 1970) ("[Adoption] is a personal relationship created between one capable of adopting and one capable of being adopted, and it necessarily requires that both the adopting parent and the adopted child be living at the time such relationship comes into being by judicial decree"); In re Adoption of Kreuger, 448 P.2d 82, 86 (Ariz. 1969).

4. 704 S.W.2d 209 (Ky. Supreme Ct. 1986).

5. See Peterson, "States Assess Surrogate Motherhood." Moreover, the New Jersey Supreme Court's holding concerning unpaid surrogacy treats it as legal but unenforceable; In re Baby M, *Family Law Reporter*, 14 (1988), 2027, p. 94.

6. U.S. Senate, *Adoption and Foster Care, 1975: Hearings before the Subcommittee on Children and Youth of the Senate Committee on Labor and Public Welfare*, 94th Cong., 1st sess. (1976), p. 6 (three-to-seven-year waiting period); "Desperately Seeking Baby," (television broadcast on "Frontline," WGBH, Boston, March 3, 1987) (three to seven years). Some commentators suggest that the waiting period is long because adoption agencies charge below market price for their services. See Elisabeth M. Landes and Richard A. Posner, "The Economics of the Baby Shortage," *Journal of Legal Studies*, 7 (June 1978), 326. Landes and Posner have suggested that the shortage might be averted by having the agencies charge higher fees and then use "the surplus income generated by the higher fees to make side payments to pregnant women contemplating abortion to

induce them instead to have the child and put it up for adoption" (!!!); ibid., pp. 347–348.

7. They are illegal in Connecticut, Delaware, Massachusetts, Michigan, Minnesota, Rhode Island, Virginia, and also in other states. Private for-profit agencies are also illegal in California, Delaware, Florida, Georgia, Hawaii, Idaho, Louisiana, Montana, New Hampshire, New Jersey, New York, Rhode Island, Texas, Utah, and others. See National Adoption Committee, *Adoption Factbook,* pp. 76–85.

8. See note 20 below and accompanying text.

9. Of the 50,720 unrelated adoptions that took place in 1982, 19,428 were arranged by public agencies, 14,549 were arranged by private agencies, and 16,743 were arranged by individuals; National Adoption Committee, *Adoption Factbook,* p. 102.

10. William R. Greer, "The Adoption Market: A Variety of Options," *New York Times,* June 26, 1986, pp. C1, 10.

11. "Desperately Seeking Baby" (discussing private adoptions in California and focusing particularly on one private adoption agency run by Mark and Bonnie Gradstein).

12. Connecticut, Delaware, Georgia, Massachusetts, Michigan, and Minnesota, for example, prohibit private placement by natural parents except in the case of family placement within the third degree of kinship; National Adoption Committee, *Adoption Factbook,* pp. 76–85. See generally ibid., pp. 12, 25, 47–53; and William Meezan, Sanford Katz, and Eva Mankoff Russo, *Adoptions without Agencies: A Study of Independent Adoptions* (Washington, D.C.: Child Welfare League of America, 1977).

13. See National Adoption Committee, *Adoption Factbook,* pp. 25, 48.

14. Fla. Stat. Ann. § 63.212(1)(d) (West 1985).

15. The problem was that the expenses were not related to the birth, care, or placement of the infant but were for living expenses (food, rent, utilities, furniture rental, and cable TV). The relevant New York statute provides that adoptive parents may reimburse the natural mother for expenses "on account of or incidental to the birth or care of the adoptive child, the pregnancy or care of the adoptive child's mother or the placement or adoption of the child and on account of or incidental to assistance in arrangements for such placement or adoption"; see In re Adoption of Anonymous, 501 N.Y.S.2d 240, 242 (1986) (construing N.Y. Dom. Rel. Law § 115[7]).

16. The Kentucky Supreme Court did that in Surrogate Parenting Associates, Inc. v. Kentucky, 704 S.W.2d 209 (1986).

17. The situation might be psychologically easier for the father because he knows that it is not his fault that he is not his child's custodian. The biological mother who was held to her contract might feel guilty that she ever agreed to give up her child.

18. I am referring to situations in which the child is shifted back and forth because custody is not shared and no custody arrangement is agreed upon, and not to situations of joint custody, in which parents have agreed or courts have decreed that the parents should share custody.

19. See, e.g., Ill. Ann. Stat. ch. 40, § 1511 (Smith-Hurd 1980): "No consent or surrender shall be taken within the 72-hour period immediately following the birth of the child." Other states also impose a waiting rule which establishes a period following birth during which parental consent to adoption and/or surrender of a child is not valid: Alabama (72 hours); Massachusetts (four days); Kentucky (five days); Virginia (ten days). See note 2 above.

20. Sees v. Baber, 277 A.2d 628 N.J. (1977). See also Louisiana (irrevocable through agency, 30 days for independent adoption); North Carolina (30 days in agency relinquishment, 3 months nonagency); Texas (public agency and some other agencies are irrevocable; otherwise 60 days); Tennessee (30 days with agency, 90 days for independent placement); Georgia (birth mother has permanent right to revoke independent placement!!); National Adoption Committee, *Adoption Factbook,* pp. 76–85.

Some statutes make a parent's surrender of a child to an approved agency "valid and binding," but allow parents who have privately placed their child with an adoptive couple to revoke at any time before final judgment of adoption (months later). See, e.g., N.J. Stat. Ann. §§ 9:3-41, 9:3-46(a) (West 1987–88); A. L. & B. L. v. P. A. & M. A., No. A-2452-85-1, slip op. (N.J. Super. Ct. App. Div. Nov. 21, 1986).

21. The reason for the state's rule is clear: the agency affords more protection against overreaching in convincing the mother to give up her child than the unsupervised independent adoption situation. Yet the rule still does not accord with the best interests of the child. It should be modified to allow the mother whose child is not in a permanent placement to change her mind concerning surrender.

22. In re Baby M, *Family Law Reporter,* 14 (1988), 2012 (quoting Sees v. Baber, 74 N.J. 201, 217 [1977]).

23. Ibid., pp. 2012–16.

24. See, e.g., In re Santore, 28 Wash. App. 319, 623 P.2d 702 (1981); Re Adoption of Trent, 229 Kan. 224, 624 P.2d 433 (1981). See generally 2 Am. Jur. 2d *Adoption* § 46, pp. 896–897 (Lawyers Co-operative Pub. 1962); and C. C. I. v. Natural Parents, 398 So.2d 220 (Miss. 1981) (biological parents were not entitled to revoke their consent to the surrender of the child to an adoption agency).

25. Moreover, doctrines requiring knowing and intelligent waiver of constitutional rights can be applied to have a similar effect. See Chapter 4, "Arguments That Enforcement of Surrogacy Contracts Is Unconstitutional."

26. 30 Ill. App. 3d 406, 332 N.E.2d 36 (1975). Perhaps the only reason for the holding was the age of the mother. In In re Adoption of Giambrone, 262 So.2d 566 (La. Ct. App. 1972), the parents of a twenty-year-old mother refused to let her return with her new baby to their home, where she had been living. But the court held that was not duress within the meaning of the consent requirement.

27. 132 Ill. App. 2d 793, 270 N.E.2d 464 (1971).

28. See In re Adoption of Giambrone; In re Surrender of Minor Children, 344 Mass. 230, 181 N.E.2d 836 (1962) (no principle of law requires that surrenders be held valid only if executed free from emotions, tension, and pressures

caused by the situation). In Massachusetts it is virtually impossible to revoke an agreement to surrender once it is signed; Sarah Snyder, "Baby Case Spurs Debate on Surrogate Mothers—Despite Custody Fight, Couples Seek Service," *Boston Globe,* February 22, 1987, p. 10.

29. See, e.g., Hendricks v. Curry, 401 S.W.2d 796 (because consent to adoption can be withdrawn at any time before an adoption decree is entered, a parent consenting to and delivering a child for adoption has the reserved legal right to withdraw consent at any time before entry of an adoption).

30. See, e.g., Warner v. Ward, 401 S.W.2d 62 (Ky. 1966) (the judge permitted a mother who was distressed when she consented to adoption to withdraw her consent before the final adoption decree).

31. 28 N.Y.2d 185, 321 N.Y.S.2d 65, 269 N.E.2d 787 (1971).

32. The New York courts awarded custody to Scarpetta, but the DeMartinos avoided the decision by moving to Florida, where they went to court and were awarded custody. The court's decision there was based in part on the theory that removal of Lenore, now thirteen months old, from the only home she had known could cause emotional trauma. The matter was ultimately resolved when the U.S. Supreme Court refused to review Scarpetta's petition for *certiorari.* DeMartino v. Scarpetta, 404 U.S. 805 (1971). See Henry H. Foster, Jr., "Adoption and Child Custody: Best Interests of the Child?" *Buffalo Law Review,* 1 (Spring 1973), 8–9.

33. Reported in "Desperately Seeking Baby."

34. See Brendon v. Titus, 22 Md. App. 412, 418, 323 A.2d 612, 615 (1974); Logan v. Coup, 238 Md. 253, 258, 208 A.2d 694, 697 (1965) (both illustrating that differences between voluntary relinquishment and abandonment are miniscule).

35. Cf. In re Baby M, 217 N.J. Super. 313, 391–395, 525 A.2d 1128, 1167–1169 (1987).

7. Giving the Mother the Right to Renounce the Contract

1. Traditionally, unilateral contracts were not binding on either party until performance was completed, but in order to prevent hardship to the offeree (the person who accepted an offer to perform) who had commenced performance, the rule was changed making them enforceable by the performing party and irrevocable by the offeror (the person who made the offer) "as soon as the offeree has started to perform the act"; Laurence Packer Simpson, *Handbook of the Law of Contracts,* 2d ed. (St. Paul: West, 1965), p. 37. The American Law Institute, *Restatement (Second) of Contracts,* § 45, abandons the "unilateral contract" terminology but also provides that the offeror would be bound when performance commences. In the surrogacy situation, the surrogate would be the "offeree," to whom the offer was made and who was expected to perform; the contracting father would be the "offeror."

The "voidable contract" characterization seems more appropriate for surrogacy, however, since the option to avoid is imposed for reasons of policy and not as a reflection of the parties' intent. Under that characterization, the offeror (but not the offeree) would probably be bound from the signing of the contract. The contractor who changed his mind about giving his semen would, however, benefit from the arguments against enforcing contracts in a very personal realm that were discussed in Chapter 2 as arguments for the surrogate who wishes to withdraw. Moreover, the unilateral contract characterization or the option contract characterization could soon come to be appropriate for surrogacy. See Chapter 5, note 30.

2. See Snyder, "Baby Case Spurs Debate." One arranger of surrogacy, when asked whether she expected the *Baby M* litigation to interfere with business, replied, "If an airplane crashes, do we shut down all our airports? As an industry, we have an incredible safety record"; Carol Lawson, "Surrogate Mothers Grow in Numbers despite Questions," *New York Times,* October 1, 1986, p. C1 (quoting Harriett Blankfield, director of Infertility Associates in Chevy Chase, Maryland).

3. Rights to custody independent of the contract are the subject of Chapters 8 and 9.

4. Kantrowitz, "Who Keeps Baby M?" p. 51.

5. For similar reasons a psychologist who screens applicants for surrogacy for a surrogacy center in California rejected an applicant whose child had been kidnapped by her ex-husband two years earlier; Goleman, "Motivations of Surrogate Mothers" (interviewing Dr. Hilary Hanafin).

6. Even if the rule were that the adopting couple had legal rights to enforce a contract when the mother changed her mind, this kind of assessment before entering a contract would be necessary, because the couple would necessarily want to avoid litigation if possible. For a description of the screening process at Surrogate Parenting Associates, one of the better-known surrogate centers, see Mellown, "An Incomplete Picture," p. 239. The author reports that as well as being tested for disease and being matched to the couple's requests for specific racial and physical characteristics, "the prospective mother . . . undergoes psychiatric interviews and a battery of intelligence and basic personality tests. This testing is designed to analyze the surrogate mother's ability to surrender her child after delivery, and to reveal personality disorders or low intelligence. The intensity of the screening process varies . . . The results of these tests . . . are sent to the couple who may accept or reject the woman."

In the *Baby M* case, the Infertility Center of New York had received a psychological report on Mary Beth Whitehead in April 1984 stating that Mrs. Whitehead "expects to have strong feelings about giving up the baby at the end." In the report, the psychologist suggested that those feelings be explored "in somewhat more depth." The center failed to inform the Sterns of the report, a fact that Mr. Stern complained of during the trial. Robert Hanley, "Father of Baby M Thought Mother Had Been Screened," *New York Times,* January 14, 1987, p. B2.

7. Keane and Breo, *The Surrogate Mother,* pp. 197–209.

8. See page 1.

9. Keane and Breo, *The Surrogate Mother,* pp. 103–12. See also ibid., pp. 191–93 (the story of "Kay").

10. See American Law Institute, *Restatement (Second) of Contracts,* §§ 8, 178–179.

11. Peterson, "States Assess Surrogate Motherhood." More precisely, the baby had antibodies for the HTLV-III virus. (About half the babies born with those antibodies actually develop AIDS.)

12. Moreover, the interests of the child would support a general rule that those who planned to adopt are responsible, even when the mother before the birth has held open the option of keeping the child.

13. Of course a still better system, at least in the case of a handicapped child with extraordinary expenses, would have the state subsidize the expenses or otherwise help out the parents. In the absence of such a system generally, however, it is difficult to see why the state should assume the expenses of children whose parents decided by contract to create them and were subsequently disappointed by a handicap.

14. See Corbin, *Contracts,* I, § 7, pp. 15–17 (distinguishing between agreements and contracts).

15. See Chapter 9, note 69.

16. Gordon v. Cutler, 471 A.2d 449 (Pa. Super. 1983).

17. Corbin, *Contracts,* V, § 993, pp. 8–9; Fletcher, *Cyclopedia of the Law of Private Corporations,* §§ 3581, 3590, 3603, 3613–14. The terminology of the Louisiana prohibition of surrogacy contracts is that they are "void and null." However, courts also sometimes give effect to contracts labeled either void or illegal. Corbin claims that a void contract properly defined is one without any legal effect—indeed it is not a contract at all; *Contracts,* I, § 7, pp. 15–17. Illegal bargains, by contrast, are sometimes enforceable by one or both parties. But he acknowledges that sometimes "void" is used loosely to cover situations in which the agreement has some legal effect; ibid. See ibid., V, § 993, pp. 8–9. Fletcher agrees that not all illegal contracts are void; § 3581. Some illegal contracts are binding when fully executed, for example, and so are not void. See also ibid., §§ 3603, 3612–14.

18. A. v. C. (1985) F.L.R. 445 (Eng. Ct. App. 1978).

19. Corbin, *Contracts,* V, § 993, pp. 8–9.

20. See Chapter 4, text accompanying note 68.

8. Rules Affecting Biological Parents' Claims to Children

1. See, e.g., Jourdan C. v. Mary K., 179 Cal. App. 3d 386, 224 Cal. Rptr. 530 (1986). As of 1985, twenty-eight states had special provisions concerning artificial insemination. Several state statutes are modeled on § 5 of the Uniform Parentage Act; they provide that when artificial insemination is performed in accordance with statutory requirements, the sperm donor will not be treated as the natural father. See Judith Bick-Rice, "The Need for Statutes Regulating Artificial Insemination by Donors," *Ohio State Law Journal,* 46 (1985), 1062, n. 80 (discussing such statutes in California, Colorado, Illinois, Minnesota, Montana, Nevada, New Jersey, Washington, and Wyoming). The Uniform Parentage Act, § 5(a), 9B Uniform Laws Ann. 295, 301–302 (1979), provides in part: "If,

under the supervision of a licensed physician and with the consent of her husband, a wife is inseminated artificially with the semen donated by a man not her husband, the husband is treated in law as if he were the natural father of a child thereby conceived." It further provides in § 5(b): "The donor of semen provided to a licensed physician for use in artificial insemination of a married woman other than the donor's wife is treated in law as if he were not the natural father of a child thereby conceived." The California, Colorado, and Wyoming statutes omit the word "married" in their statutes.

There also are statutes dealing with artificial insemination in nineteen other states. At least ten of these states require that a doctor have performed the insemination in order for the statute to apply. Most make the offspring the legitimate child of a married couple consenting to the insemination. Most statutes do not stipulate that the donor has no rights in or responsibilities to the child, but their provisions would be expected to have exactly that effect. Bick-Rice, "Need for Statutes," pp. 1062–63, reviews current provisions concerning artificial insemination.

2. 179 Cal. App. 3d 386, 224 Cal. Rptr. 530 (1986).

3. Although the request for joint legal custody and for legal recognition of de facto parenthood was denied, Mary's friend Victoria was granted visitation rights. Jourdan was also given visitation, but his request for joint legal custody was denied. Both legal and physical custody remained with the natural mother.

4. 152 N.J. Super. 160, 377 A.2d 821 (1977).

5. 224 Cal. Rptr., p. 534.

6. Bick-Rice, "Need for Statutes," pp. 1066–67, discusses the legal dilemma of a sperm donor when there is no statute absolving him of responsibility and concludes that when there is no such statute, the outcome of litigation is often conflicting and uncertain.

7. For further discussion of whether a surrogate mother who keeps her child should have this option, see Chapter 9, "When the Mother Receives Custody."

8. N.J. Stat. Ann. § 9:17-44 (Supp. 1987). The law in the state of Washington is substantially similar; see Wash. Rev. Code § 26.26.050 (1985).

In Sherwyn v. Department of Social Services, 173 Cal. App.3d 52, 218 Cal. Rptr. 778 (1985), the California Court of Appeals expressed "grave doubts" about the applicability in the surrogacy situation of state statutes denying the status of natural father to a sperm donor. The lower court had upheld the constitutionality of the statutes as applied to surrogacy arrangements. Both courts' discussions of the issues are of interest, but the court of appeals ultimately decided the case on other grounds: it vacated the trial court's judgment for failure to present a justiciable controversy.

9. See, e.g., In re Baby Girl, *Family Law Reporter*, 9 (1983), 2348 (Ky. Cir. Ct. 1983); and Syrkowski v. Appleyard, 122 Mich. App. 506, 333 N.W.2d 90 (1983), discussed in Chapter 5, note 2.

10. Of course a state that prohibited surrogacy contracts could, if it wished, deny the father any right to the child, as a means of strengthening its prohibition by making it impossible for the father to derive the intended benefit from the arrangement.

11. See Samuel Green and John V. Long, *Marriage and Family Law Agreements* (New York: McGraw-Hill, 1984), § 5.22, p 271, concluding: "At common law, there was also a strong presumption that a child born to a married woman was the child of her husband. At one time, this presumption could only be rebutted by proof of impotency or physical absence from England (*beyond the four seas*). Though modified by statute, this presumption has also been accepted in American jurisdictions." In keeping with the state's demonstrated interest in legitimizing children, twenty-four states by statute expressly extend the presumption of legitimacy to children born as a result of artificial insemination with the consent of the recipient's husband; Coleman, "Surrogate Motherhood: Analysis of the Problems and Suggestions for Solutions," p. 71.

The presumption that the woman who gives birth is legally the parent has also caused trouble in the surrogacy situation. See, e.g., Wong, "Mass. Couple Ask for Va. Ruling" (involving gestational surrogacy).

12. See, e.g., Caton v. Caton (Okla. Ct. App. March 15, 1983, unpublished), review denied, *Family Law Reporter,* 10 (1984), 1150 (upholding a statute that denies a wife the opportunity to establish her husband's nonpaternity). Historically the rule that no one could challenge the presumption was designed both to preserve family integrity and to provide a means of indemnifying the state for the expenses of child support. See, e.g., Dept. of Social Services ex rel. Sandra C. v. Thomas J. S., 100 A.D.2d 119, 130, 474 N.Y.S.2d 322, 330 (1984).

13. It is also an issue whether the child can sue to learn her true paternity. Compare Michele Marie W. v. Ronald W. (Cal. Sup. Ct. Aug. 5, 1985), *Family Law Reporter,* 11 (1985), 1526 (a child cannot sue to establish her true paternity in view of the presumption that the issue of a wife who is cohabiting with her husband is a child of the marriage), with Jones v. Robinson (Va. Sup. Ct. April 26, 1985), *Family Law Reporter,* 11 (1985), 1363 (Virginia's paternity statute denying certain illegitimate children the right to establish paternity violates the equal protection clause).

That issue would not be relevant to the surrogacy situation we are hypothesizing, unless it was applied to a guardian's action in the name of the child, because the surrogacy case involves a newborn, who is not capable of wondering about her paternity. As the child born of surrogacy grows up, however, the rule could be relevant to her.

14. See Patricia Blumberg, "Human Leukocyte Antigen Testing: Technology versus Policy in Cases of Disputed Parentage," *Vanderbilt Law Review,* 36 (November 1983), 1578, 1591; S. Joel Kolko, "Admissibility of HLA Test Results to Determine Paternity," *Family Law Reporter,* 9 (1983), 4009; and Carol Dan Browning, "The Burden of Proof in a Paternity Action," *Journal of Family Law,* 25 (October 1986), 357–372.

15. 405 U.S. 645 (1972).

16. Santosky v. Kramer, 455 U.S. 745 (1982), also establishes a due process right in biological parents. It held that biological parents whose children were removed from them on grounds of neglect were constitutionally entitled to due process at a hearing to terminate their parental rights and that it violated due

process for the state to use a "fair preponderance of the evidence" standard in determining whether the parents could and would provide an adequate home. While the case strongly supports biological parents' rights, it is not directly relevant to the situation of the contracting father in a surrogacy arrangement, because it involves the removal of children because of unfitness of parents who had been given an opportunity to act as custodians. Moreover, like *Stanley, Santosky* does not involve a contest between parents; both parents were pitted against the state.

17. In Caban v. Mohammed, 441 U.S. 380, 385, n. 3 (1979), the Court spoke of a procedural due process right, flowing from *Stanley*. In Lehr v. Robertson, 463 U.S. 248 (1983), the Court assumed the unmarried father was entitled to some degree of constitutional protection, but very little. The father in *Lehr* was deemed sufficiently protected because the state maintained a register for putative fathers. Those who registered in accordance with the state procedure would be informed of any attempt to adopt or otherwise finalize parental rights to the child, and would then have an opportunity to appear and be heard. The existence of this procedure was deemed sufficient to satisfy constitutional requirements, even though Lehr had not been aware of the register's existence and so had not registered and had not been informed of the adoption he was protesting. See also page 122.

18. Lehr v. Robertson, 463 U.S. 248 (1983).

19. Michael H. v. Gerald D., 236 Cal. Rptr. 810 (1987) (applying conclusive presumption that issue of married woman cohabiting with husband who was not impotent or sterile is child of that marriage). The California Supreme Court declined to review that holding, but the U.S. Supreme Court has granted *certiorari*. Some of the open questions on this subject may therefore soon be answered. Accord Michelle W. v. Ronald W., 703 P.2d 88 (Cal. Sup. Ct. 1985); In re Hodge, *Family Law Reporter*, 12 (1986), 1208 (Ore. Ct. App.) (applying conclusive presumption even though mother challenged it and even though blood tests conclusively showed the presumed father could not be the actual biological father). See also Happel v. Mecklenburger, 101 Ill. App.3d 107, 427 N.E.2d 974 (1981); A v. X, Y, and Z, 641 P.2d 1222 (Wyo. 1982).

20. Although *Caban* granted procedural due process, it did not reach the substantive due process argument that fathers have a right to maintain a parental relationship with their children unless they are unfit, because it decided the case on the basis of the equal protection clause.

21. See, e.g., Petitioner F. v. Respondent R., 430 A.2d 1075, 1078–79 (Del. 1981); P. B. C. v. D. H., 396 Mass. 68, 72, 483 N.E.2d 1094, 1097 (1985), cert. denied, 459 U.S. 1021 (1982). See also Market v. Behm, 394 N.W.2d 239 (Minn. App. 1986).

22. See Thornsberry v. Superior Court of Arizona, Mohave Cty., ex rel. Hunter, 146 Ariz. 517, 707 P.2d 315 (1985).

23. See Slawek v. Stroh, 62 Wis. 2d 295, 215 N.W.2d 9 (1974); Pritz v. Chesnul, 106 Ill. App. 3d 969, 436 N.E.2d 631 (Ill. 1982). See also R. McG. and C. W. v. J. W. and W. W., 615 P.2d 666 (Colo. 1980) (finding that a statute allowing paternity proceedings to be instituted by a child, her mother, and her

presumed father but not by a putative natural father impermissibly discriminates on the basis of gender and violates the federal equal protection clause and also the equal rights provision of the Colorado constitution).

24. For the history see ex parte Devine, 398 So.2d 686, 688–90 (Ala. 1981).

25. Homer H. Clark, *Law of Domestic Relations* (St. Paul: West, 1968), p. 176; Annotation, "Right of Mother to Custody of Illegitimate Child," *American Law Reports,* 2d ser., 98 (1964), 427.

26. 441 U.S. 380 (1979).

27. For nine months after the mother and father separated, the children lived with the mother and her husband. The children were then sent to Puerto Rico with their maternal grandmother. The mother and her husband were to join them after they raised some money. When the father visited the children in Puerto Rico, he took them back to New York in his custody, and then the custody-and-adoption battle between the parents began. During most of the period when they were separated and before the mother married, the children had lived with their maternal grandmother in Puerto Rico. The children were five and seven respectively when the petition for adoption was heard; three years had passed since their natural parents' separation.

28. Justice Powell wrote for the Court. Justice Stevens dissented, jointed by Chief Justice Burger and Justice Rehnquist. Justice Stewart dissented in a separate opinion.

29. 463 U.S. 248, 256–257 (1983).

30. Ibid., pp. 252, 263.

31. Ibid., pp. 259–260.

32. Ibid., pp. 259–263, 266–268.

33. Ibid., p. 265.

34. Of course parties to a lawsuit can argue both theories; Fleming James and Geoffrey Hazard, *Civil Procedure,* 3d ed. (Boston: Little, Brown, 1985), pp. 155–56. A plaintiff in the father's position would want to argue the validity of the contract, but if he lost on that theory, he would want to argue that he is the better parent and that the child's custody should be decided on that basis.

35. It appeared to the Court that the father was and had been just as involved with his children as their natural mother. The mother's case was weakened by her having sent the children to live with their grandmother; they had not lived with their mother for more than a year when Caban removed them to New York; 441 U.S., pp. 386, 388–389, 391, 394.

36. Quilloin v. Walcott, 434 U.S. 246, 256 (1978) (discussed and quoted in Caban, 441 U.S., p. 389, n. 7).

37. 441 U.S., p. 391.

38. Ibid., pp. 402–403; 407–408; 410, n. 20; 412; 414–415.

39. Ibid., pp. 392, n. 11; 416 (Stevens dissent).

40. Ibid., p. 413.

41. Ibid., pp. 404–406.

42. Many authorities believe that breastfeeding is the preferred course for the baby's development, both physical and psychological. See, e.g., Karen Pryor,

Nursing Your Baby (New York: Pocket Books, 1983). Arnold Lucius Gesell concludes that "breastfeeding may well constitute a fundamental requirement, not merely a method of choice. To be sure, the newborn can survive without breastfeeding, but only with certain very definite deprivations"; *Infant and Child in the Culture of Today* (New York: Harper & Row, 1974), p. 71.

43. Justice Stevens's suggestion would not, however, correlate absolutely with gender. See Chapter 9, page 140.

9. Custody Contests to Determine the Better Parent

1. Although one can argue that the presumption should favor mothers because they are more likely as a group to have the closer relationship with the child, one could equally argue that in order to reinforce parenting in men, courts should award custody to men who seek to parent. That rationale would lose some of its force if the father were married and planned that his wife would become the primary caretaker.

2. See Ex parte Devine, 398 So.2d 686 (Ala. 1981). Several courts have abandoned the "tender years" doctrine, although the presumption still exists in twenty-two states.

3. 278 S.E.2d 357 (W. Va. 1981). See also Derby v. Derby, 31 Or. App. 803, 571 P.2d 562 (1977), modified on other grounds, 31 Or. App. 1333, 572 P.2d 1080 (1977), review denied, 281 Or. 323 (1978).

4. 278 S.E.2d, p. 360. Several studies have shown that lawyers often advise fathers to litigate for custody even if they do not desire it, in order to reduce the level of the support they will be required to pay; "Lawyering for the Child: Principles of Representation in Custody and Visitation Disputes Arising from Divorce," *Yale Law Journal,* 87 (1978), 1131, n. 21. See also Donald N. Bersoff, "Representation for Children in Custody Decisions: All That Glitters Is Not *Gault,*" *Journal of Family Law,* 15 (1976–77), 27.

5. 278 S.E.2d, p. 360.

6. Ibid., p. 361.

7. Ibid., p. 363.

8. A father may object to such a definition and the consequent award of custody. If he supports his children and his wife, shouldn't he also be considered a caretaker? The traditionally paternal responsibilities are also important to the family unit, but the presumption described above refers primarily to traditionally maternal ones. His argument, therefore, would be that a person who spends less time with the children but contributes more money to the household should have an equal claim to custody upon divorce.

But even if the father who works outside the home and does not have extensive childcare responsibilities should not be faulted for the way he performs his obligations to his family, he does not thereby build the same kind of attachment to or relationship with his child as the primary caretaker, who takes care of the child's daily needs. From the point of view of the child's best interests, continuing the relationship with the mother is more important in those circumstances.

9. 278 S.E.2d, p. 362, n. 9.

10. Ibid., p. 363, n. 10. It may be that in some families in which both parents are caretakers it is most important, because of both parents' previous relationship with the child, to preserve both relationships, in some circumstances even to the extent of awarding shared custody. The possibility of joint custody is discussed later in the chapter.

11. The primary caretaker rule also has the virtue of avoiding some of the class bias so evident in other tests of the better parent for custody.

12. Joseph Goldstein, Anna Freud, and Albert J. Solnit, *Beyond the Best Interests of the Child* (New York: Free Press, 1973); idem, *Before the Best Interests of the Child* (New York: Free Press, 1979); Joseph Goldstein, Anna Freud, Albert J. Solnit, and Sonja Goldstein, *In the Best Interests of the Child* (New York: Free Press, 1986).

13. The presumption has been subject to criticism—most forcefully for its tendency to support removal of children from poor persons who have had to place a child in foster care and then try to get her back. See, e.g., Nadine Taub, "Assessing the Impact of Goldstein, Freud and Solnit's Proposals: An Introductory Overview," *New York University Review of Law and Social Change,* 12 (Summer 1984), 485–494; Peggy C. Davis, "'There Is a Book Out . . .': An Analysis of Judicial Absorption of Legislative Facts," *Harvard Law Review,* 100 (May 1987), 1539, 1542–46. Instead of a presumption for a caretaker, others have supported "biological essentialism" because "in a society so riven by class inequalities, here is one great simple equality"; Julia Wrigley, "Whose Baby Is It Anyway?" *Against the Current,* 2 (September–October 1987), 54. "We should see the merits of 'biological essentialism' in safeguarding the rights of poor, working-class or socially-stigmatized parents"; ibid., p. 55.

In the surrogacy situation, however, the use of a presumption for continuity to favor the mother does not carry this threat of discrimination against the poor; instead it would shield the mother from a custody contest in which her comparative lack of financial resources is likely to make her the loser.

14. The presumption might apply in the same way in a dispute between married parents who do not live together or who are separating and who both want custody of their newborn child. In any event, an unmarried father should not be in a *better* position than a married father to claim custody of his biological child. One can easily imagine arguments that the unmarried father should not be treated as well, especially if he has not offered to marry the mother. Cf. Lehr v. Robertson, 463 U.S. 248, 252, 263 (1983).

15. E.g., Mary D. Ainsworth, "Object Relations, Dependency, and Attachment: A Theoretical Review of the Infant-Mother Relationship," *Child Development,* 40 (1969), 969–1025; idem, "The Development of Infant-Mother Interaction among the Ganda," in *Determinants of Infant Behavior,* ed. B. M. Foss, 4 vols. (London: Methuen, 1961–65) II; John Bowlby, *Maternal Care and Maternal Health and Deprivation of Maternal Care* (New York: Schechter Books, 1966), p. 59; idem, Foreword to Foss, *Determinants of Infant Behavior,* I; idem, "The Nature of the Child's Tie to His Mother," *International Journal of Psycho-Analysis,* 39 (1958), 350–373; and Robert Hanley, "Bonding Is Described at

Baby M Hearing," *New York Times,* February 28, 1987, p. 34. See also Chapter 8, note 42.

16. The father's argument would be that a presumption in favor of the party who would have custody under the contract would be more fair because at least the parties agreed to this result at one point in the past; in effect this amounts to the same argument discussed above that the contract should be enforced. In addition to the considerations discussed earlier, another troublesome aspect of that argument is that it would allow unwed fathers who entered surrogacy contracts to have clearer rights to custody of newborns than even fathers married to birth mothers would have.

17. Should a court take into account the religious practices of the parties, for example, or would that involve the state in establishing or penalizing religion in violation of the First and Fourteenth Amendments? See Quiner v. Quiner (Cal. Ct. App., 2d Dist. 1967), reprinted in Judith Areen, *Cases and Materials on Family Law,* 2d ed. (New York: Foundation Press, 1985), pp. 444–451. Should the court evaluate the parties' lifestyles and exercise a preference for the one that is the more mainstream, or does that violate the parties' rights to privacy and to equal protection? See ibid., pp. 433–436; Painter v. Bannister, 258 Iowa 1390, 140 N.W.2d 152 (1966).

18. Doe v. Kelley, 106 Mich. App. 169, 307 N.W.2d 438 (1981), cert. denied, 459 U.S. 1183 (1983), involved a Michigan couple who wanted to use the husband's secretary as a surrogate. The fee was to be $5,000, plus medical and insurance expenses.

19. "The whole sorry business of surrogate motherhood is riddled with economic bias. It's rife with messages about buying and selling children, about who can 'afford' to have them"; Ellen Goodman, "The Word That's Not Mentioned in the Baby M Case," *Boston Globe,* February 17, 1987, p. 15.

20. In re Baby M, 217 N.J. Super. 313, 340 (1987).

21. Hanley, "Baby M Case Etches a Study in Contrasts: Different Social Classes and Family Relations," *New York Times,* February 17, 1987, p. B1.

22. Ibid. (quoting Mary Beth Whitehead).

23. Hanley, "Reporter's Notebook: Grief over Baby M," p. B1.

24. In re Baby M, p. 339; Robert Hanley, "Baby M's 'Best Interests' May Resolve a Puzzling Case," *New York Times,* February 2, 1987, p. B1.

25. Robert Hanley, "Baby M's Mother Examined on Her Family and Facts," *New York Times,* February 19, 1987, p. B2; In re Baby M, *Family Law Reporter,* 14 (1988), 2023–24.

26. In re Baby M, *Family Law Reporter,* 14 (1988), 2024.

27. Wrigley, "Whose Baby Is It Anyway?" p. 54. The author speaks convincingly about "middle class condescension toward the childrearing practices of poor and working-class parents." But different class values work in different ways, and Mary Beth Whitehead may have been equally judgmental toward the Sterns: when she visited, the day after she had given the baby to the Sterns, "what she saw convinced her that her baby should be with her, namely that the cradle was in the baby's own room, not in the Sterns' bedroom: 'She looked so lonely and helpless . . . wrapped in a blanket like a cocoon. I picked her up and never let

her out of my arms; she was my child, it was what was right for her, she never cried' "; Report of Judith Greif for use in *Baby M* litigation, 1987, p. 15.

28. In In re C. B., discussed above, however, the judge clearly took such factors into account in deciding to allow the surrogacy arrangement to be executed. See Chapter 5, text accompanying note 3.

29. Garska v. McCoy, 278 S.E.2d 357, 364 (W.Va. 1981).

30. People ex rel. Scarpetta v. Spence-Chapin Adoption Service, 269 N.E.2d 787, 792 (N.Y. Ct. App. 1971). Adoption is in general a process involving a transfer of children to more well-to-do homes: "adopted children enjoy more socioeconomic advantages than children who remain with their unmarried birthmothers—they have better educated, older mothers, and they live in families with much higher income"; National Adoption Committee, *Adoption Factbook,* p. 12. Accordingly, it is often important to the birth mother who wants to keep her child to avoid the comparative inquiry.

31. Not only is there less evidence available on which to make a disposition; there is also less need for a custody dispute than there may be when an older child is involved. An older child may have views and feelings about the outcome or a need to continue previous relationships, which should be examined and taken into account. Of course, there is also a risk that an older child who is aware of the proceedings may be scarred by a custody battle between her parents, a risk that the newborn does not share.

32. Report of Dr. Marshall Schechter for use in *Baby M* litigation, 1987, p. 29. Dr. Schechter was chosen as an expert witness by the guardian *ad litem.*

33. Report of David Brodzinski, Ph.D., for use in *Baby M* litigation, 1987, pp. 13, 21. The court gave particular deference to Brodzinski because he had been solicited by all the parties to serve as an expert and had chosen to serve for the child and the guardian *ad litem.* See In re Baby M, 217 N.J. Super. 313, 366 (1987). Marshall Schechter, in the report cited in note 32, used this same evidence to show "histrionic personality disorder" in Mrs. Whitehead (p. 30).

34. Michelle Harrison, "Bias Predominates in Baby "M" Expert Testimony" (Manuscript draft, March 18, 1987), pp. 7–10.

35. Mary Beth Whitehead, interview with author, Harvard Law School, February 10, 1988.

36. Harrison, "Bias Predominates," p. 6.

37. Ibid., p. 12 (quoting reports by Marshall Schechter, pp. 20 and 12, and David Brodzinski, p. 18).

38. Ibid., p. 11. Dr. Schechter also criticized Mrs. Whitehead for having four pandas of various sizes for Sara to play with; "pots, pans and spoons" would have been "more suitable"; Robert Hanley, "Experts Testify on Whitehead as a Parent," *New York Times,* February 24, 1987, p. B2.

39. For example, Mr. Stern revealed that he had never talked with his wife about the discomfort he felt in attending Christian religious services with her.

40. Harrison, "Bias Predominates," p. 15.

41. In addition to reflecting the attitudes of experts, the evidence adduced may reflect the differing styles of the lawyers for the Sterns and the Whiteheads. The Sterns' lawyer persistently attacked Mrs. Whitehead's emotional, financial,

and marital stability, trying to make her look like an unsuitable parent; the Whiteheads' lawyer, on the other hand, refused to "throw mud"; Robert Hanley, "Baby M Trial Lawyers: Two Goals and Two Styles," *New York Times*, February 23, 1987, p. B1.

42. In re Baby M, *Family Law Reporter*, 14 (1988), 2023.

43. Other instances of rules of law that appear clear but in reality leave substantial room for discretion are the doctrines of coercion, duress, and mistake in contract law and adoption law (see Chapters 5 and 6), the doctrine of abandonment (see Chapter 6), and the requirement of knowing and intelligent waiver in constitutional law (see Chapter 4).

44. Hanley, "Baby M Case Etches a Study in Contrasts," p. B2.

45. Compare the situation in Argentina, where children stolen more than a decade ago have happily adjusted to their "adoptive" families; Alan Riding, "Argentines Fight for Orphans of a Dirty War," *New York Times*, December 20, 1987, p. 1. Should the state try now to remove the children, even if their natural parents have been killed? This is a moving illustration of the pervasive conflict in family law between doing justice for innocent children and designing a system that requires people to treat each other fairly.

46. Of course if it is an ironclad rule and not a presumption, it will lead to even greater certainty. But it may nonetheless be better to have a presumption and thus to allow some flexibility to adjust the outcome to the needs and equities of the particular case.

All rules have depended upon a finding that the parent awarded custody is fit, for example; so parties always can litigate the issue of fitness. But it is difficult for a parent to prevail only by proving the other parent actually unfit, and the likelihood of losing would presumably deter many from litigating if fitness were the only issue, unless they had a strong case.

47. In re Baby M, *Family Law Reporter*, 14 (1988), 2022 (N.J Sup. Ct. 1988).

48. Ibid. and n. 17 (quoting Beck v. Beck, 86 N.J. 480, 488 [1981]).

49. Ibid., p. 2025.

50. Ibid., p. 2022, n. 17.

51. The court said that paid surrogacy was "illegal, perhaps criminal," but did not decide the issue of criminality; ibid., p. 2008.

52. To discourage the illegal contracts the court could instead simply have adopted a strict rule that a father who enters an illegal surrogacy arrangement cannot be awarded custody in a dispute with the mother. The New Jersey court considered such a rule but rejected it, pointing out that earlier New Jersey cases had declined to eliminate adoptive parents as custodians on the ground that they had participated in illegalities in acquiring the child; ibid., p. 2022.

53. Of course parties to a surrogacy contract could decide that there would be visitation, or even that the surrogate mother would pay support. The latter provision seems most unlikely, and the former is not the norm. Usually the parties opt to cut off the surrogate mother entirely, just as adopting parents have classically replaced and cut off the natural parents by adoption. But Peggy Presler of Canton, Ohio, arranged in advance for periodic visits with Adam, whom she

bore for a California couple. Presler, herself an adopted child, believed it would be better for the child if he was acquainted with her. See Peterson, "Baby M Case: Surrogate Mothers Vent Feelings," p. B4.

In the traditional adoption model the adoptive parents are the only ones with parental rights. Traditionally, unrelated adoption almost always involved anonymity between the natural family and the adoptive family, and the child was not permitted to know about her biological roots. This process is undergoing change. In some jurisdictions adoptees have acquired a right to find out about or even to meet their natural parents. Moreover, in private adoption the parties often (though not invariably) meet or know about each other; sometimes the parties arrange for the natural mother to retain some rights to visit the child, or at least to meet the child and know her as she is growing up. But these "open adoption" arrangements still are far from the norm. See Marsh Garrison, "Why Terminate Parental Rights?" *Stanford Law Review,* 35 (February 1983), 423; and John M. Stoxen, "The Best of Both 'Open' and 'Closed' Adoption Worlds: A Call for Reform of State Statutes," *Journal of Legislation,* 13 (Spring 1986), 292.

54. Wrigley, "Whose Baby Is It Anyway?" p. 55. Wrigley speculates that such an arrangement "might produce children with a depth of social understanding denied to those who grow up in one narrow social milieu." Noel Keane agrees both that surrogate mothers may be anxious for continuing contact and that most couples who hire them do not want them to have it; see Peterson, "Baby M Case: Surrogate Mothers Vent Feelings," p. B4.

55. Hanley, "Reporter's Notebook: Grief over Baby M," p. B3 (quoting Gary Skoloff, Mr. Stern's lawyer).

56. Report of Dr. Harold Koplewicz for use in *Baby M* litigation, 1987, p. 8.

57. Report of Judith Brown Greif for use in *Baby M* litigation, 1987, pp. 9, 12; Report of David Brodzinski, Ph.D., for use in *Baby M* litigation, 1987, p.14.

58. Report of Harold Koplewicz, p. 6. It is possible, of course, that their different positions on this issue reflect litigation strategy: each may have believed that the position they espoused increased the likelihood that custody would be awarded to them. Moreover, Mr. Stern's position could reflect a desire to minimize the risk that he would be responsible for child support if Mrs. Whitehead prevailed on custody. Similarly, Mrs. Whitehead's position could have reflected a desire to receive child support payments.

59. Carolyn S. Bratt, "Joint Custody," *Kentucky Law Review,* 67 (1978–79), 271–308; H. Jay Folberg and Marra Graham, "Joint Custody of Children Following Divorce," *University of California–Davis Law Review,* 12 (Summer 1979), 523–581; David J. Miller, "Joint Custody," *Family Law Quarterly,* 13 (Fall 1979), 345–412. See In re Baby M, 217 N.J. Super. 313, 367–370 (1987).

60. During the litigation Mrs. Whitehead was given four hours weekly of visitation; after the trial court decision she was allowed two hours weekly. No other members of her family were permitted to participate in the visits except at Christmas. The visits were ordered to take place at a home for wayward youths, under the supervision of a guard. Mrs. Whitehead usually fed the baby, who then slept. When the visits began, Mrs. Whitehead wished to breastfeed the baby, who was clawing at her breast, but the four guards assigned to supervise forbade

breastfeeding, under orders from the court and the guardian *ad litem*. Understandably, Mrs. Whitehead called this atmosphere for visitation "humiliating"; see Hanley, "Baby M Case Etches a Study in Contrasts," pp. B1–B2; idem, "Whitehead Outlines Her Life before Baby M," *New York Times*, February 10, 1987, p. B15.

Although supervised visits are sometimes ordered when litigation to determine parental rights is pending, such restrictions are obviously not appropriate in a final order unless there is a real risk that the visiting parent will molest the child or otherwise cause serious harm. The purpose of long-term visitation is to allow the child to develop as natural a relationship as possible with the noncustodial parent. A parent with rights to visit should be able to see the child in his or her home, or in another relaxed atmosphere, and should be able to have the child know his or her family and friends. Accordingly, after the New Jersey Supreme Court decision, Mrs. Whitehead was awarded unsupervised visitation of six hours weekly and several holidays; the visiting time is to increase over the next year, and in the summer of 1989 there will be two weeks of visitation; Robert Hanley, "Baby M's Mother Wins Visiting Rights," *New York Times*, April 7, 1988, p. A1.

61. Betsy's real name is Elizabeth, and Mary Beth's name is Mary Elizabeth. Mary Beth would like the baby now to be called Elizabeth instead of remaining Melissa to one set of parents and Sara to another.

62. Joint legal custody refers to sharing decision making about important matters in the child's life. Joint physical custody refers to sharing the child's time and to each parent's providing a home for the child. Some joint custody arrangements allow one parent to retain custody with generous visitation for the other parent; they do not necessarily split time equally between the two biological parents.

63. "After the Baby M Case," *Newsweek*, April 13, 1987, p. 23. That case is the one in which the woman from Mexico was allegedly tricked into becoming a surrogate (see Chapter 2, note 5). The ruling differed from the Yates case because it involved a permanent order of joint custody, not just a temporary disposition while awaiting the final order. States differ as to whether and in what circumstances they favor joint custody rather than awarding custody to one parent with reasonable visitation by the other, and California is more favorable to joint custody than most jurisdictions. Moreover, the fact that Alejandra and the Haros were relatives might have favored a determination of joint custody in that case.

64. Mothers can be liable for child support as well as fathers; see Orr v. Orr, 440 U.S. 268 (1979). However, it seems unlikely that the father in a surrogacy arrangement would be seeking support from a surrogate mother, because the father is likely to be much wealthier.

65. Noel Keane informs contracting couples that the surrogate might breach the contract and offers, without any increase in fee, to help them find another surrogate; Shapiro, "No Other Hope for Having a Child."

66. See, e.g., Stephen K. v. Roni L., 105 Cal. App. 3d 640, 164 Cal. Rptr. 618 (1980): a father deceived into impregnating has no cause of action in tort

because "claims such as those presented . . . arise from conduct so intensely private that the courts should not be asked nor attempt to resolve such claims."

67. In re Pamela P. v. Frank S., 88 A.D.2d 865, 451 N.Y.S.2d 766 (1982), aff'd, 59 N.Y.2d 1, 462 N.Y.S. 819, 449 N.E.2d 713 (1983), reversing 110 Misc. 2d 978, 443 N.Y.S.2d 343 (N.Y. Fam. Ct. 1981): a father who was tricked into impregnating a woman is not liable for child support as long as the mother's income is sufficient to meet "the child's fair and reasonable needs."

68. Although the issue of pregnancy by deception is raised extremely frequently in paternity suits, it is invariably a losing issue; see, e.g., Hughes v. Hutt, *Family Law Reporter,* 9 (1983), 2278 (Pa. Super. Ct. 1983); In re K. A. Y., *Family Law Reporter,* 10 (1983), 1195 (Wis. Ct. App. 1983).

69. The rule proposed for fathers in the surrogacy context is similar to rules sometimes applied to semen donors. One similarity is that contact can be established or not at the initiative of the father, and the mother cannot control whether or not contact occurs. Moreover, this system, both for surrogacy and for artificial insemination, suggests a system of layers of rights to the custody of children, rather than an approach that treats all claimants to custody as having equal rights or else eliminates the claimant altogether. Stanley v. Illinois, giving rights to the unmarried father after the mother's death but not necessarily before, is also consistent with an approach that does not put potential custodians in competition with each other, but that instead lines them up in a clear order of priority. It is not acceptable, however, for any priority to rest solely on the basis of gender; cf. Reed v. Reed, 404 U.S. 71 (1971).

Such an approach has a certain appeal, and a certain advantage over an equal rights approach. It allows for clear rules in an area in which clear rules are badly needed. It also provides maximal security for the child—not eliminating potential caretakers, but lining them up in a clear order of priority. If such a system were followed, even a donor of semen for artificial insemination might have rights *after* the inseminated woman and her spouse (and even if a doctor performed the insemination). For example, if the person inseminated was a single woman, and after her child was born she died or became unfit so that her child was taken away from her, the sperm donor might have rights against the rest of the world, though not against the mother. If he knew of this situation and asserted his rights, and if he was fit, he might have a right to custody because of his biological tie (although in some states he would have to grapple with language in state statutes cutting off his parental rights, by saying that they were not designed to cover this situation). As a practical matter, however, most donors of sperm for artificial insemination do not know about the fate of their sperm and do not assert interests in pursuing parental rights.

70. Similarly, in the discussion of adoption in jurisdictions that allow the natural mother to revoke after the baby has been placed in an adoptive home, I suggested that an exception could be made for surrogacy. There, however, it seemed that the rule proposed for surrogacy was the rule that ought to govern all adoptions. In this case, by contrast, I would not disrupt the general rule holding unwed fathers other than sperm donors responsible for child support without regard to the circumstances of the conception.

Conclusion

1. Requiring the father to be liable for child support would increase the deterrence, although surrogacy arrangements would continue to be made by couples willing to take their chances at selecting a surrogate willing to perform. Women wanting to be mothers, however, might be correspondingly encouraged to enter the arrangements fraudulently.

Appendix

1. American Fertility Society, *Ethical Considerations,* p. 67S.

2. La. Rev. Stat. Ann. § 9:2713 (West Supp. 1988); *Washington Post,* February 6, 1988, p. A5; Michigan S 228. Under the Michigan statute, it is a felony to broker any surrogacy contracts or to enter into a contract with an unemancipated minor female or a developmentally disabled or mentally ill female. The penalty is imprisonment up to five years and a $50,000 fine. It is a misdemeanor, subject to one year's imprisonment and a $10,000 fine, to enter other paid surrogacy arrangements.

3. Peterson, "States Assess Surrogate Motherhood."

4. 704 S.W.2d 209 (Ky. Supreme Ct. 1986).

5. In re Baby M, *Family Law Reporter,* 14 (1988), 2010.

6. Ibid., p. 2025.

7. See, e.g., Matter of Adoption of Baby Girl L. J., 132 Misc.2d 972, 505 N.Y.S.2d 813 (1986).

8. 106 Mich. App. 169, 307 N.W.2d 438 (Mich. Ct. App. 1983).

9. 420 Mich. 367, 362 N.W.2d 211 (1985).

10. Yates v. Keane, slip. op., Nos. 9758, 9772 (Mich. Cir. Ct. January 2, 1988).

11. A. v. C. (1985) F.L.R. 445 (Eng. Ct. App. 1978).

12. Warnock Report, p. 85.

13. Surrogacy Arrangements Act, 1985, ch. 49.

14. See *Family Law Reporter,* 13 (1987), 1260.

Selected Bibliography

Adlam, Diana. "The Case against Capitalist Patriarchy." In *Feminism and Materialism: Women and Modes of Production,* edited by Annette Kuhn and Ann Marie Wolpe. London: Routledge and Kegan Paul, 1978.

"After the Baby M Case." *Newsweek,* April 13, 1987, pp. 22–23.

American Fertility Society, Ethics Committee. *Ethical Considerations of the New Reproductive Technologies.* Birmingham, Ala., 1986.

American Law Institute. *Restatement (Second) of Contracts.* St. Paul, 1981.

Andrews, Lori. *New Conceptions.* New York: Ballantine, 1985.

——— "Removing the Stigma of Surrogate Motherhood." *Family Advocate,* 4 (Fall 1981), 20–27.

——— "Stork Market: The Law of the New Reproductive Technologies." *American Bar Association Journal,* 70 (August 1984), 50–56.

Arditti, Rita. "Surrogate Mothering Exploits Women." *Science for the People,* May–June 1987, pp. 22–23.

Arms, Suzanne. *To Love and Let Go.* New York: Alfred Knopf, 1986.

Atallah, Lillian. "Report from a Test-Tube Baby." *New York Times Magazine,* April 18, 1976, pp. 16–17, 48, 51–52.

Barrett, Michèle, and Mary McIntosh. *The Anti-Social Family.* London: NLB, 1982.

Bick-Rice, Judith. "The Need for Statutes Regulating Artificial Insemination by Donors." *Ohio State Law Journal,* 46 (1985), 1055–76.

Billiter, Bill. "State May Set Rules on Motherhood: Could Become First to Legalize, Control Use of Surrogates." *Los Angeles Times,* June 20, 1982, p. I-3.

——— "State Studies Surrogate Mother Law: L.A. Hearing Vents Views on Growing Nationwide Practice." *Los Angeles Times,* November 22, 1982, p. I-23.

——— "Surrogate Mother Protection Bill Tabled in Senate." *Los Angeles Times,* August 4, 1982, p. I-21.

———— "Surrogate Mothers Bill Dead for Session." *Los Angeles Times,* August 5, 1982, p. II-12.

Bitner, Lizabeth A. "Wombs for Rent: A Call for Pennsylvania Legislation Legalizing and Regulating Surrogate Parenting Agreements." *Dickinson Law Review,* 90 (Fall 1985), 227–259.

Black, Robert C. "Legal Problems of Surrogate Motherhood." *New England Law Review,* 16 (1980–81), 373–396.

Blair, Betty. "Surrogate Motherhood Gains Acceptance, Won't Go Away." *Los Angeles Times,* December 16, 1982, p. IV-4.

Blakely, Mary Kay. "Surrogate Mothers: For Whom Are They Working?" *Ms.,* March 1983, pp. 18–20.

Blumberg, Patricia. "Human Leukocyte Antigen Testing: Technology versus Policy in Cases of Disputed Parentage." *Vanderbilt Law Review,* 36 (November 1983), 1578–1631.

Bolick, Nancy O'Keefe. "The New Faces of Adoption." *Boston Magazine,* October 1986, p. 152.

Bonavoglia, Angela. "The Ordeal of Pamela Rae Stewart." *Ms.,* July–August 1987, pp. 92–95, 196–204.

Bowal, Peter. "Surrogate Procreation: A Motherhood Issue in Legal Obscurity." *Queens Law Journal,* 9 (Fall 1983), 5–34.

Bronner, Ethan. "Advances Elevate Status of Fetus." *Boston Globe,* July 21, 1987, p. 1.

Capron, Alexander M. "The New Reproductive Possibilities: Seeking a Moral Basis for Concerted Action in a Pluralistic Society." *Law, Medicine and Health Care,* 12 (October 1984), 192–198.

Cohen, Barbara. "Surrogate Mothers: Whose Baby Is It?" *American Journal of Law and Medicine,* 10 (Fall 1984), 243–285.

Coleman, Phyllis. "Surrogate Motherhood: Analysis of the Problems and Suggestions for Solutions." *Tennessee Law Review,* 50 (Fall 1982), 71–118.

Committee to Consider the Social, Ethical and Legal Issues Arising from In Vitro Fertilization. *Report on the Disposition of Embryos Produced by In Vitro Fertilization.* Melbourne, Australia: State of Victoria, August 1984. Cited as the Waller Report.

Corbin, Arthur L. *Contracts.* 12 vols. St. Paul: West, 1950–64.

Corea, Gene. *The Mother Machine: Reproductive Technologies from Artificial Insemination to Artificial Wombs.* New York: Harper & Row, 1986.

Crow, Carol A. "The Surrogate Child: Legal Issues and Implications for the Future." *Journal of Juvenile Law,* 7 (1983), 80–92.

Cullen, Kevin. "Law Orders Coverage for Infertility." *Boston Globe,* October 9, 1987, p. 1.

"Curbs on Surrogate Motherhood Favored by Medical Ethics Panel." *Los Angeles Times,* September 9, 1986, p. I-5.

Curie-Cohen, Martin, Lesleigh Luttrell, and Sander Shapiro. "Current Practice of AID in the United States." *New England Journal of Medicine,* 300 (1979), 585–590.

Cusine, Douglas J. "'Womb-Leasing': Some Legal Implications." *New Law Journal*, 128 (1978), 824–825.

Dart, John. "Ethicist Examines Social Issues of Surrogate Motherhood: Says Traditional Ideas of Parenthood Might Change Radically." *Los Angeles Times*, January 2, 1982, p. II-4.

"Desperately Seeking Baby." WGBH Boston television broadcast on "Frontline." March 3, 1987.

Dodd, Bette J. "The Surrogate Mother Contract in Indiana." *Indiana Law Review*, 15 (1982), 807–830.

Dunstan, Gordon Reginald. "Moral and Social Issues Arising from A.I.D., Law and Ethics of A.I.D. and Embryo Transfer." *CIBA Foundation Symposium*, 17 (1973), 52–68.

Eaton, Thomas A. "The British Response to Surrogate Motherhood: An American Critique." *Law Teacher*, 19 (1985), 163–192.

Ellis, Jane Truesdell. "The Law and Procedure of International Adoption: An Overview." *Suffolk Transnational Law Journal*, 7 (Fall 1983), 361–390.

Engram, Sara. "Doctors and Surrogate Moms: Physicians Face Ethical Dilemma over Technology." *Los Angeles Times*, April 9, 1982, p. V-14.

Erbe, Nancy. "Prostitutes: Victims of Men's Exploitation and Abuse." *Law and Inequality*, 2 (August 1984), 609–628.

Erickson, Elizabeth A. "Contracts to Bear a Child." *California Law Review*, 66 (1978), 611–622.

Fashing, Felicia R. "Artificial Conception: A Legislative Proposal." *Cardozo Law Review*, 5 (Spring 1984), 713–735.

Feldman, Walter S. "Wombs for Rent: Surrogate Mothers and Semen Donors." *Legal Aspects of Medical Practice*, 10 (May 1982), 8.

Finegold, Wilfred J. *Artificial Insemination.* 2d ed. Springfield, Ill.: Charles C. Thomas, 1976.

Fletcher, William M. *Cyclopedia of the Law of Private Corporations.* Rev. ed. Vol. 7A. Wilmette, Ill.: Callaghan, 1978.

Flickinger, Russell N. "Surrogate Motherhood: The Attorney's Legal and Ethical Dilemma." *Capital University Law Review*, 11 (Spring 1982), 593–610.

Foster, Henry H., Jr. "Adoption and Child Custody: Best Interests of the Child?" *Buffalo Law Review*, 1 (Spring 1973), 1–16.

Freed, Doris J., and Henry H. Foster. "Family Law in the Fifty States: An Overview." *Family Law Quarterly*, 16 (Winter 1983), 289–383.

Friedrich, Otto. "'A Legal, Moral, Social Nightmare': Society Seeks to Define the Problems of the Birth Revolution." *Time*, September 10, 1984, pp. 54–56.

Frug, Mary Joe. "The Baby M Contract." *New Jersey Law Journal*, 119 (1987), 337–338.

Galen, Michele. "Surrogate Law: Court Ruling." *National Law Journal*, September 29, 1986, pp. 1–10.

Garrison, Marsha. "Why Terminate Parental Rights?" *Stanford Law Review*, 35 (February 1982), 423–496.

George, Ellen S., and Stephen M. Snyder. "A Reconsideration of the Religious Element in Adoption." *Cornell Law Review,* 56 (May 1971), 782–830.

Gersz, Steven R. "The Contract in Surrogate Motherhood: A Review of the Issues." *Law, Medicine, and Health Care,* 12 (June 1984), 107–114.

Goldfarb, Carolea. "Two Mothers, One Baby, No Law." *Human Rights,* 11 (Summer 1983), 26–29.

Goldstein, Joseph, Anna Freud, and Albert Solnit. *Before the Best Interests of the Child.* New York: Free Press, 1979.

—— *Beyond the Best Interests of the Child.* New York: Free Press, 1973.

Goldstein, Joseph, Anna Freud, Albert Solnit, and Sonja Goldstein. *In the Best Interests of the Child.* New York: Free Press, 1986.

Goleman, Daniel. "Motivations of Surrogate Mothers." *New York Times,* January 20, 1987, p. C1.

Goodman, Ellen. "Surrogates Could Make Pregnancy a Service Industry." *Los Angeles Times,* September 2, 1986, p. III-5.

—— "Which Mother Is Mom?" *Los Angeles Times,* April 25, 1986, p. II-7.

—— "Wombs for Rent: New Era on the Reproduction Line." *Los Angeles Times,* February 8, 1983, p. II-5.

—— "The Word That's Not Mentioned in the Baby M Case." *Boston Globe,* February 17, 1987, p. 15.

Graham, M. Louise. "Surrogate Gestation and the Protection of Choice." *Santa Clara Law Review,* 22 (Spring 1982), 291–323.

Greenberg, Lisa J., and Harold L. Hirsch. "Surrogate Motherhood and Artificial Insemination: Contractual Implications." *Medical Trial Technique Quarterly,* 29 (1983), 149–166.

Greer, William R. "The Adoption Market: A Variety of Options." *New York Times,* June 26, 1986, pp. C1, C10.

Griffin, Moira K. "Wives, Hookers, and the Law." *Student Lawyer,* 10 (January 1982), 18–21, 36–39.

—— "Womb for Rent." *Student Lawyer,* 9 (April 1981), 29–31.

Grobstein, Clifford. "External Human Fertilization: An Evaluation of Policy." *Science,* October 14, 1983, pp. 127–133.

—— *From Chance to Purpose: An Appraisal of External Human Fertilization.* Reading, Mass.: Addison-Wesley, 1981.

"Group to Guard Rights of Surrogate Mothers." *New York Times,* November 13, 1986, p. C11.

Hanley, Robert. "Baby M Case Etches a Study in Contrasts: Different Social Classes and Family Relations." *New York Times,* February 17, 1987, pp. B1–B2.

—— "Baby M's 'Best Interests' May Resolve a Puzzling Case." *New York Times,* February 2, 1987, p. B1.

—— "Baby M's Mother Examined on Her Family and Facts." *New York Times,* February 19, 1987, p. B2.

—— "Baby M Trial Lawyers: Two Goals and Two Styles." *New York Times,* February 23, 1987, p. B1.

———— "Experts Testify on Whitehead as a Parent." *New York Times,* February 24, 1987, p. B2.

———— "Father of Baby M Thought Mother Had Been Screened." *New York Times,* January 14, 1987, p. B2.

———— "Reporter's Notebook: Grief over Baby M." *New York Times,* January 12, 1987, pp. B1, B3.

———— "Reporter's Notebook: Mother Plans to Tread Softly in the Baby M Trial." *New York Times,* February 9, 1987, p. B3.

———— "Whitehead Outlines Her Life before Baby M." *New York Times,* February 10, 1987, p. B15.

Harris, Lindsey E. "Artificial Insemination and Surrogate Motherhood—A Nursery Full of Unresolved Questions." *Willamette Law Review,* 17 (Fall 1981), 913–952.

Harrison, Michelle. "Social Construction of Mary Beth Whitehead." *Gender and Society,* 1 (September 1987), 300–311.

Hilts, Philip J. "Two Embryos Transplanted in Human." *Washington Post,* July 22, 1983, p. A12.

Hollinger, Joan. "From Coitus to Commerce: Legal and Social Consequences of Noncoital Reproduction." *University of Michigan Journal of Law Reform,* 18 (Summer 1985), 866–932.

Jacobs, Kevin. "Surrogate Mother Gives Birth to Triplets for Her Daughter." *Boston Globe,* October 2, 1987, pp. 1, 3.

Jensen, Brent J. "Artificial Insemination and the Law." *Brigham Young University Law Review,* 4 (1982), 935–990.

Kantrowitz, Barbara. "Who Keeps Baby M?" *Newsweek,* January 19, 1987, pp. 44–49.

Kasirer, Nicholas. "The Surrogate Motherhood Agreement: A Proposed Standard Form Contract for Quebec." *Revue de Droit* (Sherbrooke University), 16 (1985), 351–387.

Katz, Avi. "Surrogate Motherhood and the Baby-Selling Laws." *Columbia Journal of Law and Social Problems,* 20 (1986), 1–53.

Keane, Noel. "The Surrogate Parenting Contract." *Adelphia Law Journal,* 2 (1983), 45–53.

Keane, Noel, and Dennis Breo. *The Surrogate Mother.* New York: Everest House, 1981.

Kolata, Gina. "Multiple Fetuses Raise New Issues Tied to Abortion." *New York Times,* January 25, 1988, p. 1.

Kolko, S. Joel. "Admissibility of HLA Test Results to Determine Paternity." *Family Law Reporter,* 9 (1983), 4009–18.

Krause, Harry D. "Artificial Conception: Legislative Approaches." *Family Law Quarterly,* 19 (Fall 1985), 185–206.

Krauthammer, Charles. "The Ethics of Human Manufacture." *New Republic,* May 4, 1987, pp. 17–19.

Krier, Beth Ann. "The Psychological Effects Are Still a Question Mark." *Los Angeles Times,* March 30, 1986, p. V-1.

————— "Surrogate Motherhood: Looking at It as Business Proposition." *Los Angeles Times,* March 30, 1981, p. V-1.

Lacayo, Richard. "Whose Child Is This?" *Time,* January 19, 1987, pp. 56–58.

Landes, Elisabeth M., and Richard A. Posner. "The Economics of the Baby Shortage." *Journal of Legal Studies,* 7 (June 1978), 323–348.

Law, Sylvia. "Women, Work, Welfare, and the Preservation of Patriarchy." *University of Pennsylvania Law Review,* 131 (May 1984), 1249–1339.

Lawson, Carol. "Surrogate Mothers Grow in Number despite Questions." *New York Times,* October 1, 1986, p. C1.

"Lawyering for the Child: Principles of Representation in Custody and Visitation Disputes Arising from Divorce." *Yale Law Journal,* 87 (1978), 1126–90.

Leach, W. Barton. "Perpetuities in the Atomic Age: The Sperm Bank and the Fertile Decedent." *American Bar Association Journal,* 48 (October 1962), 942–944.

Leavy, Morton L., and Roy D. Weinberg. *Law of Adoption.* 4th ed. Dobbs Ferry, N.Y.: Oceana, 1979.

Lorio, Kathryn V. "Alternative Means of Reproduction: Virgin Territory for Legislation." *Louisiana Law Review,* 44 (July 1984), 1642–1723.

Lyons, Richard D. "2 Women Become Pregnant with Transferred Embryos." *New York Times,* July 22, 1983, p. A1.

Mady, Theresa M. "Surrogate Mothers: The Legal Issues." *American Journal of Law and Medicine,* 7 (Fall 1981), 323–352.

"Man Who Hired 'Surrogate Mother' Isn't Child's Father." *Los Angeles Times,* February 3, 1983, p. I-17.

Mandler, John J. "Developing a Concept of the Modern 'Family': A Proposed Uniform Surrogate Parenthood Act." *Georgetown Law Journal,* 73 (1985), 1283–1329.

Markoutsas, Eileen. "Women Who Have Babies for Other Women." *Good Housekeeping,* April 1981, p. 96.

Martin, David K. "Surrogate Motherhood: Contractual Issues and Remedies under Legislative Proposals." *Washburn Law Journal,* 23 (Spring 1984), 601–637.

Mason, Stephen. "Abnormal Conception." *Australian Law Journal,* 56 (July 1982), 347–357.

Mathews, Jay. "Boy's Birth Is First from Embryo Transfer." *Washington Post,* February 4, 1984, p. A14.

Mawdsley, Ralph D. "Surrogate Parenthood: A Need for Legislative Direction." *Illinois Bar Journal,* 71 (March 1983), 412–417.

McMillan, Penelope. "Natural Parents' Embryo Living in Surrogate Mother." *Los Angeles Times,* November 29, 1986, p. II-1.

Meezan, William, Sanford Katz, and Eva Mankoff Russo. *Adoptions without Agencies: A Study of Independent Adoptions.* Washington, D.C.: Welfare League of America, 1977.

Mehren, Elizabeth. "A Capital Site for a Surrogate Parent Center." *Los Angeles Times,* April 19, 1983, p. V-1.

Mellown, Mary Ruth. "An Incomplete Picture: The Debate About Surrogate Motherhood." *Harvard Women's Law Journal,* 8 (Spring 1985), 231–246.

National Committee on Adoption. *Adoption Factbook.* Washington, D.C., 1985.

"Non-Surgical Transfer of In Vitro Fertilization Donated to Five Infertile Women: Report of Two Pregnancies." *Lancet,* July 23, 1983, p. 223.

O'Brien, Shari. "Commercial Conceptions: A Breeding Ground for Surrogacy." *North Carolina Law Review,* 65 (November 1986), 127–153.

Patterson, Suzanne M. "Parenthood by Proxy: Legal Implications of Surrogate Birth." *Iowa Law Review,* 67 (January 1982), 385–399.

Peterson, Iver. "Baby M Case: Surrogate Mothers Vent Feelings." *New York Times,* March 2, 1987, pp. B1, B4.

——— "Baby M Trial Splits Ranks of Feminists: Surrogate Motherhood Stirs Exploitation Issue." *New York Times,* February 24, 1987, pp. B1, B2.

——— "States Assess Surrogate Motherhood." *New York Times,* December 13, 1987, p. I-42.

Phillips, John W., and Susan D. Phillips. "In Defense of Surrogate Parenting: A Critical Analysis of the Recent Kentucky Experience." *Kentucky Law Journal,* 69 (1980–81), 877–931.

Pierce, William L. "Baby M Decision Creates Flurry of Legislative Activity." *Family Law Reporter,* 13 (1987), 1295–96.

——— "Surrogate Parenthood: A Legislative Update." *Family Law Reporter,* 13 (1987), 1442–44.

——— "Survey of State Activity regarding Surrogate Motherhood." *Family Law Reporter,* 11 (1985), 3001–04.

Pollitt, Kathy. "The Strange Case of Baby M." *The Nation,* May 23, 1987, pp. 667, 682–688.

"Quintuplets Artificially Conceived Are Born." *New York Times,* January 13, 1988, p. A14.

Radin, Margaret Jane. "Property and Personhood." *Stanford Law Review,* 34 (May 1982), 957–1015.

——— "Market-Inalienability." *Harvard Law Review,* 100 (June 1987), 1849–1937.

Reagan, Leslie. "Surrogacy Is a Bad Bargain." *Against the Current,* 2 (September–October 1987), 56–58.

"Reproductive Technology and the Procreation Rights of the Unmarried." *Harvard Law Review,* 98 (January 1985), 669–685.

Riding, Alan. "Argentines Fight for Orphans of a Dirty War." *New York Times,* December 20, 1987, p. 1.

Robertson, John A. "Embryos, Families, and Procreative Liberty: The Legal Structure of the New Reproduction." *Southern California Law Review,* 59 (July 1986), 939–1041.

——— "Extracorporeal Embryos and the Abortion Debate." *Journal of Contemporary Health Law and Policy,* 2 (1985), 53–70.

—— "Procreative Liberty and the Control of Conception, Pregnancy, and Childbirth." *Virginia Law Review,* 69 (April 1983), 405–464.

Rothman, Barbara Katz. *The Tentative Pregnancy.* New York: Viking, 1986.

Rovner, Sandy. "Ethical Choices in Reproductive Technology." *Washington Post Weekly of Medicine, Health and Fitness,* September 9, 1986, p. 15.

"Ruling Made on Daughter Born to a Surrogate." *Los Angeles Times,* September 11, 1986, p. II-21.

"Rumpelstiltskin Revisited: The Inalienable Rights of Surrogate Mothers." *Harvard Law Review,* 99 (June 1986), 1936–55.

Rushevsky, Cynthia A. "Legal Recognition of Surrogate Gestation." *Women's Rights Law Reporter,* 7 (Winter 1982), 107–142.

Saltarelli, Joseph J. "Genesis Retold: Legal Issues Raised by the Cryopreservation of Preimplantation Human Embryos." *Syracuse Law Review,* 36 (1985), 1021–53.

Saltus, Richard. "Embryo Research Provokes Debate on Ethical and Legal Issues." *Boston Globe,* July 22, 1987, p. 1.

—— "Guidelines Urged for Fetal Tissue Transplants." *Boston Globe,* July 22, 1987, p. 9.

Sappideen, Carolyn. "The Surrogate Mother: A Growing Problem." *University of New South Wales Law Journal,* 6 (1983), 79–102.

Schmeck, Harold M. " 'Pre-Natal Adoption' Is the Objective of New Technique." *New York Times,* June 14, 1983, p. C1.

Scott, Janny. "Pair Duped Her on Surrogate Mother Pact, Woman Tells Court." *Los Angeles Times,* February 20, 1987, p. I-22.

Shapiro, Daniel. "No Other Hope for Having a Child." *Newsweek,* January 19, 1987, pp. 50–51.

Sherwyn, Bernard A. "Attorney Duties in the Area of New Reproductive Technologies." *Whittier Law Review,* 6 (1984), 799–810.

Shipp, E. R. "Death Draws Public's Eye to Adoption." *New York Times,* November 29, 1987, p. B1.

Simpson, Laurence Packer. *Handbook of the Law of Contracts.* 2d ed. St. Paul: West, 1965.

Singer, Peter, and Helga Kuhse. "The Ethics of Embryo Research." *Law, Medicine and Health Care,* 14 (September 1986), 133–137.

Slovenko, Ralph. "Obstetric Science and the Developing Role of the Psychiatrist in Surrogate Motherhood." *Journal of Psychiatry & Law,* 13 (1985), 487–518.

Sly, Karen Marie. "Baby-Sitting Consideration: Surrogate Mother's Right to 'Rent Her Womb' for a Fee." *Gonzaga Law Review,* 18 (November 1983), 539–565.

Smith, George P. II. "Australia's Frozen 'Orphan' Embryos: A Medical, Legal, and Ethical Dilemma." *Journal of Family Law,* 24 (1985–86), 27–41.

—— "The Razor's Edge of Human Bonding: Artificial Fathers and Surrogate Mothers." *Western New England Law Review,* 5 (Spring 1983), 639–666.

Smith, Ruth Bayard. "Choosing Sides." *Boston Globe Magazine,* January 3, 1988, p. 30.

—— "The Baby Broker." *Boston Globe Magazine,* January 3, 1988, pp. 20–28, 31.

Snyder, Sarah. "Baby Case Spurs Debate on Surrogate Mothers—Despite Custody Fight, Couples Seek Service." *Boston Globe,* February 22, 1987, pp. 1, 10.

Stoxen, John M. "The Best of Both 'Open' and 'Closed' Adoption Worlds: A Call for Reform of State Statutes." *Journal of Legislation,* 13 (Spring 1986), 292–309.

"Surrogate Mothers: A *Newsweek* Poll." *Newsweek,* January 19, 1987, p. 48.

"Surrogate Mothers Form Lobby Group." *Los Angeles Times,* November 12, 1986, p. II-6.

"Surrogate Parenthood, An Analysis of the Problems and a Solution: Representation for the Child." *William Mitchell Law Review,* 12 (1986), 143–182.

"Surrogate's Baby Born with Deformity Rejected by All." *Los Angeles Times,* January 22, 1983, p. I-17.

Swerdlow, Marian. "Class Politics and Baby M." *Against the Current,* 2 (September–October 1987), 53.

Taylor, Shereen. "Conceiving for Cash: Is It Legal? A Survey of the Laws Applicable to Surrogate Motherhood." *Human Rights Annual,* 4 (1987), 413–444.

Timnick, Lois. "Surrogate Mother Wants to Keep Her Unborn Baby." *Los Angeles Times,* March 21, 1981, p. I-1.

Townsend, Margaret D. "Surrogate Mother Agreements: Contemporary Legal Aspects of a Biblical Notion." *University of Richmond Law Review,* 16 (Winter 1982), 467–483.

U.S. Congress. Senate. *Adoption and Foster Care, 1975: Hearings before the Subcommittee on Children and Youth of the Senate Committee on Labor and Public Welfare,* 94th Cong., 1st sess., 1976, p. 6.

Van Hoften, Ellen L. "Surrogate Motherhood in California: Legislative Proposals." *San Diego Law Review,* 18 (1981), 341–385.

Vieth, Perry J. "Surrogate Mothering: Medical Reality in a Legal Vacuum." *Journal of Legislation,* 8 (1981), 140–159.

Waller Report. *See* Committee to Consider . . . Fertilization.

Wallis, Claudia. "A Surrogate's Story." *Time,* September 10, 1984, p. 53.

Warnock, Dame Mary. *Report of the Committee of Inquiry into Human Fertilization and Embryology.* London: United Kingdom Department of Health and Social Security, July 1984. Cited as the Warnock Report.

Warren, David G. "The Law of Human Reproduction: An Overview." *Journal of Legal Medicine,* 3 (March 1982), 1–57.

Williams, Jack F. "Differential Treatment of Men and Women by Artificial Reproduction Statutes." *Tulsa Law Journal,* 21 (Spring 1986), 463–484.

Wilson, Andrew B. "Adoption, It's Not Impossible." *Business Week,* July 8, 1985, pp. 112–113.

Winkler, Robin, and Margaret van Keppel. *Relinquishing Mothers in Adoption.* Melbourne, Australia: Institute of Family Studies, 1984.

Wong, Doris Sue. "Mass. Couple Ask for Va. Ruling in Surrogate Case." *Boston Globe*, January 14, 1987, p. II-23.

Woodruff, Elizabeth. "Irrevocability of Consent to Surrender of a Child for Adoption (*C.C.I. v. The Natural Parents*)." *Mississippi College Law Review*, Spring 1982, pp. 423–445.

Wright, Moira. "Surrogacy and Adoption: Problems and Possibilities." *Family Law Review*, 16 (April 1986), 109–116.

Wrigley, Julia. "Whose Baby Is It Anyway?" *Against the Current*, 2 (September–October 1987), 53–55.

Index